GREAT IS
THE TRUTH

GREAT IS THE TRUTH

SECRECY, SCANDAL, AND THE QUEST FOR JUSTICE AT THE HORACE MANN SCHOOL

AMOS KAMIL

with SEAN ELDER

FARRAR, STRAUS AND GIROUX   NEW YORK

Farrar, Straus and Giroux
18 West 18th Street, New York 10011

The Library of Congress has cataloged the hardcover edition as follows:
Kamil, Amos, 1964–
    Great is the truth : secrecy, scandal, and the quest for justice at the Horace
Mann School / Amos Kamil, Sean Elder.
        p.   cm.
    Includes index.
    ISBN 978-0-374-16662-5 (hbk.) — ISBN 978-0-374-71156-6 (ebk.)
    1. Sex crimes—New York (State)—New York.   2. Horace Mann School
(New York, N.Y.)   3. Preparatory schools—New York (State)—New York.
4. Social justice—New York (State)—New York.   I. Elder, Sean.   II. Title.

HV6568.N5 .K36 2015
364.15'309747275—dc23

                                                                2015010132

Paperback ISBN: 978-0-374-53650-3

Designed by Jonathan D. Lippincott

Our books may be purchased in bulk for promotional, educational, or business use.
Please contact your local bookseller or the Macmillan Corporate and Premium
Sales Department at 1-800-221-7945, extension 5442, or by e-mail at
MacmillanSpecialMarkets@macmillan.com.

www.fsgbooks.com
www.twitter.com/fsgbooks • www.facebook.com/fsgbooks

For the fellas around the campfire. And to the survivors—
the sparks of your courage have ignited a raging inferno.

Doing nothing for others is the undoing of ourselves.
—Horace Mann (1796–1859),
American education reformer
and abolitionist

CONTENTS

A NOTE ON METHODS

Over the course of writing this book, we conducted hundreds of interviews and sifted through thousands of emails, Facebook posts, media records, and other items of personal correspondence. Some quotations have been silently edited to fix the occasional typographical error.

Great Is the Truth includes several scenes, most notably during mediation, where the authors were not present. In these cases we have reconstructed the dialogue according to the recollections of multiple sources who were present.

The names of some persons described in this book have been changed.

GREAT IS THE TRUTH

INTRODUCTION:
HELL FOR SURE

A few years after graduating from college, I went hiking in the Sierra Nevada Mountains with four of my Horace Mann buddies. It had been ten years since we left the prestigious New York prep school, and we had remained in touch as our paths took us in different directions. Though we hadn't had much actual face time since high school, the bonds among us remained tight. Horace Mann had been for each of us a unique, life-forging experience. It had made us who we were.

For four days we hiked through the woods and over the streams in the mountainous region west of the Inyo National Forest, climbing mountains as we caught up on each other's lives. I was twenty-seven years old and I had packed five minibottles of tequila, limes, and a shaker of salt so that I could share a toast with my friends when I announced that I was engaged to be married.

One day "Andrew,"* our self-appointed guide, miscalculated the length of the day's hike and we raced to beat the setting sun to our next camp location on the banks of Hell for Sure Lake. We hastily set

---

* We have employed pseudonyms for those individuals who did not wish to use their real names and initials for those who did not want to use their full names. The pseudonyms always appear in quotation marks on first usage.

up our camp and scorched some vegetarian meals over the raging campfire we'd built.

After we'd eaten, and our aching joints were melting, Andrew cleared his throat. "Guys, I have to tell you something that happened to me when we were at HM." We looked up from the mesmerizing flames; this didn't sound like your typical campfire chatter. "You guys remember Mark Wright, the football coach?" We all nodded at this clearly rhetorical opener. Although Wright had "moved on" before my time, everyone knew his story, or thought he did. The rumor in the Horace Mann cafeteria was that the imposing assistant football coach and art teacher, a Princeton graduate who had reportedly tried out for the Washington Redskins, had left the school suddenly after being accused of molesting several boys.

"When we were in eighth grade, he raped me," Andrew said deliberately, his eyes now fixed on the flickering yellow-blue flames. "First he befriended me, made me feel special, and then he raped me. Not just me. There were a whole bunch of us."

The silence that ensued was brief but grave, as Andrew's own silence on a subject that had tortured him for so long was finally broken. What followed was a long night of questions and revelations. How had Andrew managed to keep all this in for so long? we wondered. We explored whether Wright's big personality—his easy laugh, his familiar manner—which made him so popular with both students and faculty, had also enabled him to hide in plain sight. Who would think ill of such a man? To echo a refrain that has been heard about countless child molesters: everybody loved him.

Andrew's confession awoke our collective memory. There were the persistent rumors about the female gym teacher who each year would pick a new football player to "have an affair with," as we tend to call it when female adults abuse male students. "Paul" told us about the times he'd been trapped in the office of Johannes Somary, the school's charismatic and wildly arrogant music department head. Behind the closed door, Somary subjected him to long, uncomfortable hugs.

"Then came the trip to Connecticut," Paul recalled. A prize pupil of Somary's, he had accompanied the maestro on a road trip for the ostensible purpose of helping him prepare for a performance there. After arriving at the hotel, he discovered that the teacher had booked one room with a double bed. When they returned to the room after the rehearsal, Somary emerged from the bathroom in his underwear, sat on the bed, and beckoned Paul to join him. "I went back outside and stood for hours in the rain, waiting for Somary to fall asleep," Paul said.

Our conversation then turned to a student who was rumored to have slept with Tek Lin, a popular English teacher known for his green thumb and his whimsical teaching style. "Wade," who had been extremely close with Lin, suddenly got very uncomfortable. "All that was just a rumor," he insisted with a passion that surprised us. When we quizzed him further, Wade admitted that he, too, had spent many hours with Tek—drinking tea, talking about Eastern philosophy and poetry—sometimes with their clothes off.

"That's outrageous!" we said. "That was completely out-of-line behavior between a teacher and a student." But the more we pushed, the more he denied that Lin had in any way acted inappropriately. Though none of us were buying that—the intimacy occurred at the teacher's house, on a weekend, there was alcohol involved, and Wade had been a minor at the time—we let the matter drop.

Denial takes many forms. After listening to Andrew's confession, and Wade's tortured explanation of his relationship with a teacher more than twice his age, Paul and I launched into a "hilarious" story we'd been telling for so long that it sounded like a well-oiled comedy routine.

When I was a senior, my mother went abroad for an extended period of time. Her absence wasn't a secret; I'm sure I bragged about it to my friends. R. Inslee "Inky" Clark Jr., the headmaster and baseball coach who had recruited me for Horace Mann, invited me and my brother Dan out for dinner. Although I trusted Inky, I didn't want to be alone with him and my little brother on a Saturday night. And I certainly had no intention of being anywhere near Stan "the Bear" Kops, Inky's creepy sidekick, drinking buddy, notorious groper of

JV swimmers and eighth-grade history students, and alleged lover. It wasn't that I feared gay men. Having grown up in a house with an openly gay brother, it simply wasn't my issue. Perhaps it was my average teenage awkwardness, my anxiety at the thought of having to make small talk with two grown men for several hours, but whatever the reason, I coerced Paul into tagging along.

The evening involved a lot of drinking, free steaks, and ultimately little more than some uncomfortable moments spent with men old enough to be our parents. We had reduced it over time to a single punch line—"I'm not taking any shit from the Bear!"—but in the context of the campfire talk I began to see the outing in a different light. Five hikers, four stories of teacher-student relationships gone somehow awry. This was starting to look like a pattern.

The stories we told one another that evening would make headlines around the world. Twenty years later, I published an article in *The New York Times Magazine* revealing an epidemic of abuse at Horace Mann. The number of teachers and students involved made it far worse than most school scandals—"Catholic Church bad," as one investigator said. Our alma mater, it turned out, was the site of perhaps the biggest sexual abuse scandal in the history of American education, a scandal characterized by denial and cover-up and an unwillingness on the school's part to be transparent about its past.

Defenders of the school have insisted on putting the matter in context: Most of the abuse took place in the 1960s, '70s, and '80s—a more lax time, they'll say, an age of sexual experimentation. Some have mentioned the repression of homosexuality that was the norm then, as if these teachers might not have taken advantage of boys (and it was mostly boys who were abused by men) if they had been able to be more open in public. And still others have pointed to the British boarding school system and its legacy of child sexual abuse. "What do you think happens in the English schools?" a bestselling novelist who graduated from Horace Mann in the 1960s said when asked about the revelations. A peer of his even suggested that sexual abuse made British schools better—an attitude some across the pond seem to share.

"Nobody said anything about it, for the same reason that people were mercilessly bullied and that wasn't dealt with," said a former student of St. Paul's School in London—where countless children were molested for decades—to a writer for *The New York Times.* "Public schools are built on the idea that it's good for you to be abused while you're young, so that you toughen up for when you go out and run the empire. That's the point."

The graduates of Horace Mann were meant to run other empires—hedge funds on Wall Street, law firms in D.C., international media companies. And while there was not any tacit understanding that abuse was good and even necessary for some, the methods used to cover it up were similar. Students who reported abuse were asked to think about what it might mean to the school, to say nothing of their future, if what they said went any farther, and teachers who relayed students' accusations to administrators had a drink poured for them while they were asked to close the door . . .

After my article appeared, the shroud of secrecy was lifted at last. Victims of abuse contacted one another, other journalists took up the story, and the scandal grew and grew. Eventually, twenty-two Horace Mann teachers and administrators would be credibly accused of abuse over a period of thirty-plus years, and former students would join together to seek redress. In Internet forums, they vented their feelings, sought consolation, and quarreled. In person, they banded together to hold Horace Mann accountable, seeking financial damages, a definitive and honest accounting of what happened, and a commitment from the school to become a leader in the fight against abuse. Their efforts were stymied by a Board of Trustees that was more concerned with protecting the institution's reputation than acknowledging the truth.

But Horace Mann did not have to handle the accusations as it did. As I came to understand, other schools and institutions have responded forthrightly and compassionately to allegations of abuse.

What happened at Horace Mann has changed the landscape of education. Just as the sexual abuse of small children became better known in the 1980s, so today we are learning about the abuse of older victims, in public and private institutions, and what we can do about it. The odds are against the victims; in most states, the statute of limitations on sexual abuse prevents serious crimes from being prosecuted. But those laws are being challenged, and today's teens and young adults are less likely to keep silent when they are mistreated. Horace Mann offers one sort of example—the wrong kind—but the importance of its story cannot be diminished. What began for us as a confession on a mountainside is now a chorus of voices, and the fire started that night is raging still.

1

A SMALL WORLD

When I was growing up in Riverdale, a middle-class section of the Bronx, my whole world was contained within a couple of blocks. From the lobby of Hudson Manor Terrace, the gray brick apartment building where my family moved when I was two, I could see my entire life: across the street was PS 24, where I went until the sixth grade; the next block over was JHS 141, my next stop; and beyond that was the park where we played ringolevio—a sort of extreme New York version of hide-and-go-seek, in which prisoners are taken.

My parents, Gershon and Ada, got divorced when I was ten years old, and my father took an apartment at the Whitehall, about three blocks away on the other side of PS 24. At the time, the Whitehall had the ultimate amenity—an indoor pool. Most important to us, it was the alleged home of the Yankees' Chris Chambliss and Ron Blomberg and even Willie Mays, who it was said lived in a penthouse apartment. Today the neighborhood is largely inhabited by Modern Orthodox Jews, though then it was made up of mostly nonobservant Jews like my parents, and a smattering of Irish, blacks, Italians, and Greeks.

My parents came up the long way. They were born into tumultuous times in Berlin. When Hitler rose to power in the 1930s, my grandparents on both sides saw the writing on the wall and escaped to the dunes of Tel Aviv to help build the fledgling Jewish state.

Although they struggled financially during Israel's lean early years, my parents excelled in the army and were well on their way to an upper-middle-class life. My father was an air force pilot, which in Israeli society is akin to NBA royalty. He went on to college and was working his way up the ranks of Bank Leumi when the bank asked him to go to the New York office for a two-year stint.

My parents jumped at the opportunity to live in the financial and artistic capital of the world.

To them Riverdale looked idyllic—a reasonably priced apartment with a stunning view of the Hudson River and the Palisades, good public schools, and easy access to the city. But beneath the lush parks and the greenery was a 1970s New York that was changing and crumbling.

As the city veered toward bankruptcy and the police were MIA, busing also shook up the city's schools. Suddenly the kids at JHS 141 were joined by much tougher youths from the South Bronx. At 141 we learned never to go to the bathroom for fear of getting jumped. My first week of sixth grade, a seventh grader in a shiny shirt held a switchblade near my stomach and demanded my lunch money, right outside the classroom's barred windows. I had nothing to give him, but the attempted mugging made an impression. Childhood was coming to an end.

Things had changed for me at home by then, anyway. My parents were in the midst of what would become a long and bitter divorce. Their battles, which had been raging for years, intensified when my father had an affair with my mother's best friend, Fran, who lived across the hallway. Her kids and me and my three brothers were all friends. Our families sometimes vacationed together. With the home fires out of control, all four of us boys began hiding: Ofer, by then out of the closet, in the discos of Manhattan; Gideon with the young tough druggies on Johnson Avenue; and Daniel, five years my junior, crawled into the TV. I spent as much time away from the constant drama as I could. Not that we were alone; almost every kid in my building had parents who were getting divorced then.

The youth center around the corner was where we went to play basketball and Ping-Pong and to crowd around the tiny black-and-white TV to watch the *Bronx Is Burning* vintage Yankees: Reggie, Munson, Nettles, Guidry. Mick the Quick . . . But by the time I was in the eighth grade, "going to the center" was just an excuse I'd yell over my shoulder to my mom, who sat, lit cigarette dangling from her lip, fretting over the crossword and how to extract the latest alimony payment from my parsimonious father. In truth, I was going out into the Bronx night to get drunk and stoned.

By ninth grade, my life was nicely divided. I was a straight-A student pretty much without ever gracing my textbooks with my shadow. Because I played sports, I got a free pass from most of the guys who were bused in; I was one of two white kids on both the soft-ball and basketball teams. And after school I was hanging with a very different crowd, Irish and Italian kids from across the highway and down the hill.

Jimmy Ryan, one of my newly acquired best friends, represented this other world. While only a decent athlete, he was a tough guy of epic proportions: in the fourth grade he challenged the entire fifth grade to meet him after school on a grassy hill known as the Fighting Grounds; I don't think he got any takers. Jimmy represented freedom and girls and the basic Fuck-You Bronx attitude I was so desperate to embrace. There was a threat of violence anywhere Jimmy went. It was like an antidote to the muted passivity and seething hostility of my mother's response to her ex–best friend living with her ex-husband.

I exploded out onto the streets and joined endless gangs of seemingly parentless teens crowding the benches, the fields, the paddleball courts, the tables, the center, the arcade, Seton Park, and Johnson Avenue. Fat city rats feasted on the open garbage that had been left in decaying piles by the budget-slashed sanitation workers under Mayor Abe Beame's flailing administration. We stood, together, denim jackets Magic Markered with the names of our favorite bands (Beatles, Doors, Stones, Zeppelin), openly smoking pot in front of what few cops we saw: they had better things to do with their time than chase off a bunch of ragamuffins getting zooted out of their heads.

Everywhere you went there were nicknames—Tootsie, Perky,

Pirate, Eggy, Ish, Fanbelt, Goich, Johnny-Boy, Gay Ray, Bend-Over Bob, the Mole, Buttons. I was the Mouse, from Amos (Ay-mos in the more Anglican pronunciation at school, as opposed to the Hebrew pronunciation Ah-mos). I was a small and scrappy middle infielder with good hands. A coach started calling me Mouse, and it stuck.

After school we'd play chicken, a game where we'd throw jackknives or stilettos into the ground, trying to get them as close as we could to our opponent's feet. One day the Mr. Yum-Yum ice cream truck pulled up, its maddening jingle a clarion call to kids all around. The guys I was playing chicken with were suddenly gathering rocks and pelting the truck, yelling, "Fuck that shit! This is Mr. Softee's territory!" The hapless vendor drove off in a hurry, fleeing in a hail of stones, while I wondered what the hell was going on. It was only years later that Ish told me that somebody was paying them to keep Mr. Yum-Yum off the block; he rewarded them all with free ice cream. "Yeah, Irish confetti," he recalled fondly.

These guys all lived across the highway, in North Riverdale or down the hill in Kingsbridge, where the streets were lined with rows of Archie Bunker–style houses and tired-looking apartment buildings that made Hudson Manor Terrace look grand. This was much more the neighborhood that people imagine when you say "the Bronx." It sure wasn't the Riverdale I came from.

One cold winter night we found an empty space in the basement of an apartment building on 238th Street, and turned it into our own private clubhouse, unbeknownst to its owners. We dragged in some derelict furniture and sat around at night drinking beer, smoking pot, snapping on each other's mothers, and making out with girls with feathered-back hair and denim jackets. We christened our subterranean clubhouse Zero.

Besides my decent grades, the biggest thing I had going for me was baseball. All those years of stickball had prepared me to become a good batter. After years of swinging at a small, curving Spalding ball with a bat the size of a broomstick, a regulation baseball looked like a grapefruit. By the age of fourteen I could hit a ball long and hard and had the arm, glove, and game smarts to match.

It was during one of my better outings that I met Inky Clark. The headmaster of the Horace Mann School was also the coach of the school's baseball team, and he had a reputation for scouting the local ball fields for promising players. I was at bat in a Pony League game at Seton Park when he pulled up in his big orange Cadillac convertible. Even if you were supposed to keep your eye on the ball, you couldn't miss Clark. He wore the plaid pants and loud sweaters of his adopted class and shouted his greetings to our coach in a braying voice that carried across the field.

When I came to the plate, the kids in the outfield moved back; that must have got Inky's attention. Then the first pitch I hit flew about 350 feet. It was caught, but it was still a hell of a rocket for a fourteen-year-old boy. I had heard Clark chattering until the moment I connected; that shot seemed to shut him up.

After that, Clark became more of a presence at our games. He was scouting talent, looking for kids to recruit to the school on scholarships and matching grants. Though I didn't know it at the time, Horace Mann wasn't just a bastion of the elite; it was already known in some circles as a place where Jews got cleaned up for the Ivy League and eventually Wall Street.

For the people I hung out with, my crew from the other side of the tracks, Horace Mann wasn't even on the radar. Though it was only about a mile from where we played stickball, it might as well have been on Neptune. The houses around the campus, in the Fieldston section of Riverdale, were mansions of the Tudor sort. Money trimmed the lawns and the hedgerows of the surrounding yards; the Beatles' last manager, Allen Klein, lived in a manse with a doorbell that played melodies by the Fab Four. John F. Kennedy had lived there as a child. The campus was gorgeous, and I can imagine that many graduates of Horace Mann felt a tinge of disappointment the first time they saw their colleges.

•

Over the course of the next few months, Inky continued visiting my games. In between he'd send typewritten letters on Horace Mann letterhead. "I have heard you are a fine student, which combined with your athletic interests means that Horace Mann might be a great spot for you," he wrote in one letter. "Let's plan to get together fairly soon . . . In that way, we can start the necessary procedures."

Although two of Fran's kids went to Horace Mann, my parents knew little more about the place than my friends and I did. When Inky's offer to join its student body came at the end of ninth grade, it was like finding a message in a bottle on the seashore, albeit one written in a tongue none of us understood.

Soon enough, I found myself sitting, arms folded, in the admissions office in a building on the Horace Mann campus they called the Cottage. If Inky was famous for his lime-green pants and plaid jackets, he was outdone only by Gary Miller, the glad-handing director of admissions. Miller was a Thurston Howell III caricature of a WASP. Ambivalent about losing my friends, I let my Bronx accent do my talking for me ("Yeah, how you doin'?"). But if I meant to queer the deal with my attitude, it didn't work. Miller had probably seen enough of Inky's diamonds-in-the-rough to take my tough guy street act in stride. Clark, I came to understand, was on a mission to change Horace Mann, one kid at a time, and I was just a small part of his master plan. I had a lot to learn—about Inky, his mission, and the school itself.

When I was summoned alone to my father's apartment for our weekly Sunday-at-one conference, my mind was made up: I didn't want to go to Horace Mann. That day, I walked through the PS 24 playground to the Whitehall steeling myself for his wrath. I walked past the doorman and stole a look around for Chambliss, Blomberg, or Mays. I stepped out of the elevator on 8 and pressed Father's doorbell, expecting to be met in battle, or maybe to find him relieved that he wouldn't have to pay even a small portion of the steep tuition.

Instead, I found him in a conciliatory, almost concerned mood. He asked me about the offer and even my "five-year plan." At fourteen, my immediate plan included nothing more than sports and girls, and it certainly didn't extend half a decade into the future. He asked me what my objections to Horace Mann were. I shrugged like Jimmy Ryan and told him I just wanted to be with my friends.

"You will make new friends," he said.

"I just don't want to go," I whined. "That whole place is filled with a bunch of snobs."

"Snobs!" He repeated the word, raising one eyebrow and sticking out his lower lip in an exaggerated expression of surprise. He stood and limped to the bookcase by his desk. He picked up a thick dictionary and lumbered back to his chair to continue our interview.

"Snob," he said, as he leafed through the pages before stopping at the definition. "'Snob: one who blatantly imitates, fawningly admires, or vulgarly seeks association with those regarded as social superiors.'" He looked up at me. "This is who attends Horace Mann?"

"Well, not exactly," I said, fumbling my response. "I don't know."

He continued. "'One who tends to rebuff, avoid, or ignore those regarded as inferior; one who has an offensive air of superiority in matters of knowledge or taste.'" He looked at me again, like a chess player who has just maneuvered his opponent into checkmate. "These are the students you will meet?"

I dug in. "I don't care! I'm not going."

He closed the big book, smiled at me, and said kindly, "Why not try it for a year? If you don't like it, we can talk about it then."

2

THE CITY ON THE HILL

Pink is for pussies.

That's the thought that crossed my mind as I stood in the Breezeway wearing the pink Lacoste shirt my brother Ofer had given me to wear on my first day of summer school at Horace Mann. This was before Ralph Lauren ushered in the prep school era of fashion by aping the style of the yacht club set. My brother meant well with his fashion-forward statement; he thought it would help me blend in.

But first I had to pass biology. The only condition on entering as a sophomore was that I take a summer science class that made my studies at 141 look like kindergarten. I'd gotten straight As there without breaking a sweat, and only after arriving at HM did I understand how low the bar had been set. I was in the major leagues now.

The summer of 1979, I shuttled between HM's pristine campus and my mother's apartment, my backpack stuffed with enough books for a semester's worth of classes. Our teacher was Michael "Doc" Passow, himself a graduate of Horace Mann. He was quick-witted and broke down the material in a way that made biology come alive for me. He bantered with the students in a familiar, collegial fashion that was unlike any student-teacher interaction I'd ever witnessed. Compared with him, most of the teachers at 141 were like prison guards.

The student labs were state-of-the-art. The hallways were free of the graffiti and litter I had come to regard as normal; the food in the cafeteria, which I couldn't afford, was comparable to what I was bringing from home; and the stalls in the restrooms had doors on them. For a 141 kid who had trained himself to hold it in all day, this was a major deal.

By the end of the second day, I was racing home to scarf a quick dinner before throwing myself into a full evening of memorizing information about mitochondria and cell organisms—just the kind of thing that used to make my eyes cross. My brothers were astounded by the overnight change in my behavior. My two best friends, Lance and Pat, were mostly just annoyed.

The buzzer would sound and one of my brothers would yell out my name. I'd tear myself away from protoplasm and answer the intercom.

"Yo, Mouse, we're going to the benches," Lance would say. "You wanna hang out?"

"I gotta study, man."

"In the summertime? What the fuck?"

When I got tired of explaining, I'd walk away from the intercom. As the summer wore on, I just stopped answering. One night, August 2, 1979, to be exact, we sat in the 141 arcade mourning the death of Thurman Munson, the Yankees catcher and captain who had been killed in a plane crash that afternoon. As we passed a bottle of blackberry brandy and the booze set in, I remember promising Lance and Pat that nothing would ever change between us. They were skeptical. "You'll forget us," Pat said as he took a deep hit off the bottle. That was the last time I ever hung out with any of that crowd.

Suddenly my life on the street—getting high, hanging out on Johnson, chasing girls at Zero—didn't seem to matter much. Between the college-level bio course and the homework, I didn't have much time to worry about what my old friends thought of me, and the life at Horace Mann had its own appeal, unimaginable to my 141 pals. The other HM students seemed to *want* to be there. I found them lounging like lazy cats in the sun on the perfectly manicured outfield grass, using their book bags for pillows. They spoke of where their parents would "summer," a word I had never heard used as a verb; they told tales of the exotic places their older siblings had gone to after Horace Mann, not just Ivy League schools but places with names that conjured far-off British castles and dragons—Bryn Mawr, Tufts, Williams, Haverford, Swarthmore, Vassar. I don't remember any of my old gang talking about college, let alone the Ivy League.

I battled through biology, and the week before my sophomore year began I took the bus up to the John Dorr Nature Lab in Washington, Connecticut, for orientation. The school's Nature Lab—275 acres of fields, streams, and ponds—was used as an alternative campus for overnight visits and tougher, extended Outward Bound–type trips.

In our orientation session, we worked together to prepare meals, clean the lodge, and perform trust exercises, all in the name of teamwork and becoming capable self-determining individuals. This was a place that challenged both the mind and body, and I loved every minute of it—the hiking, the games, even singing around the campfire.

I left the Nature Lab with friendships I carry to this day. Andrew, who on the hike years later would tell us about Mark Wright's abuse, was a budding intellectual and a proud vegetarian. And there was Matt, a squat joker from Jackson Heights who always seemed to be at the center of a group of laughing students.

More important, by the time I returned to the Riverdale campus I had my first Horace Mann girlfriend—Jodi Breckenridge. Jodi was from a different world from the girls I knew at Zero. She played soccer and was an avid downhill skier and softball player. Her father, Alan, was a taciturn English teacher and administrator at the school, and he would become a meaningful figure for me. My new life had begun in earnest, and the old one seemed as distant as the childhood cries of "Ringolevio!"

For all its aura of privilege, Horace Mann belonged to an educational movement that aspired to make schooling less exclusive, as well as less remote, by encouraging students to blend college preparatory learning with their home life.

Though Horace Mann did not begin as a "country day school," the ideals of that movement came to reinforce the thinking behind its birth. In the late nineteenth century, Anne Galbraith Carey, the wife of a prominent Baltimore attorney, began a series of conversations about how to educate boys in a way that combined the best aspects of the world's top boarding schools with the clear advantages of having those boys live at home, within their family and community, during their formative years. The upshot of the conversations was a plan for a "school in the country near town," an idea that caught the attention of Dr. Daniel Coit Gilman, the celebrated president of Johns Hopkins University. In 1897, the Country School (today the Gilman School) opened the doors of its Homewood Mansion location, off North Charles Street in Baltimore, to thirty-two boys between the ages of nine and thirteen. "It is proposed to establish a country boarding and day school . . . designed for the education of those boys whose parents wish them to be trained from the beginning of their school education under the best methods approved by modern educators and with surroundings which will protect their health and character," read the school's first prospectus. Within the next few decades, dozens of such "country day schools" were established around the United States, and many city schools transformed themselves accordingly.

Horace Mann did not become a country day school itself until 1914, but it started out as a revolutionary educational experiment in its own right.

In his 1881 annual report to the Columbia board of trustees, Dr. Frederick A. P. Barnard, the president of Columbia College, drafted a curriculum for the ideal elementary school. Barnard approached Nicholas Murray Butler, a brash (some said arrogant) and promising senior. Butler had been considering a career in law and politics, but he was intrigued by Barnard's proposal. A few years later, as a Columbia graduate student, Butler began giving lectures to teachers about Barnard's theories. The lectures were so well attended that Columbia's largest lecture halls had to turn away hundreds of eager teachers.

In 1887, Barnard's dream of a school where teachers were trained was realized when Butler cofounded, and became president of, the

New York School for the Training of Teachers, which later affiliated with Columbia and was renamed Teachers College. As part of the program, a coeducational experimental school was established with the aid of $10,000 from George Vanderbilt. The Model School, as it was originally called, was set up at 9 University Place in Manhattan's Greenwich Village "to provide students in the Teachers College the opportunity to practice and observe high-level teaching." Two sets of parents registered their two children for a total enrollment of four. Butler renamed the school Horace Mann after the mid-nineteenth-century progressive Massachusetts legislator and educational reformer who is widely credited as the father of public school education in America.

By 1894, Butler's school had outgrown its Greenwich Village building and moved north to the countryside of Morningside Heights on 120th Street in Manhattan. Grazing goats accompanied the boys and girls as they walked from the trains to their new school. The rest of the city soon caught up with the pioneering move. In 1896, Columbia University moved its campus from 49th Street and Madison Avenue, and today the bustling neighborhood is home to St. John the Divine, Union Theological Seminary, and the Jewish Theological Seminary.

The move north was accompanied by an effort to reexamine the traditionally formal and authoritarian teacher-student dynamic. Relationships between students and teachers were remarkably friendly. *The Country Day School*, published on the occasion of the school's seventy-fifth anniversary, quoted one celebrated Horace Mann graduate, the physician and poet William Carlos Williams (HM '03), on his experience with an English teacher named William Abbott: "The nonchalance of 'Uncle' Billy's approach to his class, the almost lounging way he deported himself gave me a feeling that won me completely. He was gentle without giving the impression—I don't know whether or not he was lame, but in memory, I think he was. Something made me almost sorry for him—which added to his attractiveness . . . His voice was as gentle as his manner, but when he wanted to be cruel, he could do it with a smile."

In 1894, Dr. Virgil "Prit" Prettyman, an exceptional Latin teacher, was named principal. By 1912, the school had, once again, outgrown its building, and Prettyman, an ardent foe of coeducation, used the opportunity to convince the board to split the school into one for boys and one for girls. His plan was to move the boys up to the Riverdale section of the Bronx, where Teachers College owned a piece of property that Horace Mann teams used for athletics.

One day, as the story has it, while strolling through Van Cortlandt Park, Prettyman met what today we would call a homeless man. When the man, clearly drunk on hard apple cider, told Prettyman of his troubles, the headmaster responded in kind, detailing his search for a proper location for the boys' school. The man said he knew the exact spot and dragged Prettyman across Broadway, up a steep, heavily wooded hill, across Old Albany Post Road, to a tract of land that had once been a Native American fortress. The land had originally belonged to the Van Cortlandt family, beginning in 1694, and had changed hands several times. When Prettyman arrived in the clearing, he saw before him a run-down building, once a public schoolhouse, now inhabited by a group of Italian farmers. Next to it was a tract of land big enough for a baseball field. Prettyman paid the man a dollar for his assistance and scurried toward Manhattan to secure money for an option to purchase lots for the campus.

The physical move from Manhattan to the Bronx also signaled a move away from Teachers College. Not only would the school be educating only boys, it would also join the growing trend of schools adopting the country day school philosophy. Prettyman retooled the curriculum to prepare boys for either business or college. He implemented longer school days with ample time to include both athletics and extracurricular activities. Although a friendly rivalry and fierce competition for students developed between the country day schools and traditional boarding schools like the Phillips Academy, Exeter, and Deerfield, Horace Mann adopted the boarding school nomenclature of forms—with the seventh grade being the first form and the twelfth grade being the sixth form.

In 1914, the renamed Horace Mann School for Boys moved to the Riverdale campus it still occupies today. The Horace Mann High

School for Girls remained at Teachers College on 120th Street until it merged with the Lincoln School and finally closed in 1946.

At the dedication of the first building, now known as Tillinghast Hall, Dr. James E. Russell, the dean of Teachers College, proclaimed, "American leadership calls for initiative, self-control, and self reliance." He stressed that "knowledge is no substitute for character—that what a boy *is* is of far more consequence than what he knows."

In the 1920s, Dr. Charles Carpenter Tillinghast succeeded Prettyman as headmaster. Under his watch, the school would sever its ties with Teachers College. In keeping with the "city school in the country" philosophy, all Horace Mann boys were required to take part in vigorous athletic play. They were also encouraged to form student groups, and dozens of clubs burst forth: the Print Club; the Debating Club; the Modern Railroad Club; the Science Club; the Current Events Club; the Ski Club; the Latin Society; *The Mannikin*, the school's yearbook; and a quarterly literary magazine for which the boys wrote prose, poetry, and drama.

Perhaps the most prestigious affiliation was to be on the staff of *The Record*, the school's newspaper, which was published every week during the school year and was consumed within the community with the same passion accorded to *The New York Times*. *The Record*, structured and printed as though it were a professional newspaper, routinely won first place in Columbia University's annual competition among school newspapers. Although under the supervision of a member of the English department, *The Record*, with a budget of its own, went largely uncensored.

"We of the administration of the school," Tillinghast said in *The Country Day School*, "were frequently asked by principals and headmasters of other schools how we dared permit the paper . . . [to] cause some readers to raise their eyebrows and to wonder just what might be happening on the hill."

Horace Mann, under Tillinghast, gained national prominence, and HM graduates were routinely accepted into the country's most prestigious colleges and universities. A list of prominent alumni, then and now, reads like a who's who of American political, business, and cultural life. It includes Orvil Eugene Dryfoos, the publisher of *The New York Times*, whose wife, Marian Sulzberger, was the daughter of the publisher Arthur Hays Sulzberger, himself an HM graduate; Anthony Lewis, the longtime *New York Times* columnist and two-time Pulitzer Prize winner credited with creating the field of legal journalism; Robert Caro, the author of comprehensive biographies of Robert Moses and Lyndon B. Johnson; Ira Levin, the author of *Rosemary's Baby* and *The Stepford Wives*; James Schlesinger, who served as secretary of defense in the Nixon and Ford administrations and as secretary of energy in the Carter administration; the media mogul and philanthropist Si Newhouse, whose properties include Condé Nast (publisher of *Vogue*, *Vanity Fair*, *The New Yorker*, and other magazines); Jerry Speyer and Robert Tishman, who built Tishman-Speyer into a billion-dollar global real estate empire; Roy Cohn, an aide to Senator Joseph McCarthy and a member of the prosecution team in the Julius and Ethel Rosenberg trial; the political pollster and Microsoft chief strategist Mark Penn, whose clients have included Bill Clinton and Tony Blair; Renée Richards, the transsexual tennis star who graduated as Richard Raskind; Barry Scheck, a member of the legal team that successfully defended O. J. Simpson as well as founder of the Innocence Project; and Eliot Spitzer, former governor and attorney general of New York.

Jack Kerouac, the celebrated author of *On the Road*, was another graduate. Born and raised in working-class Lowell, Massachusetts, the future Beat icon was offered a football scholarship from Columbia on the condition he spend a year polishing his education at Horace Mann. Kerouac, who also played football at HM, arrived on campus in the fall of 1939. The school would figure in some of his later works, including his last novel, *Vanity of Duluoz*, published before his death in 1969. Kerouac's main character, Jack Duluoz, dubbed the school "an academy of wits." The Beat legend seemed to authentically enjoy his time there, aside from the two-and-a-half-hour subway ride each way from his grandmother's house.

Looking back at his tenure, Tillinghast claimed in a reminiscence in *The Country Day School* that during his thirty years, fewer than five boys were punitively dismissed from the school. "Real crises were uncommon indeed; and the majority of penalties were imposed for thoughtless and hence unfortunate conduct in classroom, corridor, library, auditorium or dining room; and in each such instance the attempt was made thoroughly to understand all the circumstances, to listen carefully to both the boy and any other teacher involved, and then to take action which all agreed was fair and commensurate with the gravity of the misdemeanor."

In 1950, Dr. Mitchell Gratwick was appointed Horace Mann's third headmaster. In many ways, Gratwick embodied the Horace Mann ideal of the scholar-athlete. As a boy, he had attended the Nichols Country Day School in Buffalo and graduated from the Phillips Academy in Andover, Massachusetts, before attending Harvard. At Harvard, he had been a champion boxer and made the varsity football, hockey, and track teams. He later became an assistant dean of freshmen.

"It is our responsibility at Horace Mann to start the minds of young men working and simultaneously to toughen them with discipline," Gratwick was quoted as saying in his 1982 *New York Times* obituary. "Call us a college preparatory school, if you will, but perhaps more accurately in the broadest sense, we are a school to train boys for living."

By the time Gratwick retired in 1968, the world outside Horace Mann had changed. Everything was now up for discussion—women's liberation, gay rights, race relations, desegregation, the environment, even school uniforms.

If Horace Mann was to retain its relevance and maintain its status as one of America's elite schools, it would need to change. It would need a leader who could delicately balance the academic rigor and Ivy League entrée HM parents had come to expect with the new realities and mores the era was demanding. With his Yale credentials and connections, his Kennedy-compound good looks, and his proven passion for school reform, Inky Clark, who was chosen as Horace Mann's headmaster in 1970, seemed to be sent from central casting, if not the gods themselves.

Arriving at Horace Mann from Yale was a natural trajectory for Inky. Having been instrumental in changing the student body of one school, he was looking to alter the face of another.

Russell Inslee Clark Jr., a graduate of a Long Island public school, went on to Yale, where he became an exceptional undergraduate, even by Yale standards. Varsity golfer, president of his fraternity, editor of the yearbook, and, perhaps most notably, a member of Skull and Bones, that legendary symbol of WASP secrecy, Clark was the very model of the Yale man. "His blood ran deep blue," the *Pittsburgh Quarterly* wrote of him; "he was an insider, but he had an outsider's perspective."

In 1965, Kingman Brewster, Yale's seventeenth president, appointed the twenty-nine-year-old Clark to the position of dean of admissions. Brewster himself, despite his excellent pedigree (he was a descendant of one of the founders of the Massachusetts Bay Colony), was *not* a classic Yale man himself. As an undergraduate, Brewster had turned down a membership in Skull and Bones (very few recruits have been known to decline "the Tap"), and as president he wanted the school to reflect the changing order that events in the 1960s heralded.

Inky would prove to be the perfect man to execute Brewster's wishes. After graduating from Yale, he hadn't been idle. As Jerome Karabel noted in *The Chosen: The Hidden History of Admission and Exclusion at Harvard, Yale, and Princeton*, "By 1961, when he joined the Yale admissions staff at the age of twenty-six, Clark had in four short years discharged a two-year military commitment, acquired two master's degrees, and gained two years of teaching experience in a boarding school." He shared Brewster's passion for change, and as a first order of business, Inky fired all the Yale men who worked in the office of admissions ("They were very, very stuck in their ways and they were very, very sure about the kinds of people that should be at the University," he later said) and replaced them with public school graduates, including the school's first black admissions officer. Then he set about changing the actual admissions process, eliminating from interviews all references to physical characteristics and family finances. The number of private school and legacy admissions dropped dramatically under Clark, and the number of non-WASP kids—black, Jewish, other—who got in rose just as precipitously.

Not all Yale alumni were pleased by the changes Inky wrought. In *God and Man at Yale*, William F. Buckley Jr. (a former Bonesman himself) famously complained that "a Mexican-American from El Paso High School with identical scores on the achievement tests, and identically ardent recommendations from their headmasters, had a better chance of being admitted to Yale than Jonathan Edwards the Sixteenth from St. Paul's school." In a story recounted in *The Chosen*, Clark was called before the Yale Corporation board and quizzed about his zeal for reforming the admission process. "You're talking about Jews and public school graduates as leaders," an unnamed banker told Clark. "Look around . . . these are America's leaders. There are no Jews here, there are no public school graduates here."

To the former feeder schools with which the Ivies had such a cozy relationship, Inky had a message of his own. If Choate wanted to get more boys into Yale, he suggested to the prestigious prep school when its leaders complained about their change in status, it should be "beating the bushes" for the country's most talented students and thus become "a great national high school."

Perhaps that was part of the draw Horace Mann held for him. It was one of those feeder schools Clark had learned to do an end-run around as head of admissions at Yale. Horace Mann, for its part, viewed Inky as a man who could get their students into Yale. When he arrived at HM in 1970, it was still a boys' school. But times were changing and the women's liberation movement rendered the idea of an all-boys school quaint, perhaps even a little silly. Inky stepped into this change-or-die atmosphere and made HM coed in 1975.

Despite some grumbling from the old guard, a new era had been ushered in at Horace Mann. Having broken the male boundary, Inky wanted to further alter the composition of the student body by looking for athletes outside of the prep school norm.

Which is where I came in.

When my sophomore year began in earnest that September, I

still felt out of place but I didn't think that anybody was judging me. I certainly never used the word "snob" again. Sure, Horace Mann had its cliques, and many new students have felt ostracized over the years. Andrew Solomon, in *Far from the Tree: Parents, Children, and the Search for Identity*, describes in painful detail the hazing he received at HM for his effeminate behavior: "Homophobia was ubiquitous in the 1970s, but the smug culture of my school delivered a sharply honed version of it." But I was a straight, decent-looking athlete with a sense of humor at a school where that stood for something.

The prowess of the Lions, Horace Mann's baseball team, was another of Inky's accomplishments. Inky was not only a master recruiter; he was also an educator who insisted we understand the intellectual aspects of the game. To that end, he made us study and tested us on the San Diego Padres' official playbook. Although not the strongest bench coach or teacher of fundamentals, Inky wanted to make sure we grasped, with the thoroughness of the future leaders we were expected to become, our fielding responsibilities in any given situation. If a ball was hit down the right-field line with two outs and a man on second, where was the second baseman supposed to be? The left fielder? It didn't matter if you were the catcher; in order for the team to perform at its peak, it was incumbent upon every player to know, at all times, what was expected of the other eight. Inky's rigor paid off, and my junior year we were 22–1 (that one loss, to Poly Prep, still stings), and I proudly walked around wearing my maroon letter jacket and baseball cap.

Horace Mann was dedicated to the idea of building well-rounded individuals, and it said a lot about the school that the headmaster was the team coach, and that Bruce Weber, one of my favorite English teachers, was an assistant coach. The guiding philosophy was not the either/or dogma of most public schools and their cliques—jock, brainiac, artist, dweeb—but something more like "all of the above."

Inky increased my confidence in my intellectual abilities too. He taught an urban studies class that was better than most college courses I later had. Among our assignments was *The Other America: Poverty in the United States*, by the socialist author Michael Harrington. The book, Inky informed us, had had an enormous impact on both the Kennedy administration and Lyndon Johnson's subsequent War on Poverty. Inky invited Harrington to speak to the class. His presence had an enormous impact on me. It was probably the first time I realized that ideas, important ideas, are the product of flesh-and-blood people—some of whom even take the time to share their insights with high school students.

Inky also showed us that much was to be learned outside class. As part of our urban studies curriculum, we were required to do a field assignment.

Senior year, Paul, who was to become my lifelong best friend, convinced me that we needed to pose as runaways. We were prepped by Inky and his close friend Kops on what might happen and how we could pretend to be street kids. We assumed fake identities—I was "Greg Pierce"—and spent the night at Covenant House, a shelter for homeless youth located in midtown Manhattan.

When we reported our experiences to the class, Inky and Kops, whom we had invited for our presentation, were quite pleased. (Ironically, Covenant House suffered from its own scandal years later when its president, Father Bruce Ritter, was forced to step down after being accused of sexually abusing boys at the shelter.)

I later learned that "Inky's boys" was what they had called the new recruits Clark had helped usher into Yale. Being one of Inky's boys at HM didn't seem to hold any particular stigma, and I soon learned to fit in well enough at Horace Mann.

It was about then that I met Ion Theodore, the sculpting teacher who became a mentor to me. "Theo," as we called him, was well into his eighties then. His body was still like a work of sculpture itself, and he had a mane of long, flowing white hair. Theo had been an Olympic torchbearer, representing his native Greece, in the infamous 1936 Berlin Games. "I found myself with my arm raised in a fascist salute to Der Führer," he recalled years later in a video Kate Geis (HM '87) and I made about him. "Good God!"

After coming to America, Theo had acted onstage with Marlon Brando. When I met him, he had been teaching sculpture in his basement studio at Horace Mann for decades. I spent hundreds of hours in that dank space while Theo, a scratchy classical record playing in the background, expounded on what it meant to create a masterpiece, all while scraping away at a block of stone. "You have an image in your head, my boy, of the perfect statue, of a life well lived, but the reality can never match the mercurial vision you have in your head." After school, he grappled with the wrestling team and played tennis, often barefoot, on the courts at Four Acres, overlooking the campus.

My one regret about being a baseball player was that the season coincided with Alan Breckenridge's Searchers program. I watched with envy as students spent months preparing for their solo expeditions, where they were dropped for three days to forage for their own food and water in a remote section of Vermont. You'd see them swimming two lengths of the pool underwater and rappelling up and down the walls of Gross Hall, HM's cafeteria building. I'm sure it built character; one graduate, Beth Kissileff (HM '85), recalled "72 hours to think about who I was and where I was going at this pivotal time," armed only with matches and a Bible. One boy caught and ate a squirrel, or so he claimed.

"Why are you walking around looking like you're going to a fight?" my new friend Matt asked me one day. "No one here is looking to kick your ass." It was true, I had to admit; my new peers were more interested in debating each other after class, exchanging witty repartee in the cafeteria, and trading bons mots with teachers and coaches both in and out of class. I wasn't prepared for that; the idea that teachers and students could have an egalitarian relationship may have been a by-product of the 1970s, but nowhere had I seen it in such sharp relief. Soon I began to learn there was another side to that familiarity.

It was Matt who first told me that there were certain teachers I should try to avoid.

"What, like hard graders?" I said.

"No," he said, "like pervs. Stay away from them."

I didn't think much of his admonition then. I had heard about some teachers, like Joe Klein, the driver's ed instructor, who supposedly had a habit of groping female students, and others who had their eyes on the boys. I had heard the same rumors as everyone else—that Mark Wright had left the school the year before under mysterious circumstances. I was warned to avoid Kops, who had some unusual pedagogical methods, and to steer clear of Bill Clinton (not *the* Bill Clinton), the pasty dean of guidance, who seemed to know the most intimate details of what transpired at weekend parties he hadn't attended. Even Inky came in for some snickering: he had no family of his own, and he had a noticeably closer-than-average relationship to Kops, another "confirmed bachelor." (One student swore she had rung Inky's bell once, to be greeted by the headmaster and Kops clad only in towels.)

But like a medieval sailor confronting a map with certain areas marked "Here be monsters," I was more interested in wending my way home and tending the fast friendships I had made with boys like Matt.

Tough and tender tutors like Theo were the embodiment of the seemingly contradictory style of the school. "Iron" Mike Lacopo, a no-nonsense ex-Marine, imparted a love of Shelley and Keats that I carried into my college studies.

But my favorite English teacher probably remained Bruce Weber, the man who introduced me to *The Great Gatsby*. He was an amiable curmudgeon with a wry smile, born with three fingers on his right hand. And while he taught Fitzgerald's great book to all his sophomores, I like to think he knew it held special significance for me. An outsider in paradise, I was as agog in the face of conspicuous wealth as Nick was ogling Gatsby's estate.

"Mr. Kamil, what's Fitzgerald driving at in this scene?"

"You mean, like what's it about?"

"We can certainly start there."

"Um, it's about life."

"Can you please be a little more vague?"

Weber's Socratic, if at times sarcastic, methods made me feel as though he and I shared a little joke about the new world in which I'd just landed. Like Nick, I was invited to lavish parties in places I could not have imagined just a few months earlier. My new friends and I devised a system to make the seemingly endless string of sweet sixteens more affordable. Together we'd enter some of New York's finest restaurants, hotels, and clubs armed with Bic pens and make a beeline for the gift table groaning with lavishly wrapped presents. As the others stood guard we'd take turns signing our names to various cards. Later we'd delight in the cafeteria when the sweet sixteen's tongue-in-cheek thank-you note included something along the lines of "Thanks, Amos, for the diamond earrings. I never knew you were so friendly with my Uncle Elliot and Aunt Judy."

Beyond Theo and Weber, there were other teachers, even more beloved, who were legends on campus. Though I never had classes with them, their reputations loomed large, their quirky behavior defining what made Horace Mann unique.

Tek Young Lin was a small, almost delicate physical presence, with a light, deft sense of humor (one admiring former student calls him "a sprite") and a deep love of language. His students remember his absolute passion for grammar, the cherry trees he planted all over the Horace Mann campus (carefully selected from different strains, so they didn't all bloom at the same time), and his classroom, unlike any other in the school.

Located on the top floor of Tillinghast Hall, Lin's room was not large to begin with, and he filled it with tall potted palms, their fronds flopping over students' heads and drooping down toward their book bags. Some years he accessorized that blackboard jungle with a fairly large lizard that would stalk its way around the branches and occasionally topple onto a desk with a thud.

Dressed simply, in a collared shirt and slacks, with rubber-soled canvas shoes, Lin addressed the class from a swivel stool, on which he often perched with crossed legs. From there he loved to tell the story of Rollo, his imaginary friend who collected holes and placed them just behind his ear for safekeeping:

What I want to do is to whimsy you into collecting holes. Impossible? Not a bit. You, too, can collect holes. I still do. Occasionally, I am embarrassed by a contretemps. One day, having duly forgotten that I had already pocketed a hole, I subsequently poured in a whole new collection of holes, which naturally fell through the original hole.

Suppose I give a workshop in collecting holes? Will you come? No money-back guarantee. Some of you may not be disposed toward collecting holes, but it's fun trying.

A Buddhist and a runner, Lin coached the boys' cross-country team as well as teaching literature and writing. He also served for some years as the school's chaplain. In those varied capacities he attracted a large and devoted following of grateful students. Many of them stayed in touch with him after graduation, even visiting him when he retired and moved to California. On a Facebook page called Fans of Tek Young Lin (where the hole collector story was preserved until the page was taken down), they talked about their admiration for his intellectual gifts, their gratitude for what he taught them, and their fond recollection of his eccentric tales. Their comments suggest a feeling of gentle protectiveness toward him. One was even making a documentary about him.

Then there was Johannes Somary, the beloved Swiss music teacher. His favored students were familiar with him in ways exceptional even then. They babysat his kids, accompanied him on choral trips to other states, and were encouraged to call him "Hannes." To me he seemed almost a caricature—the brilliant conductor with wild hair and Continental mannerisms. Not being a music student, I was perhaps impervious to his charms. My only encounter with him occurred when I was in the teachers' lunchroom, a guest of Theo's. Theo was in the midst of lecturing me about some classic thing or another when Somary placed his cafeteria tray on the table between us, inserting himself into the conversation. After a few moments, apropos of nothing, he interrupted Theo's monologue to say, in his thick Swiss accent, "If you don't have class, I'm afraid you don't have much of anything. Class is the most important asset one can have."

I was underwhelmed.

My junior year, Crawford Blagden joined the English faculty. Blagden defined himself in contrast to Horace Mann. Room Ten, on the first floor of Tillinghast Hall, was filled with old slouchy couches instead of neat rows of chairs. He wore flannel shirts and jeans and work boots instead of jackets and ties. And he groused openly about the school's overprivileged students, mocking them for their fancy cars and shallow interests.

He himself was deep, he let you know: a poet (unappreciated), a pipe smoker (in class), a lover of music (which he often played on a phonograph—Ry Cooder was one of his favorite musicians). And he insisted that his students be deep, too. He had them keep journals, but not just about their reading. He pushed them to open themselves up in those pages, to talk about what they were *really* feeling, about hardships in their lives and families, about their inner selves. By senior year I'd pulled Blagden out of more than one bar and deposited him into the basement apartment he rented about a half block from the baseball field where I'd first laid eyes on Inky.

Rumors about teachers' strange behavior swirled ceaselessly around the campus. We would speak openly about Inky's drinking and his love for Kops, about how Somary liked boys, about that female teacher who would pick a male football player each year to have sex with.

The eccentricities of teachers like Somary, Kops, and Tek Lin weren't just tolerated: they were celebrated. The cult of personality that surrounded some of our best teachers was a large part of the appeal of a Horace Mann education. These teachers were not merely characters—they possessed specialized knowledge, had highly refined tastes, and with their Ivy League degrees and connections, they held the golden keys to our future.

And with the promise of the Ivies followed by a successful career of our choosing at the upper echelons of finance, law, or media, we did as we were told. Either because our parents paid good money for us to do so or, like me, we felt privileged just to be able to breathe the same rarefied air as the intellectual giants who were our teachers. This, after all, was Horace Mann.

•

Through it all was Inky, my personal savior and the man who wore the big hat at this particular circus.

Even before I took a class with Inky I would drop by his office, its walls lined with pictures of his favorite baseball players, put my feet up on his desk, and kibitz about everything from my classes to the state of the Lions. He was not just a coach; baseball was an obsession with him, as it was with me. If our victories were legendary, in our minds at least, our few losses were like wounds that neither of us could keep from picking at.

I recall those years at Horace Mann as being sunny and filled with the kind of laughter that made my sides hurt; it is only in retrospect that the shadows lengthen. Life was easier then, in every sense. I gathered proudly with my classmates in the auditorium and sang with more gusto than comprehension the words to our school's alma mater:

> *We were strangers met in friendship, now we're kin to one and all*
> *Who have passed their youth 'neath the guiding hand . . . of our Noble Horace Mann . . .*
> *Great is the truth and it prevails; Mighty the youth the morrow hails.*
> *Lives come and go; stars cease to glow; but great is the truth and it prevails.*

3

OUT OF THE PAST

Jerry Sandusky was everywhere. It was 2011, nearly twenty years since we'd traded stories of Horace Mann around the campfire in the Sierras, and suddenly the Penn State assistant coach was looking out at me from every newspaper and magazine, shielding his eyes on every TV screen. The Sandusky trial wouldn't begin for months, but the evidence was already mounting in the press. After a grand jury investigation, the seemingly lovable doofus had been charged with fifty-two counts of child sexual abuse. Most of his victims he found through the Second Mile, a charity he founded for at-risk youth in his native Pennsylvania. The stories were appalling—and consistent: grown men spoke of having been groomed by the coach when they were kids, of being taken on special trips and being given gifts before Sandusky tried to get them into the shower, or asked them to touch his erect penis. The combination of the horrific stories and the happy-go-lucky man accused of being a rapist—a rapist charged with the task of taking care of defenseless children— was deeply disturbing. And it made me think of Horace Mann.

Child sexual abuse had been much in the news before then, of course, most notably in the Catholic Church scandals that seemed to reach a boiling point in 2002. That year, *The Boston Globe* ran an extraordinary series investigating the Boston Diocese, which later admitted to having moved dozens of predatory priests from parish to parish after they'd molested young boys. As hundreds of men (and some women) found the courage to come forward and recount their suffering, the district attorney's office began its own investigation. Church members organized protests, and even clergy members began to call for the ouster of Cardinal Bernard Law. After more evidence of a church cover-up emerged, including decades of "passing the trash" (as it's called when a known predator is moved from one parish or school to another), Pope John Paul II accepted Law's resignation on December 13, 2002.

It was an extraordinary event with enormous implications. *The New York Times* reported the same year that more than twelve hundred priests had been accused of abuse in the United States alone, and similar scandals were erupting in churches around the world, culminating in the resignation of bishops in Argentina, Ireland, Germany, and Canada. The *Globe* won a Pulitzer Prize for its reporting, and the nation was riveted by the sight of grown men, many in their forties and fifties, weeping at the memory of the torment they had endured. The aftershocks are being felt to this day. In 2014, a UN committee grilled representatives of the Vatican over its handling of pedophile priests, and Pope Francis met with victims of sexual abuse, sounding (according to one witness) "like a sinner in confession."

I was aware of the story when it was breaking but had not paid that much attention: I'm not Catholic, and the doings of the church had always been a mystery to me, shrouded in incense, inasmuch as I thought of them at all. But the Sandusky story resonated. Maybe it was the revered school with its emphasis on sports that rang a bell, or the revelation that the abuse had gone on for so long and so little had been done to prevent it.

The pretrial coverage of Sandusky convulsed the nation: Many college football fans worshiped Penn State and Sandusky's boss, Joe Paterno; they accused the accusers and, of course, the media of sensationalizing the case. (Sandusky himself didn't help matters when he did a phone interview with Bob Costas. When the NBC reporter asked him if he was sexually attracted to young boys, he didn't deny it. He said he "horsed around with kids" and "showered after work-outs; I have touched their legs.") Then came the graphic testimony at the trial itself and the ensuing debate about the school's responsibility to stop Sandusky (there had been many complaints over the years) and the damage its complicity did to its reputation. Who was at fault? was a question that hung over the proceedings, even after Sandusky was sentenced to thirty to sixty years in prison. And what could the school have done differently?

I couldn't help thinking: Hadn't we at Horace Mann lived through something similar? What if the stories I'd heard around the campfire twenty years before were only a small sampling of a much larger problem? Although we'd unearthed examples of inappropriate behavior that night, we had not pursued the conversation much since then. But now my mind raced. Like Sandusky, Mark Wright had left the school and the football program under mysterious circumstances. There were rumors everywhere back then about him and a handful of other teachers. Were all the rumors that swirled around the cafeteria true? Why had Stan Kops been let go after some incident up at John Dorr? Did his suicide a few years later have any relation to his firing? Was Tek Lin, the English teacher and would-be guru, as saintly as he seemed?

I called Andrew, whose confession at the campfire still rang in my ears, and asked him how he was doing. We spoke less frequently than we had as young men; time, distance, career, and family had simply put too much space in between us. It wasn't as if either of us—or anyone on that trip—had ever forgotten what was revealed that night, but it wasn't a subject that came up naturally when we did catch up.

But Sandusky brought it all back. Andrew was thinking about Horace Mann, too—about his own experiences and those of his class-mates. And about Mark Wright.

"I'm not doing too well, Mousey," he told me. "This whole Penn State thing is really fucking me up." We talked for about an hour about Wright and the similarities we saw between his story and what was coming to light about Sandusky.

"I just wish someone would write about Horace Mann," he said. "They could call it 'Horace Mann Horror Story.'" It wasn't clear if he meant it as a joke.

The next day I found myself on the train headed for Washington, D.C. I took out my laptop, opened a new blank document, and typed "Horace Mann Horror Story" at the top of the page. I wrote and wrote and wrote on the three-hour ride, pausing only to save my work. By the time the train pulled into Union Station, I had written twenty-seven pages based on my own recollections, time-ravaged rumors, half-remembered innuendos, and a handful of harrowing stories I had heard firsthand.

I emailed my first draft to Andrew and two other Horace Mann friends. Andrew was thankful and said that I should try to get it published. Paul, taking issue with my characterization of the murky night at Inky's mansion, angrily said, "This isn't your story to tell. It's interesting, but it didn't happen to you." Ariel Kaminer, another HM graduate, was an editor at *The New York Times Magazine*. Before I knew it, I was sitting in front of Ariel and the magazine's editor Hugo Lindgren. He loved the idea of the piece but said that I'd need to do a whole lot of reporting and fact-checking before they could even think about publishing it.

The afternoon I got the assignment from the *Times*, I ran into Bruce Weber, my tenth-grade English teacher, in the paper's cafeteria. Bruce had been working for the paper since the 1980s and I had gotten used to seeing his byline. He greeted me warmly and asked what I was up to.

"I'm working on something not unrelated to Penn State and Horace Mann," I said.

"You mean Inky, Kops, and Mark Wright," he said, as though decades hadn't passed. It was more of a statement than a question.

So it was true. Here was a teacher who knew exactly the same rumors I'd heard. That didn't make the rumors true, of course, but it meant the stories had circulated among the teachers as well.

I started by interviewing Andrew in more depth about Mark Wright. In many ways, Wright was the ultimate Horace Mann success story. People remember him as tall and extroverted, with an easy smile and a huge laugh. He graduated in 1972, a time when African American students like him were a rarity, then went to Princeton, where he majored in art and archaeology and played right tackle for the football team. A glowing article in *The Daily Princetonian* described him as "a Picasso in cleats" and speculated on whether he could have gone pro or would get a Ph.D. "I think Mark lives life to the fullest," the head of his department told the paper, noting that he "exudes enthusiasm and versatility." After college, he came back to Horace Mann to teach art and to coach football.

"I first had him as an art teacher," Andrew told me, in the steadied voice of someone who had worked through the story in therapy. "He was a great guy. Funny, gregarious, everyone loved him. He had this aura of success around him, and I was so happy that someone like him would take an interest in a skinny underclassman like me. I felt special.

"One night he called my house and asked my parents if he could take me to the museum," Andrew continued. "My parents were so excited that a teacher would take such an interest in me." And this being Horace Mann, he added, "it didn't hurt that he had also gone to Princeton." Still, Andrew didn't feel comfortable hanging out with a teacher on the weekend, so he turned down the invitation. A little later Wright had another idea: he asked to draw a portrait of Andrew.

"It was the night of the eighth-grade dance," Andrew told me, "and instead of going to the gym, I went to meet him in his art studio on the fourth floor of Tillinghast. He locked the door and told me to undress." As he got to this part of the story, Andrew's pace slowed and his voice lowered.

"He'd told me to bring a bathing suit, but when I got there he said not to bother putting it on. I was really uncomfortable but did it anyway since he was across the room. I remember exactly what he said: that he needed to see the connection between my legs. The next thing I knew, he had my penis in his hand. I was so scared. He was a pretty intimidating guy. He began performing fellatio and masturbating," Andrew said, now breathing with effort.

"I left the room and walked to where the dance was. I saw all these kids doing normal eighth-grade things. I tried being present at that party, but I was horrified." Afterward, Andrew said, "it was really hard being at Horace Mann, knowing that if I ran into him, he would get up really close to me and say stuff like: 'What's wrong, little buddy? You're not still mad about that time, are you?'"

I began calling around. I started with my inner circle of friends and ex-teammates and slowly expanded, reaching out to every HM alum I could think of who might want to talk.

My phone work quickly led me to G. "You should ask him," his high school girlfriend told me. "I bet he knows something."

I knew G. from the rocky Little League fields of Riverdale, where he had been a formidable lefty catcher. A burly kid with piercing blue, almond-shaped eyes, he was a tough guy and an intellectual and had gone through a dark period when we were juniors and seniors. I remember him then as angry, distant, and hyperintellectual—the type of kid who read Strindberg, listened to the Dead Kennedys, and smoked enough pot to numb his adolescent pain. A punk rock kid heading for the Ivies. Today G. is a lawyer, married with children, and though he and I had never been particularly close and despite the thirty years that had passed, he immediately took my call.

I told him what I was doing and asked him what, if anything, he knew about Mark Wright. There were a few minutes of exchange before the phone went silent. Then he said, "I'm about to tell you something I haven't even told my wife." He proceeded to describe in graphic detail how Wright "examined" him in a windowless training room that I'd heard others talk about. "I was fourteen and recovering from a football injury," he said, in an almost jocular tone, "when Wright used the purported physical exam to try to engage me in a sexual encounter by touching my penis. Although nothing further happened, I was speechless, and I never said anything to anyone. I don't think he looked me in the face when he was doing what he did, and I certainly didn't look him in the face either."

G. spoke in an even tone as he told me he never felt like a victim. We began tossing around the names of some of the other kids Wright might have "examined." When we hit upon T., a kid in our class widely rumored to have been abused by Wright, G.'s voice suddenly cracked. "I wish I had told someone what happened to me. Then he wouldn't have been able to do it to other kids."

"We were just kids," I offered lamely. But G. was now openly weeping into the phone.

I was struck by the similar approach Wright took to both Andrew and G.: find a vulnerable kid, befriend him, gain his trust and that of his parents, then strike.

"The whole goal of the grooming process is to wrap the child close," Paul Mones, an Oregon-based lawyer who has been representing victims of sexual abuse for more than twenty years, told me. "The affection and trust is to make the kid complicit in the act. Make them feel like it was their fault, so it won't even occur to them to talk."

Wright seemed to fit Mones's description of a classic groomer. He wasn't some monster lurking out there in the darkness. He was affable, popular, and garrulous. Almost all the victims described his magnetism and how they felt honored that an older man, a guy who had tried out for the Washington Redskins, no less, would take an interest in them. Wright hid in plain sight, often enlisting parents as part of the elaborate smoke screen that normalized his seemingly endless encounters with young boys. The victims' silence also ensured Wright could keep pursuing other victims. Until I introduced them, with their mutual consent, Andrew and G. had not known for a fact that the other had also been abused by Wright. Although they had certainly known each other while at HM, and had heard the rumors about Wright's victims like the rest of us, they could not be certain who else had been victimized and which rumors were true.

I learned that in the winter of 1978, one of Wright's examination subjects, a football player, spoke up. "I reported that Coach Wright was performing limited but inappropriate physicals on team players," the former student told me, "and that I was concerned that he was going to do so on others. The contact was very limited, to about thirty seconds. It was a 'private-parts inspection.'"

Ron Lombardi, HM's aptly named football coach, confirmed that the student had complained and that Lombardi himself had brought the matter to his boss, Chet Slaybaugh Sr., head of the athletic department. According to Lombardi, Slaybaugh brought the issue to Inky. When some time had passed and Wright was still on campus, Lombardi marched back into Slaybaugh's office and demanded that Wright be terminated. "If I see that creep on campus when we get back from winter vacation, the shit's gonna hit the fan," Lombardi threatened.

When students and faculty returned to campus after the 1978–1979 winter break, Wright was gone. One teacher remembers being told he resigned, but no one I spoke to recalled being told why.

Wright's victims might have appreciated the opportunity to talk about their experiences—if not with school officials, then with counselors or psychotherapists. Students in general might have welcomed an explanation, however limited, of why a teacher whom so many looked up to simply disappeared from their lives. And the entire school might have benefited from a more open discussion of student-teacher boundaries, the danger of abuse and the right to resist it, how to report it, and how the school would respond. But several faculty members of that era said that, to their knowledge, the school said nothing—not to the students, not to their families, and not to the police.

After Horace Mann, Wright lived for a while in Washington, D.C., and worked at TIAA-CREF, the financial services organization. Then the trail grows faint. His Horace Mann classmates didn't keep up with him after college, and of the dozens of Princeton classmates I contacted, none had any information to share. Wright died in 2004 while living in a bayside condo in the South Beach section of Miami Beach. The cause of death was never announced.

As more people spoke up, the more I marveled at Wright's relentless pursuit of boys. He was seemingly everywhere. Sleeping over at students' houses, taking others to the movies, examining them in dark basements, drawing them into closed art studios, approaching them in the library, showing up in empty hallways and pinning them up against their lockers. Had no grown-up on the tiny campus noticed this behavior? It didn't seem plausible that the students all spoke about it and the teachers didn't.

When I met Bruce Weber again a few weeks later to ask for a list of people I might talk to, he softened my assumption that "all the teachers knew"; he'd certainly heard some of the same rumors but had no direct knowledge.

"You have to remember I was only twenty-four at the time," he said. "I wasn't exactly in the inner circle." He then stopped and looked at me with tears rimming his eyes. "How are the guys?" he asked.

"Some of them aren't doing so great," I said. "It was pretty bad, Bruce."

Stan Kops, like Wright, was another alumnus who went to Princeton before returning to HM's classrooms. He was a popular eighth-grade history teacher and coached the JV swim team. Stories about "the Bear," almost universally told in the forgiving, eyebrows-arched tones reserved for the oddball uncle or kooky neighbor, floated freely through the cafeteria.

The stocky, awkward Kops also had unusual disciplinary methods. Rob Boynton was a blond-haired, blue-eyed "typical HMer" a year ahead of me. He recalled an incident in which Kops punished a boy for misbehaving in class by forcing him to take his shirt off and stand by an open window in the middle of winter. There were other stories: when students didn't answer Kops's questions quickly enough, he would put them in a headlock or playfully twist an arm. The objects of his attention were all the same—male, athletic, and handsome.

Another former student, who asked not to be named because his child currently attends the school, said, "Mr. Kops would occasionally cancel class in favor of something called 'frolic.' Basically, he would allow kids to run amok in the classroom and kind of joined in the action. I was new in seventh grade and remember thinking that this was a different kind of school where a teacher was physically 'handling' me. I can remember him being kind of red and breathless after a particularly vigorous frolicking."

Alan Ampolsk (HM '78), a former student of Kops's who was never subjected to any abuse from him, and remembered him primarily as a good teacher, said, "I also remember him as a bizarre, clearly damaged person who did borderline abusive things in public." Writing in response to my reporting, Alan continued, "I do remember the time he used a classmate of mine to demonstrate how the classic asphyxiation method of crucifixion worked. This went a little far, and I remember him saying to the student in a worried way, 'Are you all right? Put your head down on the desk . . .'"

It was in the context of Kops's coaching the swim team that I came into contact with his long, creepy touches—always accompanied by pointers about stroke or form. His postpractice entrance would clear the steamy communal shower room in a hurry. But Kops had been nothing but nice to me. Or had he?

When I was a senior, a family emergency took my mother abroad for several weeks, and my siblings and I were left to take care of ourselves. It was then that Inky Clark invited me and my twelve-year-old brother Dan out for dinner, and I brought along my friend Paul. On the designated night, we walked up the steps to the headmaster's house, where Inky greeted us at the door. Photos of Horace Mann athletes—mine included—lined the walls of the foyer, as they did the walls of his office. In the living room, by the fire, sat the Bear—nursing a cocktail.

"Can I offer you boys a drink?" Inky called out from behind the bar. This certainly didn't happen every day, but the suggestion didn't sound so jarring in 1982, when the state drinking age was in the process of being changed from eighteen to nineteen. Like any self-respecting seventeen-year-olds, Paul and I said sure, as we all kidded my little brother about being left out of the fun. Gin and tonics were poured, consumed, and refilled. Talk loosened up. Still, something about sharing fireside cocktails with Stan Kops was making me uncomfortable.

At one point in the evening, making some point I can no longer remember, Kops left his hand on my shoulder for a nanosecond too long. I still had enough of the old Bronx in me to shrug his hand off and pointedly asked Inky, "Coach, where are we eating?"

Boys in one vehicle, teachers in another, we swerved to the Riverdale Steak House. As Paul climbed out from behind the wheel of his blue van, he muttered a line that we still repeat to this day: "I'm not taking any shit from the Bear." Then we stumbled into the restaurant, where we consumed steaks and many more gin and tonics. When we'd had our fill, we uttered some prearranged exit line, thanked our hosts, grabbed my brother, and drove off drunk into the night, leaving the two grown men to pay the bill and finish out the evening as they might.

Despite all of Kops's idiosyncrasies, many of his students—boys and girls, athletes and not—were as devoted to him as he was to them. He made students feel that he cared deeply about their education and their well-being. In return, a pretty sophisticated student body and a lenient faculty chose to view his behavior as merely odd, when in many other contexts it would have been deemed outrageous or even threatening.

All that changed in the fall of 1983 with an incident at the John Dorr Nature Laboratory. Kops accompanied one of the seventh-grade orientation trips that year and slept, as visiting faculty often did, in a cabin with the students. At some point in the night, one of the boys, whom I'll call by his middle name, Seth, woke up.

"I was on the top bunk," Seth recalled matter-of-factly when we spoke on the phone. "Middle of the night, my sleeping bag fell to the floor. I climbed down to get it, and as I bent over to pick it up, Kops came up from behind me and pressed up against me. It was pitch-black. He then helped me to pick up the sleeping bag even though I didn't need any help." They were fully clothed, he said, and he didn't feel assaulted, just uncomfortable. "I probably wouldn't have said anything except for what happened the next morning."

After breakfast, Seth told me, as the group assembled for activities, Kops took him aside behind a building, grabbed his own crotch, and asked, "What were you doing last night?" Seth says he was in shock. "I freaked," he said. "I started screaming, 'You're calling me a homo? You're the homo. You're the homo!'" Listening to Seth, I wondered if that was really what Kops was getting at—perhaps he was making a crude masturbation joke? But more to the point, I wondered if, from Kops's peculiar perspective, that bizarre encounter with a twelve-year-old looked all that different from twisting students' arms or making them partly undress in full view of the class.

Seth said he was unsure of what happened next, but according to the story that circulated around campus, he took off running, screaming something about Kops. Seth says his father, an active parent in the Horace Mann community, demanded the school take immediate action.

After the incident, Kops was forced to resign from HM, where he had spent the better part of his life as a student and a teacher. One student called what happened at Dorr Horace Mann's *Rashomon*—everyone seemed to have a different theory or story or reasonable explanation for how and why Kops was fired.

Michael Lacopo, who was the headmaster at the time (Clark had been promoted to president), is now retired and living in Colorado. When I reached Lacopo, he told me that he could not discuss any case by name but that he presided over only one such allegation. Speaking in clipped sentences, he gave me a very limited report. "The act was never consummated, but it was an issue of concern, and it became clear it was time for him to move on. And he didn't deny it. And the kid's parents were satisfied," he said. "Everyone knew where I stood on the matter."

Horace Mann says faculty members received a letter about Kops's resignation, but Lacopo made no announcement to his students, their parents, or the student body in general.

Kops called some of his favorite students at home and asked them to meet him at school the next day for an announcement. One was Kate Aurthur, who'd taken his ancient history course the previous year. When they assembled, she said, he told them he was leaving. "He didn't say why he was leaving, and I didn't know why yet," she said. Regardless, the news came as a shock. "It was very emotional. He always had a red face and a soft voice, but he got redder than usual and choked up."

Alan Ampolsk was the only alum I heard from who recalled seeing Kops after he left Horace Mann. "In October 1983," he wrote, "after I'd graduated from college and just a few weeks after the *Horace Mann Record* article [about Kops leaving HM] ran—I was walking west on 12th Street from the Strand bookstore to catch the West Side IRT home. I looked up and there was Kops, walking toward me, coming from the opposite direction . . . He crossed the sidewalk to greet me and launched into a conversation—wanted to know how I was, what I'd been doing, and so on. I asked him how he was doing, and he said, with way more than even his usual degree of heavy solemnity, 'Well, I'm no longer at Horace Mann. And I've been seeing a therapist and trying to put the shattered pieces of my life back together.'"

The next time students heard anything about Stan Kops, it was at the end of the next school year, and the news was far more shocking: he had committed suicide. The rumors ran quickly through the Horace Mann student body. Some said that he shot himself in a car, with a Bible nearby. Others said he shot himself on a baseball field as some sort of coded message to Clark. The school, as usual, said nothing.

After Kops left Horace Mann, he landed at Rutgers Prep, a private school in Somerset, New Jersey, where he taught history while taking classes at New Brunswick Theological Seminary. A former Rutgers Prep official, who was involved in Kops's hiring but did not have permission to comment on it, said the school always checked applicants' references. "No one from Horace Mann said anything that indicated Stan would be anything other than a safe bet at Rutgers," that official said. "Rutgers had no idea about any potential allegations of sexual impropriety against Stan at HM. If they had, they never would have hired him."

Kops finished the year without incident, the Rutgers Prep official said, but because "he had strange teaching habits" his contract was not renewed.

Shortly after the school year ended at Rutgers Prep, Kops drove across the Raritan River to Piscataway and shot himself—not standing on a baseball diamond but sitting in his car, the police told the school administrator. Today Stan Kops's name appears on the honor roll of the Tillinghast Society, which recognizes alumni who made provisions for Horace Mann in their wills.

If Kops was the awkward bit player lurking on the periphery of student life, Johannes Somary, the legendary head of the arts department, was the larger-than-life star of the show. Somary, with his thick Swiss-Austrian accent, wild hair, and mad eyes, always seemed to be followed by a gaggle of well-heeled students—the music theater crowd.

They were perfectly nice boys and girls who seemed cut from an entirely different, more expensive, cloth than me. Guys like Andrew Solomon, a skinny, bespectacled intellectual who seemed a polar opposite of the kids I'd known at 141. He was picked on for his looks, his manner, even his walk, and teachers like Somary were a godsend. "The music teacher awarded me concert solos," he recalled, "let me call him by his first name and hang out in his office, and led the Glee Club trips that were among my happiest adventures." Solomon wore bow ties and spoke with a slight British stage accent. I didn't like or dislike Andrew. I feared him. His wealth, his intellect, and his fancy Manhattan address. He made jokes I didn't have the background or sophistication to understand.

Or Rob Boynton, the blond-haired boy who remembered Kops's strange discipline methods after all these years. Boynton was an HM lifer who grew up on the other side of Riverdale, farther north and closer to the river. He wore preppy clothes and always seemed to be smiling or shouting something witty across the baseball field to some teacher. He had a keen intellect and a quick wit. As president of the Glee Club, he could probably identify the signature atonalities of the Pulitzer Prize–winning composer and HM alumnus Elliott Carter. Mostly he could enunciate. I was more of a Springsteen guy.

These distinctions, it turned out, were mostly in my head and said more about my own insecurities than about anyone's social status. The truth is I had nothing to do with most of the students who surrounded Somary. And to the extent they knew I existed, they probably never thought much about how my parents paid my tuition. I never had a bad moment with Solomon or Boynton or anyone from the so-called theater crowd, not one. Some, like Solomon, came from wealthy families, and perhaps their fortunes, and the sense of belonging those fortunes implied, reinforced my insecure teenage suspicion that everyone save me came from unimaginable wealth.

Somary himself fit that picture. "He had a formidable arsenal for impressing students," recalled Edward Bowen (HM '74), when I met him for dinner. "He was fabulously wealthy, had priceless art on his wall, drove a shiny green Jaguar, and was a world-famous conductor."

The son of a famous Austrian-Swiss banker, Somary enjoyed a prominent international reputation and was celebrated for reviving lost choral works. He had guest-conducted numerous orchestras, including the Royal Philharmonic in London and the Vienna Philharmonic. The walls of Pforzheimer Hall at Horace Mann were lined with posters from his concerts.

"He was a hero to me," said Bowen. "But he was also a monster."

Bowen, the director of accounts receivable at the New York City Human Resources Administration, with thirty people reporting to him, struggled for years with alcohol and drugs. It was only after years of sobriety and therapy that he could admit to his therapist and himself that Somary had breached his trust when he began to sexually abuse him. In 2011, Bowen, writing under the pseudonym "Samuel Survivor," started a blog called *Johannes Somary, Pedophile*, on which he detailed his memories. "Though Mr. Somary brought the gift of music to many and had a long and celebrated career, he was also a molester of children," he wrote. "It took many years for me to remember the two instances of my molestation by him. Those events had a devastating impact on my life." He wondered if there were other victims and hoped his blog might encourage them to gather together. At first, he heard very little.

As Bowen recalls, Somary had slowly groomed him; the teacher befriended him, encouraged him to call him Hannes, talked to him about his sexual interests, and then hired him to babysit his children. It was at Somary's Riverdale home, where he lived with his wife, Anne, and their three children, on a fall night in 1973 that the teacher first abused the student. Bowen was sixteen at the time, and he grew agitated forty years later as he described how Somary sat next to him on the couch, unzipped his pants, and started handling his penis.

"I wasn't scared," says Bowen, "just stunned. The primary emotion was revulsion. I told him to stop and he did." But a few weeks later, Somary molested him again. "I was such a good victim," he told me, as the meal in front of him grew cold. "Shy, trusting, unsophisticated." Worse, Bowen's mother, Joan, a well-loved math teacher and administrator at Horace Mann, was a colleague of Somary's at the time he was abusing her son.

"There are so many of us," Bowen told me right before he rushed out the door to catch a symphony at Avery Fisher Hall. That, too, was part of Somary's legacy: introducing young people to the music that would stay with them all their lives.

Before he left, Bowen referred me to Joseph Cumming (HM '77), another victim of Somary's sexual attentions when he was at Horace Mann. When I reached him on the phone, he said, "I talked to Eddy Bowen. I know why you're calling, and everything you've heard is true." Joseph wanted to remain off-the-record but had already become an informal clearinghouse of information as more and more survivors started coming forward.

M. would speak to me only from a blocked number. His pseudonym is not the first initial of his first or last name; it is one letter in his middle name. He would call at midnight and frantically tell me his story until the wee hours of the morning. He called Somary "a manipulator par excellence"; after grooming him as he had Bowen, the teacher suggested one night they take a drive. They parked in a lot near a club where the two had often played tennis together.

"He then pulled me close to his chest," said M. "I'm thinking, *This is weird. Uncomfortable.* Then he starts kissing my lips. I'm thinking, *Oh, my God, this can't be happening.* I didn't know what to do. I was just a child. I didn't have the ego strength to say no. I was shocked, uncomfortable, but I let it persist. He unzipped my pants and started to masturbate me." M. was fifteen.

Somary took him on Glee Club trips, wined and dined him at a yacht club across the river in New Jersey, and brought him on excursions to Europe. "We stayed at the best hotels," M. recalled. "I met with the great classical musicians of the time and ate at the finest restaurants. I was expected to have sex with him and did, even though it repulsed me every time. It was all very confusing."

When Somary found out that M. no longer wanted to room with him, "he drove to my house and sat in my living room like a jilted lover, begging me to stay in the same room with him—right in front of my father!" M.'s mother, who later confirmed his account, said she and her husband didn't understand their son's discomfort. They thought he was just being a teenager, preferring the company of his peers. He couldn't bring himself to tell his parents the truth.

This arrangement continued for three years, even after M. left for college. "I don't know why I let it go on for so long; I've been asking myself that for decades." I would hear a lot about these kinds of confused feelings as I kept talking to people, and I came to appreciate how, as much as anything, perpetrators of child sexual abuse contaminate their victims' ability to love, to even understand what it means to love another person.

"Part of me thought I was in love," said M. of Somary. "Part of me still *is* in love with him."

The school's Glee Club trips were legendary. I heard about so much debauched behavior that I wondered what else anyone had seen. I got my answer from Holly Thomas (HM '80), who recalled,

"When I was a sophomore—on the Europe trip; England, France, Germany—we were in Heidelberg. I heard there was a party in the hotel, older kids were drinking and partying. I went upstairs and saw how drunk kids were. I went back downstairs and I saw one boy, very, very, very drunk. As I was coming downstairs, I heard Hannes. He was carrying the boy down and then I saw him trying to kiss him and the boy vomited on him. I held this in my whole life."

She told me of another girl on the trip who had seen the same thing, and said the two of them never spoke of it to anyone but each other. "On the same trip, there was a jazz band, which was a cool thing in that whole world," recalled Holly. "While we were on that trip to Europe we ended up in a group with Hannes. One of the members of the jazz band shut the door and said we all have to try hash before we can leave the room. Hannes was there, with a girl sitting on his lap, and was not protesting. Then the boy said, "No one is going to leave before you kiss Hannes." *Why is this kid doing this?* I remember thinking. He has now come out as a survivor. We kissed Hannes like you kiss your dad and then left fast."

In the early 1980s, Dr. Kathleen Howard joined Horace Mann. She was a popular, engaging science teacher, and both of her sons, Benjamin and Charles Balter, went to school there as well. In 1993, she learned that Ben had been sexually abused by Somary—twenty years after he had molested Ed Bowen.

The summer before Ben's senior year, he accompanied the Glee Club on a European tour. When he returned, his family said, something had changed. "He was always really smart," Charles told me. "He was a really nice guy but he was always a bit socially awkward—one of those kids who could perform at the highest levels of math and science but couldn't do the basic things like tie his shoes." After the trip, "he was withdrawn, angry and secretive." (The family was already in turmoil: Charles was in Nyack Hospital wearing a neck brace after a swimming accident, Ben had been in the process of coming out of the closet, and their parents had just split up. Although everyone was aware of Ben's unhappiness, there were too many possible causes for them to link it to his European trip.)

That fall, Ben took private music lessons from Somary at St. Jean Baptiste, a Catholic church on the Upper East Side of Manhattan. Kathy Howard asked if she could observe a lesson; impossible, said the maestro. Perhaps he knew she was preoccupied with her other son, Charles, who was in the hospital. For that fall he repeatedly abused Ben.

It was during that period that Ben's father found him hidden in a crawl space in their home, passed out after swallowing pills. He was admitted to Nyack Hospital, where his brother had recently been, and placed under a suicide watch.

The day after he was released Ben Balter wrote to Phil Foote, Horace Mann's headmaster. In a letter dated September 29, 1993, Ben accused Somary of "grossly inappropriate sexual advances." He outlined the abuse and pleaded with the school to do the right thing. "It is unfair to me and to other students to have such teachers in our midst," he wrote, "for they compromise not only the goals of the Horace Mann school, but also the integrity of education in general."

Foote brought the letter to the board, and "people came out of the woodwork to protect Somary," he recalled. Foote's tenure as headmaster lasted only three years. It was by all accounts a tumultuous period; he was an outsider, and some with knowledge of the school at the time suggested he had been brought in to clean things up. Since that time he had suffered a stroke, but he agreed to speak with me in his home on the Upper East Side. He was the first person to talk to me and was able to recall both the letter and the surrounding events. "Somary came into my office with the mother and strenuously denied everything. His vehemence made a lot of people put off doing anything about it." He later told me he didn't know why Ben Balter's mother "gave up so easily" in her quest to see Somary fired. "I always wondered why she didn't pursue it," he told me. "Maybe she just got defeated."

But Kathy Howard *had* tried to pursue the matter. She claims Michael D. Hess, chairman of the Horace Mann Board of Trustees, told her at the time that unless she had a videotape of the abuse, there was no proof and she should let the matter drop. Who was she compared with Hess, who in addition to being the chairman of HM's board was the corporation counsel for the City of New York and later a partner at Giuliani Partners? (It was while working at Giuliani Partners that Hess received a lot of press for defending Monsignor Alan Placa, "the pedophile priest," in his own sex abuse trial.) Hess was a seasoned veteran; in 1971, as chief of the Civil Division of the United States Attorney's Office, he had argued on behalf of the U.S. government against the publication of the Pentagon Papers. Those documents, which were being printed in *The New York Times* and *The Washington Post*, exposed America's war in Vietnam as a sham and a failure. When I spoke to Michael Hess, he told me he had no recollection of the incident, or of any incident involving Somary. He adamantly denied saying anything about a videotape.

I asked Phil Foote why he himself didn't try to remove Somary, or at least investigate the charges more thoroughly. Why didn't he go to the police? "The structure of HM was not easy," he said. "There were groups and groups within groups. It was a time with different values and different systems. You didn't have the access you do now. It was hubris. HM was sure it was above everybody else. Nobody wanted anything to change."

I was stunned. I now had an HM administrator on record saying that he and others knew of Somary's abuse, or at least had heard the accusations.

Later that year, overcome with rage and grief at her son's worsening depression, Kathy confronted her colleague Somary at school, pushing him against a locker. "How dare you stick your tongue down my son's throat!" she said, to which he spluttered, "That's how we Swiss kiss!"

Ben graduated from Horace Mann, meandered through Brown University, and went on with his troubled, drug-addled existence, until he finally took his own life in 2009.

I asked Foote if he knew what became of Ben. He said no, then paused to study my face. "He committed suicide?" he guessed, before I could say it. He turned away and, staring into the middle distance, said, "Oh, my Lord."

Ben's letter was addressed to Foote. But his mother said that she also spoke to Eileen Mullady, the head of the school immediately following Foote, to make sure she knew about her son's letter. I reached out to Mullady, as well as the former Horace Mann administrators Larry Weiss and Ellen Moceri; none responded to my questions. Neither did the Board of Trustees, the body responsible for those school officials. One former longtime member told me, "No one will talk to you. They are all lawyering up."

Somary continued to teach at Horace Mann until 2002, retiring after thirty-three years at sixty-seven to accolades and bouquets.

As I dug deeper into the Horace Mann story, I became convinced that these were not isolated incidents of abuse but a pattern of assault that had been covered up by the institution. How could so many incidents have occurred on a tiny campus with no more than six hundred students without the school being aware of them?

As I reached out to my ex-teammates and told them what I was discovering, they invariably asked if I'd heard anything negative about Inky. "We all assumed he was gay, Mouse," said Rich Smyth, another Riverdale player Inky recruited to play center for the Lions. "And he was a terrible alcoholic, but I don't think he was like that." I agreed and assured him that I'd not heard anything inappropriate about Inky and felt pretty sure that after nearly hundreds of interviews I probably never would.

But the more I learned, the more I kept thinking about Inky. Where was he in all this? (Where the hell were any of the grown-ups, for that matter?) Was he not on top of the staff that ran around the campus? Hadn't he hired Wright out of Princeton? Hadn't he mentored Wright when he was a teacher at HM? Were the rumors true that he and Somary had known each other at Yale? Was his alcoholism so advanced by that point that he simply didn't notice or care? I knew the power of Inky's denial firsthand. There was a chilling moment in my mother's living room about a year after I'd graduated from college. My mother had invited him over for lunch. Kops's recent suicide sat like a heavy, unaddressed presence in the room. So, yearning for a deeper connection, I took a swig of my drink and found the courage to say that I was sorry to hear about the death of his friend.

Inky looked at me with his watery blue eyes and slowly wiped his mouth. "Strangest thing, Mouse," he said, as though from far away. "I heard about Stan Kops, too." It was as if the two had never met.

When I had all I needed to know to write my piece, I sought a meeting with Tom Kelly, the school's current headmaster, and Steve Friedman, then the chairman of the board. I wrote letters to every single board member asking for their side of the story. I was met with silence and then referred to Douglas Kiker, HM's representative at Kekst and Company, a New York–based communications firm that specializes in crisis situations, to whom I submitted a long list of detailed questions: Why was Mark Wright fired? What complaints had the administration heard from students? At what points during his tenure did the administration address questions about Kops's teaching style? To what degree (and how) was the administration aware of or concerned about his drinking? Why were Somary's unorthodox travel arrangements permitted? How did the administration respond to complaints about his behavior? Were they investigated? Did the school at any point contact the police about any of these accusations?

Kiker sent me "a statement from Horace Mann School in response to your inquiry." In it he wrote, "As it relates to your specific questions it is the School's longstanding practice not to comment in any way on current or former students, members of the faculty or other employees." (Despite many attempts to speak to current Horace Mann board members, administrators, and teachers, this policy continued throughout the research and writing of this book.) A wall of silence that none shall scale.

Only one member of the board, a former baseball player who is now a partner at Goldman Sachs, answered my call, only to tell me he wouldn't speak to me because he was on the board. From January 2012 to June 6 I begged, along with the magazine's editor, for someone to speak with me.

After I submitted my questions to Kekst, Kelly showed Kathy Howard a copy of Ben's 1993 letter, which she had never seen. Kelly's timing was, to say the least, strange; the school was determined not to talk to me, and later claimed that all evidence relating to Somary's tenure had been destroyed in a fire, and now he was sharing a dead boy's letter of accusation with his mother?

They say stories are never finished, only abandoned. As my deadline approached, I had two major frustrations: Tek Lin and women. The teachers I named as perpetrators were by now all dead, and I felt it was important to get the perspective of a living one. But even though I knew about Tek Lin's improprieties from two different men, no one was willing to go on record to speak about his experiences with the beloved English teacher. I wasn't willing to out a survivor who wanted to remain in the shadows.

And although a number of men came forward to speak to me, no woman had shared her story by the time we went to press. Statistically women suffer more sexual abuse than men and are more likely to speak of it. I had tried to get women to talk with me and had certainly heard rumors of at least one teacher and his "special" girls. I didn't want my piece to be viewed as a sensational man-boy story— in our homophobic society, sexual abuse often gets conflated with homosexuality. I frantically reached out to two women but did not secure their testimony. Because of the absence of women in the original *Times* article, I was later called a homophobe; others called me a closeted homosexual.

The day I received the magazine assignment, Ariel Kaminer, who'd become my editor, walked me out of the Times Building. We paused at the subway entrance before she descended to catch her train. "You're brave to take this on," she said.

"Or just stupid," I replied. "I'm about to be slammed by some serious negativity."

"That's not what I meant," she said. "I'm not sure you're prepared for the tsunami that will ensue when you publish. Everyone who has been abused—not just at Horace Mann—is going to seek you out to tell you their story, too."

4

THE STORM UNLEASHED

I think you broke the Internet," said the editor of the *Times Magazine*'s comments section.

"Prep-School Predators" ran on the cover on June 10, 2012 (it was published online a few days before), but even before publication the story had been making waves. For months people in the school administration, while refusing to speak to me, were weighing their response and discussing the effects the negative press might have. Board members put their individual lawyers on alert to shield them from any possible fallout. Some parents had been suiting up for battle without having read the piece. (One HM mom called the wife of a regular contributor to the magazine and asked her if her husband could do anything to stop "this horrible story.") Upon publication, the piece received more than a thousand comments from readers, many of them Horace Mann alumni. The most painful were those from victims of abuse: some were coming to grips for the first time with what had happened to them.

"I was abused by Mark Wright as a seventh grader in 1978," posted one anonymous commenter. "It's funny but only now, reading all this material, did it occur to me that I could have reported him to anyone. As it was, I kept the incident to myself for nearly twenty years, not even telling my parents."

A former HM athlete from my era wrote to me privately that he thought he had been "Mark Wright's only little buddy." He has still to come forward publicly.

I received a phone call from J., who'd been one year ahead of me at HM and is today a Washington, D.C.–based political consultant. He was still close with Jodi Breckenridge and her family and had told Jodi that he hoped my article would never get published, as it would put the school in a negative light. He then told me that when my article did appear, he joked with Rob Boynton about not being good-looking enough for Wright to molest. He was no longer joking. Wright had, in fact, "examined" him. "I never didn't know it happened," he said by telephone as I paced around my backyard. "It was always there, but I was able to watch the priest thing on TV and distance myself from it. I would never dwell on it for more than a few seconds. And before this week I had never told a single person."

I received letters and emails from beyond Horace Mann. I heard allegations about other schools—the Landmark School in Beverly, Massachusetts; Yeshiva University High School for Boys in New York City; the Hackley School in Tarrytown, New York—and stories of sexual abuse from readers in Norway and Germany, California and Alaska. One thing I was learning quickly was that the stories of child sexual abuse were virtually identical, no matter what the culture. The victims were often the product of broken homes or neglectful parents; the perpetrators were trusted figures who tended to hide in plain sight, making themselves conspicuous in school life; and the process of solicitation had a nauseating familiarity, from small favors to little gifts to special outings. Although the bait might have been different— an athletic scholarship, a starring role in that year's play, or the threat of some perceived loss of prestige—the grooming was something like fishing. Find a promising fishing hole, sort through the larger catches, discard the ones who might cause trouble, ingratiate yourself, and strike.

Of course, intimate relationships between teachers and students date back a long time. The example of Socrates established a powerful ideal of how Eros and education can commingle. In a scholarly article on student-teacher relationships in academic medicine, Gregory Luke Larkin and Michael J. Mello note,

> Teachers have fraternized with their students since antiquity. Moreover, there are levels of attraction within academe that promote the learning process itself; students learn better from teachers they genuinely like. At Plato's *Academy* and later at Aristotle's *Lyceum*, young Greek men studied and recreated in close proximity to their masters. In the *Symposium*, Plato asserts a strong love between Socrates and his admiring male acolyte, Alcibiades. This love was deep, masculine, and sometimes seductive. The idea of a higher spiritual love in interpersonal human relations gave birth to the very notion of *platonic love*, a strong counterpoint to any rumors of *Eros* in the ancient Athenian Academy.

The Dutch classicist and translator Hein van Dolen notes that Plato depicted the teacher as

> in Plato's own words . . . boy crazy. When Socrates was in the company of beautiful boys, he lost his senses. Some sort of *mania* (divine madness) took possession of him and he was almost unable to resist it. He often complained about the fact that he was helpless towards adolescents, and said that he could only cope with the situation by asking difficult questions to these beautiful boys and teaching them philosophy. So, according to Plato, Socrates sublimated his passion.

(Another student, Xenophon, paints a similar portrait of Socrates. "He informs us that his master, when challenged by the presence of a good looking adolescent, remained capable of self-control, but took some measures," writes Van Dolen. "He did not allow the boy to embrace him, comparing his kisses to spider's bites. Sexuality and other physical contact between teacher and student were simply unacceptable.")

Of course, such passions did not always end in sublimation. The sexual abuse of male students at British preparatory schools is often taken for granted, as if it were a venerable tradition. "You had deference and the attitude that this sort of thing happens," said Alan Collins, a lawyer who represented a former student at Aldwickbury School, in a story in *The New York Times*. In Britain, as in the United States, teachers were often allowed to move on quietly (frequently to another job at another school) to avoid damaging the institution's reputation. "Sexual abuse is a taboo subject," Collins said. "People do not want to talk about it for the obvious reason that it's really gruesome, and in this country there has been a tendency or a temptation to sweep it under the carpet." In recent years, the taboo has weakened. Men who were molested as far back as the 1970s have brought legal action against their former teachers and their employers.

"Boys craved your attention and strove for your praise," the British judge Johannah Cutts said in sentencing Roland Peter Wright, a former headmaster at the prestigious Caldicott Preparatory School. "From those you picked out boys for your individual sexual attentions." Wright got eight years in prison; he was eighty-three years old.

Though Horace Mann is not a boarding school, it strives to be a closed environment where teachers wield considerable power and their force of personality is to be reckoned with. For a lot of young students seeking substitute parents or just a sense of being special, that kind of hermetically sealed world can be dangerous. Teachers like Somary knew how to exploit a student's wish for praise. "In my mind, Hannes was one of the great musicians of our time," recalled Joseph Cumming, one of Somary's victims. "At the time I thought it was generally understood that he was one of the top three choral conductors in America." As with many of the boys who would later accuse the maestro of molesting them, Joseph had been told that he had great talent, and he wanted to follow in his mentor's footsteps. "He was opening doors for me, introducing me to famous and influential musicians. That was very thrilling for me." Now he says he knows he was good, "but not that level of good. I should have realized it, but Hannes made me believe that."

In the realm of competitive athletics, young men and women literally put themselves in the hands of older coaches. In 2011, the former WBC world champion Sugar Ray Leonard made headlines when he revealed that he had been abused by "a prominent Olympic boxing coach" at the age of fifteen. A few years later, he wrote in his memoir *The Big Fight*, the same man fondled him as he explained how important a gold medal could be to Leonard's career. Since then, Leonard has offered himself as a "poster child" for victims of childhood sexual abuse and urged others to speak out and seek treatment.

In his 2012 autobiography *Wherever I Wind Up*, the major league pitcher R. A. Dickey describes how as an eight-year-old child he was abused by a thirteen-year-old female babysitter, and later by a teenage male. In the book, Dickey elaborates on his struggles with suicidal thoughts as an adult. That same year he set career personal season bests in games started (33), wins (20), completed games (5), shutouts (3), innings pitched (233⅔), strikeouts (230), ERA (2.73), walks plus hits divided by innings pitched (1.05), and batting average against (.226). He was named the year's National League Cy Young Award winner, becoming the first knuckleballer in MLB history to win the award.

Female athletes have come forward as well, notably Bridie Farrell, a former national speed-skating champion, who spoke out about her abuse at the hands of Andy Gabel, her teammate and trainer. Farrell, a former women's American record holder in the fifteen-hundred- and three-thousand-meter individual and three-thousand-meter relay competition, first revealed details about her sexual abuse when she stopped skating to enter Cornell University. Ever since, she has continued to discuss it publicly. Gabel went on to become the president of U.S. Speedskating, a position he resigned after Farrell and others came forward with stories of abuse. After a radio interview in which she identified Gabel, he publicly apologized in a newspaper story. In doing so, he ran no legal risk—the statute of limitations in New York had expired in 2005.

In the weeks after my article appeared, I heard from many who felt that I didn't go far enough and had been too selective.

At least one name kept coming up that I hadn't heard in my reporting. "That intellectually arrogant, shaven headed English teacher Robert Berman had his boys try and enroll me in his sex ring," a doctor wrote. "I was too ashamed to tell my parents who would have EXPLODED in fury and been in [HM headmaster] Dr. Gratwick's office the next day."

I received a call from "Gene," then in his fifties, who said he read my article with rage, anticipating he would see the name of his abuser in print. "I graduated from HM in 1973," he told me. "I was abused by an English teacher whose name did not appear in your article. I kept looking for the name Robert Berman and got angrier and angrier when his name didn't appear. For over thirty-five years I thought I was the only one he ever abused." Gene mentioned one other student he knew who had been abused by Berman. "Another committed suicide his first year in graduate school. Robert Berman is alive."

I had spoken to roughly one hundred people, and Berman's name simply did not come up. I vaguely remembered the rumors I'd heard about him as a student and had heard of his cult of personality, but no one I'd spoken to had accused him of anything. I learned later that some of the alumni who read the piece felt that there had to have been a kind of cover-up, or a threat of legal action from Berman.

Berman left Horace Mann the year before I arrived. The whispers about him came in two varieties. When HM was still an all-boys school, students were required to swim naked in the pool. According to one rumor, Berman would sneak into the pool's balcony to snap pictures. According to another, Berman stole into the boys' shower room to take his photos.

Everything about Berman gave the impression of control, from his physical appearance—shaved head, thick black-framed glasses, and dark suits—to the quiet, almost weary manner in which he addressed his students. He went out of his way to make it clear that his classroom was an environment with its own rules, where genius, as defined by the teacher himself, was paramount. Frost, Melville, Dostoyevsky, Freud, Leonardo, Michelangelo, Mozart, Bach, even Berman himself, were all in his pantheon of genius. You, a lowly Horace Mann English student, were not.

Some of the boys were mesmerized and, either to survive or out of genuine awe, lined up to achieve the one thing that was unachievable—impressing Berman. They would cast off the cultural detritus of sports and TV; they would imitate his strange way of speaking as they argued passionately about the nature of genius. A small group even began to dress like him, walking the campus in dark suits, thin ties, and shaved heads. Some of the other students derisively called them "Bermanites."

In his memoir, *The 13th Boy*, Stephen Fife (HM '71) writes of the way Berman lured his students by lowering them. "Your work is boring," Berman told Fife with disgust. "To write an interesting story, you have to start with an interesting subject. *Moby-Dick*, on the most basic level, is about the hunt for the greatest of Great White Whales. God looked down on it from heaven, and He approved."

In another encounter, Fife reports Berman telling a group of aspiring writing students, "You will not write anything worth reading for at least the next twenty years." When Fife pointed out that writers like Rimbaud, Fitzgerald, and Keats all did their best work before forty, Berman snapped, "Those writers are not your concern. They were geniuses. They're in a category all their own. Much better for you to put in the work now in the hope that you'll write something interesting in the distant future."

If genius was to be worshipped, pop culture was to be loathed. Berman would call students "fools" and "peons" if they expressed the slightest interest in the latest rock band or, worse, in girls. "If the Second Coming were being broadcast on television," he bragged, "I still wouldn't watch."

After talking to some of his fellow classmates, Marc Fisher (HM '76), now an editor at *The Washington Post*, approached his former college roommate David Remnick, the editor of *The New Yorker*, who assigned him a profile of Berman.

Fisher had graduated from Horace Mann before I arrived. "My class," he wrote in *The New Yorker*, "was the last to exclude girls, and, inside the ivy-covered stone and brick buildings, the social up-heavals of the seventies were wearing away some of Horace Mann's British-boarding-school trappings." They still called their teachers "Sir," and the teachers referred to the boys as "Mr.," but the dress code was vanishing and the peculiarity of each individual instructor was only more pronounced. The custom of having teachers deeply in-volved in a boy's life was entrenched and well beyond suspicion.

"This is what private schools sell," said Fisher in an interview, "a level of intimacy and teacher involvement in the lives of the kids that in a healthy fashion can be inspiring and life-changing but that can fairly easily cross the line." Fisher was assigned to Berman's tenth-grade English class and described the first day's session in his story:

> We waited in silence as he sat at his desk, chain-smoking Benson & Hedges cigarettes and watching us from behind dark glasses. Finally, Mr. Berman stood up, took a fresh stick of chalk, climbed onto his chair, and reached above the black-board to draw a horizontal line on the paint. "This," he said, after a theatrical pause, "is Milton." He let his hand fall a few inches, drew another line, and said, "This is Shakespeare." Another line, lower, on the blackboard: "This is Mahler." And, just below, "Here is Browning." Then he took a long drag on his cigarette, dropped the chalk onto the floor, and, using the heel of his black leather loafer, ground it into the wooden floorboards. "And this, gentlemen," he said, "is you."

Fisher asked to be transferred out of Berman's class the next day, and he was not alone. He was to learn that many of the teacher's stu-dents quit, and it says something about the school at the time that no one thought that unusual, or a matter of anyone else's concern. Didn't the administration or the other teachers think there was anything odd about Berman's pedagogical methods, to say nothing of the num-ber of boys who fled his class?

"Information was so compartmentalized that no one really put it all together," said Fisher. "For me personally, the compulsion to do the story was that I knew what this looked like from an adolescent perspective but I had no clue and was just dying to know what this all looked like from an adult perspective."

Gene, who would become one of Fisher's early sources, wanted to meet with me in the wake of the *Times* piece. I drove the short distance to the apartment he had been renting since his recent divorce. As we sat at the kitchen table, he shared a file he had on Berman. "He was like Eichmann," he told me as he nervously recounted his story of Berman's mental and psychological abuse.

From his dossier he pulled out letters he'd exchanged with the teacher over the years and described the slow and steady way Berman had groomed him and the devastating, long-lasting damage the abuse had caused in his life. Gene had for many years been attending meetings for adult survivors of sexual abuse, but the scars and anger were visible as he pulled out one damning letter after another. Writing to Berman and confronting him was part of the slow and painful process of getting his life in order.

In 2005, Gene approached Eileen Mullady, Horace Mann's headmaster, and formally accused Berman of abusing him. When it was clear Mullady would not pursue the matter, Gene approached the board members Robert Katz and Peter Sloane in Katz's law office. "This is not Horace Mann's bill to pay," Katz told him.

Katz was more than just a board member; he was also Gene's second cousin. This last bit of detail made me physically ill.

I swiftly concluded the interview and raced to my car. As I opened the driver's-side door, I turned my head and threw up in the street. It was something I thought happened only in Hollywood movies.

I would hear more accounts of students attempting to report abuse before I was done. In 1970, Doug Osserman (HM '71), who later committed suicide, reported in graphic detail Somary's abuse of another student to Harry Allison, the head of the Lower Division. According to a friend of Osserman's, Allison pooh-poohed the account, telling the boy "not to worry about such ridiculous stories."

Several victims had reported Mark Wright's abuse to Gordon Newcombe, an Upper Division head. Alan Breckenridge and Dick Warren, another popular English teacher, told Inky Clark that one especially vulnerable kid came to them and said Wright had made sexual advances. Warren told me he had reported the incident to Inky, whose first reaction was to say nothing about damaging children but rather that "we have to protect Mark." Wright was fired only after a third or perhaps fourth report of abuse. To this day, there is still no real clarity about which incident finally sealed Wright's fate at Horace Mann.

Fife reported being abused by Robert Berman on four occasions—on one occasion he notified the head of the Upper Division, Philip Lewerth, that Berman had kissed him in D.C. Fife says that Lewerth told him that in the absence of eyewitness testimony, the school's policy was for administrators to side with teachers. Lewerth eventually talked Fife out of pursuing the matter.

In 1994, at a time when he was thinking about writing a fictionalized narrative of his high school experience, Fife returned to campus. He met with Bill Clinton, and, over shots of scotch, the two discussed Berman's abuse at length. Clinton, nearing retirement, urged Fife not to stir up the past, saying that he would ruin the school for future generations. Fife reported Berman a final time, on May 10, 1996, when he spoke to Headmaster Eileen Mullady. According to Fife, Mullady concluded the meeting by saying, "If you care anything about the school, you won't repeat this."

There were more revelations to come.

Ariel Kaminer called excitedly. "You are not going to believe what Tek just told my colleague," she said, referring to a follow-up piece Jenny Anderson was doing for the *Times* on the revered English teacher. I wasn't surprised that revelations were coming out about

Tek, but what was shocking was his cavalier attitude. Anderson's piece, with the straightforward headline "Retired Horace Mann Teacher Admits to Sex with Students," described Tek as

> different from other teachers—a Buddhist who carefully tended to his elaborate gardens, a chaplain and a cross-country coach. He was so beloved that the English department chairmanship was named in his honor.
>
> But there was something else about Mr. Lin: a focus he placed on certain students, a fascination that some said looked like infatuation.
>
> Last week, in an interview, Mr. Lin, now 88, acknowledged that there was something to those whispers. He said he had had sex with students, "maybe three, I don't know," crossing boundaries he said were not so clear years ago.
>
> "In those days, it was very spontaneous and casual, and it did not seem really wrong."

Tek's claim to be surprised that some of them still remembered was as outrageous as it was sickening. He presented his past actions as both consensual and casual. Some shrugged the story off as the ramblings of an old man; others echoed his view that his "transgressions" took place in another era when opinions about consensual sex—even between adults and minors—were quite different. Andrew Solomon, on *Charlie Rose* to promote his book *Far from the Tree*, was caught off guard when the host asked him about the headlines concerning Horace Mann. After acknowledging how saddened he had been by the revelations, Solomon concluded that the late 1970s were "a morally blurry period."

But to many people within the school and beyond, Tek's delusional confessions were scandalous. Joyce Fitzpatrick, a onetime colleague of Tek's in HM's English department, captured the outrage of many in a letter to me.

After a rundown of her impressions of various teachers, she arrived at Tek, "whom I would have said I knew pretty well," she wrote. "I'm flabbergasted by the revelations about his pedophilia.

"There was no license then for a 48-year-old man to abuse a 15-year-old," she continued. "That boundary was crystal clear to us then just as it was in the Roaring '20s or in any period where a child's sensibilities were recognized. Just why, do we suppose, Tek kept his predations so discreet when he was teaching? Statutory rape laws protect minors: no consent is possible from those too young to give it freely."

The *Times* story quoted three former students of Lin's who said he had sexually abused them. Many of them remained conflicted about his behavior; long after my article appeared, I interviewed an HM alumnus who had been victimized by Lin.

"I had a problem with my parents so I stayed with Mr. Lin," "Xander" told me. "That started the week when I turned fifteen. I had just helped him plant pachysandra on the hill at Barnard before the first time I stayed at his house. It was late May, early June. I'd say I was there about one-third of the time as a student at Horace Mann. I was at his house for graduation."

Xander's father had gone to Horace Mann—in fact, he is one of the school's many celebrated alumni—and saw nothing unusual in his son's relationship with the teacher. "My parents figured it was a safe place to go," he said. "What could be safer than staying at the house of a Horace Mann teacher?"

"He did sexually abuse me," Xander admitted. "Although I have to say he did understand the word no. He took pictures of me naked or when I was sleeping. I was passive. He would jerk off on my butt and clean it up. But it wasn't all the time."

There was a moment before I could ask him what I had been wondering. "So how are you not angry at him?"

A pause. "He really was a great teacher. He taught me so much about so many different subjects. Non-Western cultures, plants, Eastern philosophy. He was a wonderful teacher."

There were myriad press reactions, some of them written by

alumni who'd been abused. In *The Daily Beast*, the HM graduate Kate Aurthur accused the school's driving instructor, Joseph Klein, who died in 2006, of groping her as she drove—while another student sat in the back. "Everyone knew that he had been a math teacher but because he was such a lech, the school had demoted him to driver's ed," she wrote. Aurthur asked a number of peers for their stories. "I was reminded by one that a math teacher had upgraded a C− she'd gotten to a B+ because, he said, 'she was cute.' Another told me she'd been given drugs by an English teacher. A third reminded me that a different male English teacher had had an affair with a female student we knew."

Around the same time "Rebecca," several years younger than me, published an anonymous account in *The Daily Beast* of the years of progressively violent abuse she suffered at the hands of another popular HM English teacher. It was harrowing to read.

> The situation with my teacher continued, on and off, into my high-school years, but took a new turn—toward violence. Sometimes, when we were about to have oral sex, I would get a nervous grin on my face, which he interpreted as mockery. He would slap me, hard, one time knocking me to the linoleum floor. He dragged me by my hair and hit me on my back, leaving bruises in the shape of handprints. I think part of his rage was knowing I would inevitably end up with a younger man, and it infuriated and scared him, making him feel that fate and time were against him.
>
> He repeatedly tried to have anal sex with me, and I would push him away.

I recognized that she was referring to Crawford Blagden, the popular English teacher whom I knew well when I was at school. He was one of the cool teachers, the guy who would take you out barhopping. Now I was learning about another side of the man.

Several of Rebecca's former classmates corroborated her claims in the article's comments section. "Swear to God, went over to the dude's house, in his basement, and she was sitting sniffling in his easy chair, with 2 empty beer bottles in front of her, drinking a third one," posted someone calling himself or herself only "Princeton 1993." "The dude was offering me a joint, and I said 'dude when are you going to move out of this basement? and isn't that a condom on the floor?' and she [Rebecca] hides her face and he shoved me."

"I probably sustained brain damage from some of the blows to my head," Rebecca wrote in a subsequent post in another forum. "I was dragged around by my hair while my abuser said, 'I'm so glad I finally found a way to hurt you that nobody can see.' I was raped, and sodomized, and brainwashed. I was convinced to keep it a secret, and silenced, and emotionally hurt. I asked for help from the guidance department; nobody helped me."

Rebecca said her parents reported Blagden's abuse to Headmaster Foote. Years later, in 2005, when Tom Kelly replaced Mullady as headmaster, Rebecca said her parents told him about everything that had happened to her.

In June 2012, in response to "Prep-School Predators" and a request by the New York City Council, the Bronx District Attorney's Office set up a hotline for Horace Mann victims and others to report allegations of abuse directly to its Child Abuse and Sex Crimes Bureau. Assistant DA Jill Starishevsky, working closely with Lieutenant Austin Morange and Detective Daryl A. Sims of the NYPD Bronx Special Victims Squad, began to gather information and investigate the allegations.

Starishevsky had dedicated her career to seeking justice for victims of child abuse and had prosecuted thousands of sex offenders. She and her team established communication with Kelly and began to review the school's child abuse reporting policies and procedures. The effort would last for ten months and would result in more than sixty separate interviews, more than twenty-five of which were with victims of alleged abuse. While the majority of the interviews were conducted in the New York area, investigators traveled to California, Colorado, Vermont, and other states. Meanwhile, the school administration remained silent. Some board members, backed up by parents who had sunk significant funds and social capital into purchasing the Horace Mann education and brand, took the position that the school that exists today had nothing to do with the Horace Mann of the 1970s (though the evidence was mounting daily that teachers at the school had abused kids well into the '90s).

Tom Kelly tried to put a friendlier face on the school's posture. In a letter to alumni dated June 10, 2012, he expressed empathy ("Words cannot describe how sad and upset I am at the thought of any harm coming to any member of our community while attending Horace Mann School") even as he reassured all concerned that such things could never happen today. "In fact," Kelly wrote, "an employee in today's environment would be immediately removed for a range of behaviors far less severe than those represented in the article." He asked for support and patience as the school formulated a more complete response, and ended his letter on a strangely passive note: "Please keep talking and please allow Horace Mann School to be part of the conversations."

Some parents felt Kelly was the right man at the right time. Holly Thomas has one kid at the school today. She says, "He's the reason from the top down there is such a great climate in the school. It's an academically challenging and nurturing place where kids feel comfortable going to advisers if feeling stressed. His daughter goes to the school. He has boundaries, but people are always coming to his house. He creates a nice, positive environment for kids, his wife as well. They are accessible, nice people. He cares. That's the climate of the school."

Throughout the controversy engendered by the revelations, Kelly remained the smiling face of Horace Mann. It would become a challenging job.

5

A SAFE SPACE

Within hours of "Prep-School Predators" appearing online, Dr. Alice Swenson (HM '89) established a private Facebook group called Processing Horace Mann. It began as a small support group with a narrow focus: a few dozen people were working through the shocked disbelief—or the anger, empathy, or contempt—that the stories of abusive teachers and oblivious, sometimes outright hostile administrators stirred up in them. But then it went viral. Within forty-eight hours, the number of Horace Mann alumni sharing opinions and revelations had mushroomed into the thousands. The discussions got more intense—and more personal.

Some said they couldn't believe all this had gone on right under their noses. Many expressed outrage but not complete surprise. "On some level," Nicholas Chen (HM '75) told me, "we knew on a DNA level what was going on."

It was a place to share secrets. Holly Thomas had seen a boy vomit on Somary when the teacher was trying to kiss him during one of their European Glee Club trips. She had not spoken of the incident before, besides comparing notes with another girl at the time who'd seen the same thing. "When I posted that [story] on PHM, the boy, now a man, contacted me and said, 'I think it was me and I want you to know I'm OK and nothing ever happened,'" she recalled. "He told me he didn't want either of us to hold that anymore. It was a huge relief."

It was all just a bunch of lies, some insisted. Scurrilous gossip from unnamed sources. *I know the accusations are not true*, some said. *I studied with that teacher and he never laid a hand on me.*

Conspiracy theories abounded: Weren't Clark and Somary roommates at Yale? Was Skull and Bones at the heart of it all? Hadn't Michael Hess defended the pedophile priest? But throughout it all the tone remained remarkably, even astonishingly, civil. As though every member had attended some intensive workshop on fostering good group dynamics—which in a sense we all had. Such comity was a crucial part of the Horace Mann educational experience. When someone stepped out of bounds (accusing the accusers of being mentally ill, in one notorious instance), group conscience asserted itself, gently but firmly reestablishing a tone of civility and productive discussion.

As the group grew, I sat riveted to my screen for weeks. Everyone did. The discussion was more than a distraction; it caused us to question an experience we all cherished and to wonder what our own roles were in the growing scandal. "Was this *my* school?" we asked one another.

One by one, victims of abuse came forward, using their own names. Others posted anonymously with the help of friends.

As Processing Horace Mann grew, and some people started to wilt from sheer emotional exhaustion, the subject matter broadened. Participants were processing every part of their high school experience, from rapist teachers, to the weird cafeteria worker who sold Ecstasy on the side, to the great parties some kid threw, to inside jokes that no one should have been able to remember but everyone did. Thousands of graduates, from the 1960s to the current era, all joined together in some kind of spontaneous group therapy to reevaluate their adolescence.

"This is so high school," Ariel Kaminer's husband, David, complained as she logged countless hours on the page. "You don't understand," she replied, "this *is* high school."

People began attacking almost every aspect of the school, as if we had all reverted to our prepubescent days trading gossip in the HM cafeteria. Everything seemed up for grabs. There was intellectual one-upmanship and mannered repartee; it was like a convention of smarty-pants with everyone trying to outduel everyone else. There were attacks on teachers veering into the libelous, squabbling between old school rivals. There were heated conversations about why there was mandatory nude swimming when the school was still all boys, and whether teachers were allowed to photograph it.

Jackie Lowey (HM '82) gave us a glimpse of what it felt like to be female at the school when it was going coed:

> I have wrestled with trying to get my hands—or at least my words—around the experience of being a young woman at Horace Mann in the 70s and early 80s . . . We were visitors in those early years—walking into classrooms with old-school boy prep teachers—many of whom did not know what to make of us. We were aliens who rocked their boats and got their used hand-me-downs (the shabby "girls'" gym) . . . There were virtually no female teachers whom we could look to for guidance or to as role models . . .
>
> Normal was the sisterhood advising you to bend forward in Mr. Juka's French class so he could cop a glance. Normal was watching Crawford flirt with your friends and wondering whether you weren't pretty enough to be flirted with. Normal was listening to Kops pruriently and graphically describing ancient females being sodomized by inanimate objects and giggling nervously in class. Normal was laughing about how gross Klein's drives were. Normal was Tek openly flirting with male students and treating female rivals with enmity. Normal was watching [a female teacher] flirt with and, purportedly, fool around with your male friends . . .
>
> And our weekends . . . well that was a whole different crazy normal. Drinking at the West End at 14 years old. Studio 54 and Limelight at 15 . . . I don't know whether it was the environment or the times. But we all wanted so desperately

to grow up fast. And that played perfectly into the hands of the predators who had inserted themselves into our community. We had nobody to tell us that when much older men take an interest in you (male or female)—it doesn't mean they think you are particularly sophisticated, witty, or unusually mature—it means that they have a perversely inappropriate attraction to young girls and/or boys and know how to manipulate their way into their lives.

Many users said that their experience with Processing Horace Mann was the single most emotionally significant one they'd had with the school. Soon those emotions coalesced into plans to act, precipitating the first direct showdown between enraged alumni and the administration.

On August 16, 2012, school administrators met with the Alumni Council to address the backlash caused by my piece. As they arrived on campus, they were greeted by a vigil for the survivors. Roughly a dozen alumni, many of them members of the newly formed Horace Mann Action Coalition (HMAC), gathered in the allocated section of the parking area on the corner of Tibbett Avenue and 246th Street, just west of the baseball field. Reporters circled and about ten security guards and New York police officers nervously told the protesters that both sides of 246th Street were off-limits. Despite the security precautions, Alumni Council members Bill Irwin (HM '74) and Peter Brown (HM '53) stopped to converse and express their solidarity.

The demonstrators sang protest songs, carried posters with the *Times Magazine* cover on one side and talking points on the other, and wore T-shirts saying HM ACTION COALITION and I SURVIVED HORACE MANN. They gave out T-shirts, candles, and a handout with questions for Steven Friedman, the hedge fund manager who served as chairman of the Board of Trustees.

As night fell, and the Alumni Council assembled in the auditorium, Justin Lerer (HM '95), president of the council, kicked off the meeting

by handing out HMAC's questions as well as the group's main statement. Kelly offered brief introductory comments and then yielded to
Friedman, who read a prepared statement. The crux of Friedman's
statement, according to notes circulated by Bill Irwin, was that
"there is no book on how to handle a situation like this and that the
Board of Trustees has struggled for the past two months in determin-
ing what can and should be done and coming to a consensus." (Friedman was ignoring the example of Pennsylvania State University,
which launched an independent investigation of abuse in the wake of
the Sandusky trial. In October 2013, Penn State settled the case
brought by victims of Sandusky for nearly $60 million.)

The remainder of the two-hour meeting was dedicated to answering questions. Friedman and Kelly took turns emphasizing that their
primary concern was to safeguard the best interests of the current
school. They spoke at length about what the school had done to protect the current students from abuse. Bill Irwin stood to ask the next
question. Although he was satisfied with the school's handling of
present-day dangers, he made it clear that he and many other alumni
were not satisfied with the rest of the board's response. Specifically,
why was the board not establishing an independent investigation in
the manner of Penn State? "Supporting the police and DA will only
go so far, as most of the abuse is likely not prosecutable due to the
statute of limitations," Irwin said. He then quoted from Friedman's
August 6, 2012, letter, which stated, "Those who can be held accountable must face the consequences of their actions . . . Our goal is
that Horace Mann School will be the standard in New York on this
vitally important issue."

Irwin insisted that the community needed information beyond
what could be gleaned from media, Facebook, or email. "We can
lead by doing an investigation, uncovering the truth per our school's
motto"—*Magna est veritas et praevalet*, Great is the truth and it
prevails—"and thereby holding people accountable, not only for
abuse but potentially for cover-ups as well, even if they can't be
prosecuted."

Friedman replied with a list of reasons the board did not support an investigation: many of the accused were deceased, there would not be an opportunity to challenge witnesses, and there would be no subpoena power. He then stated that the cost would be prohibitive: Penn State had spent $12 million (in reality, it had spent $8.1 million) on the Freeh report, an internal investigation led by the former FBI director Louis Freeh, and an HM investigation would cost even more, given the wider scope of abuse. In this Friedman was spot-on.

Friedman defended the school's position as best he could, even the slow start at responding to the story. It was difficult for thirty-five board members to agree on anything, he maintained, much less something as complicated as a scandal of this magnitude. Why not more of an apology? one council member asked, citing the example of another school's letter of apology following a different sex scandal. An open apology opened the floodgates to litigation and liability, Friedman replied.

He asked to be judged on what HM did after a couple of years rather than after a couple of months.

Friedman came across as "very genuine, very bothered by the abuse," Irwin reported on Processing Horace Mann. He added, "We should treat him not as an enemy, but a thoughtful advocate for the school. He appears willing to listen and debate, and I encourage everyone to do so in a positive manner."

As more allegations arose, Tom Kelly's primary response seemed to be removing any sign with a tainted name on it. When they took Inky Clark's name off the baseball field, it struck me as strange. I hadn't written or even heard anything about Inky other than he was probably gay and definitely an alcoholic. It got me wondering what else the administration knew and what the source of its information was. A file? A board member? A victim?

And then I met Jon Seiger (HM '79). Seiger, a jazz musician, was a self-described troubled kid who had been sexually abused by an uncle at an early age. The tale he told me sounded outlandish, and I did not know whether to believe it fully—but it could not be dismissed.

Seiger says that on an evening strikingly similar in its inception to the one Paul, my brother, and I shared at the headmaster's Tudor mansion, Inky invited him over. When he arrived Kops was there, and the two men plied him with drinks. But then, Seiger claims, they took him out to a Manhattan club where older men purchased the sexual services of young men. Later that evening, after more drinks, Inky and Kops convinced two male prostitutes to come back to the headmaster's house for more drinks before instructing them to "get things going" before Clark and Kops continued to abuse Seiger all night.

Following that incident, Seiger says, Kops "would look around and make sure no one was there and grab my ass or crotch or something. Just boldly—quickly, of course, to make sure no one was looking. And then Mr. Clark a couple of times had sent notice for me to come to the office and would say, 'I want you to stop . . . at my house after school' or something, on a Friday, and I really didn't know how to say no anymore at that point."

To check their control over him, Seiger says, Inky and Kops would come up behind him or put him in a choke hold. While it may have looked playful to everyone else, Seiger said that "kind of public thing was exactly what they intended it to be. We can do this right out in public, and let everybody see this, and nobody's going to say or do anything."

I met with Seiger over ten hours on three occasions. In these meetings, he recounted, in nauseating detail, being sexually abused by eight different teachers. I was not in the business of accusing people or of doubting survivors, but Seiger's tale severely tested my tolerance for knowing the truth. Particularly when he named Ion Theodore as one of his abusers. Seiger claims that Theo had masturbated him in a hotel room while another boy watched TV in the next bed.

I pushed him and said it was difficult to believe that one boy could have been abused by so many people in one institution. "How do you explain it?" I asked.

"I've been asking myself that question for thirty years," he said.

"The truth is I believe they were talking to one another. No, I know it. After Inky and Kops abused me in the headmaster's house, Somary approached me and said, 'I heard about the great time you had the other night with Mr. Clark and Mr. Kops. I'm glad you are getting to know them so well.'"

Fisher quoted Seiger for his story in *The New Yorker*; his experience with Berman, Fisher wrote, "mirrored others in many details." He was asked to stay after class, given special assignments, told he was better than the other boys—and then corporally and sexually abused. After spanking him in his classroom with a wooden pointer, Berman "told Seiger to give him oral sex. Seiger complied and Berman repeated his demand every few weeks for the rest of that year—between seven and eight times in all, according to Seiger."

Fisher spoke to Berman late in his reporting; he had already been working in tandem with the police and *The New Yorker*'s fact-checkers. "Seiger's story was so fantastic and shocking that it raises alarms to anyone about his credibility, what memories we trust and don't," said Fisher. "His appearance on the scene threw everybody because it sort of ratcheted the story up to a very different level."

I called the Bronx DA and Fisher. They both confirmed that although it seemed far-fetched, they believed Seiger's account.

Seiger's story put me in a dilemma. When he made his experience public within the HM community, I received dozens of emails and calls asking if I believed him. I didn't know how to counter the doubts his story raised. I was struggling with his accusations, like everyone else. He was the only person to make accusations against either Inky or Theo. It wasn't precisely that I didn't believe him. It was more that I didn't *want* to believe him. Of course, the fear of not being believed is what keeps many genuine survivors from ever speaking out.

Although false reports do occur, it seems the percentage of people who lie about being sexually assaulted is lower than anecdotal evidence might suggest. To date, the Making a Difference (or MAD) Project is the only attempt to evaluate the percentage of false reports made to U.S. law enforcement officials. Of the 2,059 cases included in the MAD study, 140 (7 percent) were classified as false. Two other methodologically rigorous studies, both conducted outside the United States, produced results between 2.1 and 2.5 percent. Put simply, the overwhelming majority of people reporting that they were sexually abused or assaulted are telling the truth.

Setting the statistics aside, it was hard for me to hear Seiger's accusations about Inky and Theo. Inky changed my life; Theo had enriched it in countless ways. Theo, the gentle man with the shock of wild white hair who was for many years the multifaceted head of the arts department. The sculptor, athlete, philosopher, historian, thespian, and naturalist. I loved him and simply couldn't square the accusations with the man I knew. Theo wasn't only a teacher and a mentor to me—he was like a family member. In fact, he almost *became* a family member when, years after I'd graduated from HM, he asked my mother to marry him. She declined his offer, but the two remained close until his death in 1997. I even named my son Abraham Theodore in his honor.

I was stunned by Seiger's claims and fell into a mini-depression. I had naïvely thought I was writing about what had happened to a few friends and that the story would end with Wright, Somary, and Tek Lin, and perhaps we'd all finally get an explanation as to what happened with Stan Kops. But if I was going to shatter the idols of so many others, I suppose it was only fitting that a few of mine would be smashed in the process.

Perhaps the truth isn't so great.

6

THE TURNING
OF THE TIDE

E ven as more and more survivors came forward and told their
astonishing stories, others were skeptical.

"It makes me think of the Salem witch trials," said a
prominent lawyer whose wife had sung with Somary's Glee Club when
she was a student at Riverdale. "All of these people coming forward
with stories that sound so similar." The lawyer didn't consider the
possibility that victims' stories sound so similar because the modus
operandi of their predators doesn't change. The boys and girls they
abused were different, but the abusers stayed the same.

I wondered if the Horace Mann scandal would help push the
country to a tipping point. The Catholic Church's large settlements
(more than $3 billion in total, mostly in the last decade) had had an
impact; so had the spectacle of grown men and women, former altar
boys and devout believers, bravely discussing the emotional and psychological distress that abuse had caused them. A national movement was under way to change the statute of limitations so that child
sexual abuse could be more readily prosecuted.

Research on sexual abuse in schools was gaining traction as well.
In 1990, the educational researcher Charol Shakeshaft began to an-
alyze cases of child sexual abuse in U.S. schools. Her first paper ("In
Loco Parentis: Sexual Abuse of Students in Schools," written with

Audrey Cohan) was the result of a four-year study of 225 sexual abuse cases, and it came up with the headline-making conclusion "All of the accused admitted sexual abuse of a student, but none of the abusers was reported to the authorities, and only 1 percent lost their license to teach. Only 35 percent suffered negative consequences of any kind, and 39 percent chose to leave their school district, most with positive recommendations. Some were even given an early retirement package."

Shakeshaft's work led to a job in the Department of Education under George W. Bush and the publication of *Educator Sexual Misconduct: A Synthesis of Existing Literature* (2004). In this report, she claimed that nearly 10 percent of U.S. public school students had been the victim of sexual harassment or sexual abuse at the hands of teachers or other school employees. While her critics (notably the teachers' unions) complained that the study did not differentiate between rape and verbal intimidation, her study and subsequent work helped bring the issue to the fore. Shakeshaft, who today is a professor in the Educational Leadership Department at Virginia Commonwealth University, said, "When I first started talking about this as an academic and going to schools to talk about it, people used to say that can't be true, it doesn't happen. Now nobody says it doesn't really happen. We're seeing more awareness and more action in terms of teaching people what is appropriate."

As Processing Horace Mann grew and became a regular forum for those HM alumni who would not let the scandal die, the smaller HM Discussion Group (and its Web corollary, HoraceMannSurvivor.org) offered a safe space for those most affected by abuse. The discussion group had been started a few days after the publication of my article, by Joseph Cumming, who'd been abused by Somary beginning when he was fifteen years old until the end of his senior year. "I'd been very deeply grateful to Hannes for all the good things he'd done for me, which I now recognize was grooming for abuse," said Joseph. "He had mentored me, given me opportunities in the music world, helped me financially, helped me get into college. And ultimately, during my senior year in high school when I needed a place to live, he and Anne took me into their homes to live with them.

"At the same time he was touching me in ways that caused me extreme distress and ultimately led to me attempting suicide," he continued. Joseph was sitting in the book-filled office at his home in New Haven, not far from the International Church at Yale, where he serves as pastor. Like a lot of victims of sexual abuse, he had tried to put the memories of what had happened between him and Somary behind him. He describes his teacher's seduction as beginning with hugs that slowly escalated to kisses and fondling. Ultimately, on one of the school's many musical excursions, Somary got in bed with him and rubbed his genitals against the boy's buttocks.

After graduation, Joseph had problems with drugs and alcohol (he claims Somary introduced him to binge drinking on a school trip to Poland and had another of his protégés turn him on to pot and hash). It was only in the '90s, after his call to the ministry, that he told his fiancée, Michele, about what had happened to him in high school. "I wanted her to have no surprises about me after marriage," he recalled. "I was very surprised she still wanted to marry me after I told her all kinds of bad stuff about myself. Though I didn't give her all the details . . . It wasn't until 2011 that she said, 'Describe to me exactly what he did.'

"For many years I tried to convince myself that what he had done had an innocent explanation," said Joseph. "That what he had done could somehow be construed as not really sexual abuse. And that maybe this was how Swiss artists expressed innocent affection; they're more passionate, more physically demonstrative than uptight Americans." Now he was speaking with his wife. "Hearing my own voice out loud I thought, Oh, my goodness, how could I have ever thought this had any innocent explanation?"

Encouraged by his wife, Joseph began searching for other victims of Somary's. "I said if I ever find one other person who says, 'Hannes abused me,' then I will denounce him—I'll go to the police, Child Protective Services. But if I don't I'm going to try and believe [what happened] was innocent" or at least an aberration. Using Yahoo and later Google, he typed in combinations of "Johannes Somary, sex abuse," "Johannes Somary, pedophilia." "Because he [Somary] worked with Catholic churches, there were a million stories that would come up that had his name and sexual abuse in them" but none relating the teacher to accusations.

In March 2011, a year before my story appeared, he found Ed Bowen's then anonymous blog, *Johannes Somary, Pedophile*, and knew he was not alone. "We had known each other superficially in school," Joseph said. "Ed was a few years older but his brother was a classmate of mine, his mother was one of my teachers." Both boys had been in the Glee Club.

"We went through this 'I'll tell you my story if you'll tell me yours' thing," Joseph recalled. "In his case it was totally clear-cut; there was no ambiguity about what Hannes did to him. I said, 'Ed, if there are two of us, there are probably ten of us. Between us we came up with seven or eight names of people who might have been abused." Within a few days, Joseph called Tom Kelly, who was sympathetic, though the timing was inauspicious: Somary had died a month earlier. Using what resources he could find, including the school's alumni record, Joseph began cold-calling some of the names he and Bowen had come up with.

"Every single one I reached said, 'Yes, Hannes initiated sexual relations with me.' I felt terrible. I had known enough to wonder if they had been abused and had not done anything about it."

In one dramatic instance, Joseph could find only a street address for one of the men he thought might have been abused, the person I called M. "I sent a note saying, 'Blast from the past, your old friend from thirty years ago. There's something I'd like to ask you about, could you give me a ring? Here's my number.' He called immediately and the first words out of his mouth were, 'I know exactly what you want to talk about and it's all true.' And I thought, after all these years, how could you possibly know what I want to talk about?"

•

"On the Facebook group and website, I posted that I was in touch with other survivors," said Joseph. "I did not at that time say I was abused myself"—at least not to anyone outside of the small group of survivors he had already found. "And I said if you or someone you know was abused and would like to talk confidentially with others, you can contact me. Instantly I was getting three hundred emails a day, my phone was ringing forty to fifty times a day. A couple times a day someone would say, 'I've never told anyone this, not even my wife, but I was sexually abused at Horace Mann.'"

Among the numerous books on his shelves are many in Arabic. "These are all of the major commentaries on the Koran over the centuries, medieval and modern," he explained, pointing at various titles. "And these are the most influential treatises on Islamic systematic theology through the centuries, and these are some books in which I wrote chapters." Joseph is a devout Christian who works with Muslim, Christian, and Jewish leaders. His family was not particularly religious and most of his friends growing up were Jewish. ("I probably went to thirty bar mitzvahs but the only Christian confirmation service I ever went to was my own confirmation after my conversion.") He had a religious awakening when he was seventeen.

"When Hannes was abusing me, I came to a place where I attempted suicide," said Joseph. "And I believe that God intervened very dramatically to rescue me from taking my own life."

He was a mess his senior year; he went from being an almost straight-A student to nearly failing. "What was happening sexually caused me to go into a paralysis academically, where sometimes I couldn't bring myself to set foot on campus," he recalled. "I couldn't bring myself to go to class, and frequently couldn't bring myself to do my homework." Aside from the guilt he felt about his relationship with Hannes, he was ashamed of letting down his parents, who had gone into debt to send him to Horace Mann.

"Although there are a lot of rich kids at HM, the kids who were abused were mostly from families of modest means," said Joseph, echoing something I would hear from experts in teacher-student abuse. "We were also mostly from families where either the parents were going through a divorce or one of the parents had just died or was in the hospital, or we were in serious conflict with our parents . . . In a lot of cases kids were so alienated that they were no longer welcome to live in their parents' home. The abusers didn't just screen the victims; they screened the victims' families for those kids who would be unlikely to tell their parents what was going on. And if they did tell their parents, their parents would be unlikely to feel like they could take any action. They did not mostly go after kids of trustees who could get them fired."

One day Joseph went to the top floor of his parents' four-story house with the intent of jumping out the window. "I began to jump off—and it wasn't like I was thinking of jumping off, one of these cry-for-help things where I really wanted to be rescued—and just as I reached the point of no return I heard a voice in the room behind me speak out loud. And I was utterly astonished because I thought I was alone. I was so startled I fell back, it almost felt like a hand had pushed me back. I looked around and it was a dark room, no-body there. I was really weirded out. And the voice said, 'Go get your Bible.'"

He found one on his shelf, a relic of a ninth-grade HM English class, and then heard the voice say, "Open it and read."

"I just opened it randomly and landed on Psalm 38, and I felt as though King David had somehow got in a time machine and read my mind and then went back in a time machine and wrote about it three thousand years earlier," said Joseph. "He described exactly what I was feeling." What he read was, "O Lord, do not rebuke me in your anger nor discipline me in your wrath. Your arrows have pierced me, and your hand has come down on me. Because of your wrath there is no health in my body; there is no soundness in my bones because of my sin. My guilt has overwhelmed me like a burden too heavy to bear. My wounds fester and are loathsome because of my sinful folly. I am bowed down and brought very low."

"Then I thought to myself, that's probably just like random chance. I bet if I close it and open it again I'll land on 'Methuselah begat,' that kind of verse. So I closed it again and opened it randomly and this time I landed on Psalm 6, which says the same thing but slightly differently. 'O Lord, do not rebuke me in your anger or discipline me in your wrath. Have mercy on me, Lord, for I am faint. heal me, Lord, for my bones are in agony. My soul is in deep anguish. How long, O Lord, how long?'

"For me this was a huge breakthrough moment," he said. "It was as though I had been in the depths of a dark dungeon and a ray of light had shone into it. And because of the simple knowledge that there was somebody, meaning God, who knew exactly how I felt and did not reject me because of it, and who cared. Now, God did not intervene to rescue me from the situation; the abuse did not stop, my academic problems didn't go away. I was still just as much of a mess as before. But just the knowledge that someone knew everything about me and cared and wanted to lead me out of this—and both psalms go on with a prayer for deliverance and an expectation that God will deliver the psalmist—that was all I needed. It was transformative for me."

He righted himself at school, and while the abuse went on, he "began pulling away from the relationship with Hannes. Not completely withdrawing but putting a little bit of distance. And Hannes perceived it and was angry about it." The following summer he accompanied Somary on a trip to London, where the abuse continued. "But I was beginning to develop some emotional space from him."

By the time he got to Princeton, Joseph had not worked through his feelings about what had happened at Horace Mann, nor had he spoken to anyone about it. "I had been planning a career in music," he said. "That's what Hannes had encouraged me with." He played piano, sang, and took up the trumpet for a while, with less success. "I wanted to conduct and compose like Hannes; I wanted to be like Hannes. He had said to me, 'You have the potential to become one of the great composers of your generation if your talent is properly nurtured, and I'm going to nurture you.'"

He arrived at Princeton and was placed into an advanced music theory course, and his assignment was to write a sonatina in the style of Mozart. The class was impressed, "and the professor pulled me aside and said, 'This is the best work I've ever seen from a student. You have the potential to become one of the great composers of your generation if you're properly nurtured and I'd like to nurture you if you want that.' He had no way of knowing. I just totally freaked out. I went cold as a stone; I had to leave. He said, 'What did I say?' I couldn't talk to him, I couldn't go to his class. I became obsessed: Is he gay? Is he trying to come on to me? I think he probably was gay, but I don't think he was coming on to me. He was just trying to take an innocent interest in a student and I just totally freaked out."

Joseph never returned to class despite the professor's continued entreaties—and even the threat that he'd have to flunk him if he didn't turn in some work. "That was the end of my musical career."

As he spent long days listening to victims' stories, interviewing lawyers, and fielding media requests, Joseph's work as director of the Yale Center for Faith and Culture's Reconciliation Program suffered. But he was a man with a mission, and as the group expanded, so did his sense of purpose.

Once Joseph felt that the group was large enough, he arranged for them to meet face-to-face. He invited me to join what would become the Horace Mann Survivors' Group for its first gathering, on the evening of Wednesday, June 13, 2012. We met in a bare-bones conference room in Ed Bowen's apartment building, on East 125th Street.

I asked my wife, Madeline, to accompany me. I also cajoled Paul into coming along—much as I had on that night in 1982, when I persuaded him to come to dinner with Inky and the Bear. He had been through it all—from my first year at Horace Mann, to the campfire ten years after graduation, to my wedding, where he stood under the chuppah with Madeline and me. We were friends for life, in every sense.

Paul grew up on the Upper East Side, and when I met him at school he represented a world that was still foreign to me. His father was a soft-spoken, gentle man—but a fierce and brilliant litigator, the first Jewish lawyer to become a partner in a prestigious non-Jewish New York firm.

Our friendship began when Paul invited me to a Stevie Wonder concert in 1979. When we returned from Madison Square Garden that night, we climbed up to his room on the fourth floor of a brownstone on Eighty-Fourth Street and lay down to sleep for the night with the light on. Paul asked me to turn it off because I had been the last one into bed. I countered that he should turn off the light since he was closer. We kept up this argument for hours and, both of us being stubborn mules, finally fell asleep with the light on. We have continued some form of this running argument for thirty-five years.

When we were both doing the postcollege flounder, Paul suggested we go to his parents' house on Martha's Vineyard for a few months to get girlfriends, find some menial jobs, and figure out the rest of our lives. For six months we lived in their Chilmark house, where we did a lot of theater, wrote plays, and spent hours engaged in deep soul-searching talks late into the night.

Today, I could think of no one better equipped to lend a sympathetic ear and empathetic soul to a survivor of sexual abuse. Paul's radar was so fine-tuned that he seemed to be able to pick up messages and nuances others couldn't see or hear. His professional life as a rabbi and drug counselor had been spent listening to people at their most vulnerable moments. Though he hadn't become a lawyer, Paul had learned the intricacies of the legal game at his parents' dinner table. In short, he possessed a perfect mix of qualities for the upcoming battle with Horace Mann.

As we entered the conference room, I met Ed Bowen, whom I hadn't seen since I'd interviewed him for the *Times* article a few months before. He seemed both relieved that his tale was finally out in the world and exhausted by what the last few weeks had wrought.

Soon after, Kathy Howard, Ben Balter's mother, arrived. I hardly recognized her: she seemed lighter than the person I'd met that cold February night at the Riverdale Diner, as if the burden of her guilt had been slightly lifted when Ben's story was shared with the world. More men of various ages slowly appeared. Ron Klepper, who would have graduated my year but had left Horace Mann before I arrived, wore all black. He seemed fidgety and distant, his eyes darting nervously around the room.

When Joseph called the meeting to order, there were roughly a dozen people seated around a U-shaped table. There was an open laptop for F., who was participating via Skype from Northern California. The attendees ranged in age from their early thirties to their late sixties, and their experiences spanned nearly four decades of Horace Mann's history.

There was no set agenda, but the evening began dramatically. Though Joseph had told most of the men individually that he had been abused, he had not spoken of it in a group setting. After welcoming and thanking them for coming, he found his voice.

"My name is Joseph Cumming and I was abused by Johannes Somary," he said, choking back tears and holding his wife's hand. Then we went around the table, introducing ourselves. Some told their stories.

The group's dynamics were as complex and wide-ranging as the stories that had brought its members together. Some were abused hundreds of times while others were mildly harassed once or twice. Some wanted an independent investigation; others demanded financial restitution. Some had suffered so badly that the damage was clearly visible on their faces. Others, though externally whole and successful, had buried a toxic pain that leaked out in other aspects of their lives. Some had never set foot on the campus of Horace Mann since the day they'd graduated. Others, despite their abuse, sent their own kids to the school or served on the Alumni Council.

After the personal stories had been told, there was the question of what to do next. What did they want from one another? Would this group serve as anything more than a healing circle where victims would share their stories and offer support? Was that enough? Were there others out there and, if so, was it the group's responsibility to identify and reach out to them? And what exactly did the group want from Horace Mann? Was the mission of the Survivors' Group to retain lawyers together and sue their alma mater?

This was the beginning of a dialogue that would continue, in one form or another, for months. The larger question was this: Should the members of the Survivors' Group take a reconciliatory or legal approach in dealing with Horace Mann?

Joseph, who had been meeting and speaking with Headmaster Tom Kelly for weeks, tried to convince the others that Kelly was an ally who would do right by them. Kelly, after all, had apologized to him and Ed Bowen when it was announced the school would host a concert to honor Somary after his death; the memorial was ultimately held elsewhere. And Kelly did engage in dialogues with many of the survivors and repeatedly expressed his willingness to talk to anyone who would listen.

F., via Skype, passionately argued that Kelly was just a tool. "It doesn't matter if he is a good guy or not," he said. "He is going to do what the school tells him to do."

The group broke up that night with promises to continue the conversation. The next day Klepper posted on Facebook and argued for restitution. "I DO want remuneration" he wrote, "and I'll tell you why: our parents sent us to HM, because they wanted us to have the best possible education and leg-up we could possibly have . . . It HAS left irrecoverable scars . . . My trust in most people is very low (an example is how I'm here on F'book: U.N. Owen—'unknown'). In my personal life, I'm incapable of developing any meaningful relationship with someone—I can't give of myself, emotionally, and never have."

Over the next few weeks, the group had several more conference calls. It was agreed from the first meeting that they should contact the school as a group, and after some back-and-forth, they sent the Board of Trustees what they called "an early draft of a 'working document.'"

We believe the Horace Mann community has an historic opportunity to show leadership on this issue—to set an example of the right way to handle a crisis of this kind in order to promote healing, reconciliation, justice and truth. We

welcome a dialogue with the current Horace Mann administration and Trustees on how to realize these goals.

We believe work must be done in four areas: 1) protecting
potential future victims, 2) ensuring "never again" at Horace
Mann, 3) healing and assisting past victims based on their
legitimate needs, and 4) changing the wider system [to assure
adult victims of sexual abuse in New York State could seek
redress].

When it seemed that no new members would be coming forward,
the Survivors' Group began to focus on trying to get Kelly, Friedman,
and the board to speak with them. Joseph and Paul, acting as liai-
sons for the group, had made several overtures, but their requests
for face time were answered with silence. Despite Kelly's assurances
that a meeting was close at hand, Friedman and the board were in
the midst of messy internal arguments over how the school was going
to respond. Many of the individual board members were bringing
their own personal lawyers into meetings as they convened to discuss
what to do next. Should the school pay damages? Would that open it
up to more liability? How many more victims were out there? Would
payment open the door to other claims? Could current or former board
members be held liable? Would admission place the school on the
brink of financial ruin? The fact that it was summer, and many board
members were at their houses in the Hamptons or vacationing elsewhere, only added to the chaotic atmosphere.

The board's silence was extremely painful to the group members,
many of whom just wanted to be acknowledged. Finally, after much
internal debate about what tone to take with the school, the group
drafted a new letter:

Three weeks have passed since we presented a letter to the
Board of Trustees, and we have still received no response.
We have received no acknowledgment of our letter, nor any
indication of when or whether we will ever receive a personal
response. We have received no gesture of compassion or car-

ing from the Board of Trustees . . . In our first letter, presented to Dr. Kelly on June 20 and to the Board on June 21, we sought to open a constructive dialogue with the Trustees and Administration to find solutions good for the school and for us. So far the Trustees appear to be stonewalling us.

"We worked obsessively on the letter," Paul said. And though it would have been easiest just to email it, Joseph felt strongly that he and Paul should deliver the letter to Kelly in person.

Around eleven o'clock on a sticky New York summer night, Paul jumped on his motorcycle and retraced the route he had taken from the Upper East Side to Horace Mann when he was a student. He drove north on the FDR Drive, over the Willis Avenue Bridge, and onto the Major Deegan. He exited at Van Cortlandt Park, crossed over Broadway, and ascended the winding, tree-lined hill onto the campus.

He found himself standing on 246th Street, in front of the headmaster's house, where Kelly lived with his family in a classic Tudor mansion that evoked the power, wealth, and gentility of an estate somewhere in the English countryside. The headmaster's house squarely faced the rest of the HM campus across the street.

As he waited for Joseph to arrive, Paul wandered the campus. New modern buildings had joined the old stone structures he remembered from his days as a student. When Joseph and Kelly finally arrived in separate cars, the headmaster introduced himself in his usual jovial manner as if they were there for homecoming week.

Inside, Paul found the house virtually unrecognizable from the place he'd visited decades ago. Kelly had remodeled the headmaster's residence, as had others before him. Gone was the gallery of photos of boy athletes that Inky favored. Kelly offered them drinks from his well-stocked fridge. By the time they sat down to talk, it was close to midnight.

Though warm and affable, Kelly tried to run the meeting with a rapid-fire monologue. Intentionally or not, he bombarded them with so much information that it was impossible to absorb it all. He wanted to make sure Joseph and Paul knew that he was doing everything he could to make the situation right. He listed all the things he'd done and all the unilateral steps he'd taken—like contacting the sibling alumni Regina Kulik Scully (HM '81) and Dominic C. Kulik (HM '82) about changing the name of the Tek Lin chair in English that they had endowed in their former teacher's honor. Kelly also spoke of taking down any signs with the perpetrators' names on them—he'd even removed Inky Clark's name from the athletic field that had been like a second home to him. At the time it seemed a strange admission; Jon Seiger's revelations about Inky and Kops were not yet public and no one else had named Inky as a perpetrator.

Kelly also said that he had not yet renewed his contract with Horace Mann. Since the board didn't want him walking away from this mess, he implied he had enormous leverage. Paul thought this notion a bit naïve, but he was encouraged when Kelly promised to make notes of their meeting and share them with the board. Kelly also promised that there would be a meeting between the survivors and the entire board.

"It was a chaotic time, and Kelly seemed, at that point, like an honest broker," Paul said. "He came across as sincere, shell-shocked, and devastated. I do believe he was a man trying to do the right thing."

As Joseph and Paul stood up to leave, Kelly said, "I'm so sorry for what happened to you."

There were tears in his eyes.

Despite their promises, Friedman and the board kept putting off any meeting. Finally, on July 30, 2012, after nearly two months of radio silence, Paul and Joseph received an email from Friedman:

> As Board Chair of Horace Mann School, I sincerely regret it has taken time to establish a meeting with you and anyone else you would like to include. Dr. Kelly and I would be pleased to meet with you in the early evening at HM or at the Columbia Club in NY, or at another location that you prefer, on any

of August 14th, 15th, 16th, 20th, 21st or 22nd. I hope one of these dates work. If not, please suggest others. Please confirm that no lawyers will be in attendance. As challenging and heart wrenching as these issues are, I hope we can have a conversation or series of conversations that lead to healing.

A meeting with Horace Mann administrators was set up at the Harvard Club in Manhattan. The survivors perceived it as an opportunity to meet with the school's administration for the first time and hear what they had to say.

"We'd all heard various rumors about what the school planned to do," said F. "But very few of us had been addressed directly."

A minority of survivors wanted the meeting to be focused on reconciliation and didn't want lawyers present, but most believed it was appropriate to bring lawyers. The question of whether they would seek financial restitution was unsettled. But they all wanted the school to address the demands they had made in the original letter— an independent investigation and the school's support of a bill in the New York legislature, known as the NY Child Victims Act or simply the Markey bill, after its author, the state assemblywoman Margaret Markey.

It was Markey's intention to dismantle the state's strict statute of limitations on child sexual abuse cases. That law made it all but impossible to hold Horace Mann or the abusive teachers legally responsible for what happened. Statute of limitations laws vary from state to state. In New York, a five-year clock starts ticking from the moment an abused child turns eighteen or the case is reported to law enforcement or a state agency, whichever occurs first. There are no statutes of limitations for murder, kidnapping, treason, or fraud—but in New York at least, sexual abusers of children get a free pass after a victim turns twenty-three.

This is what Markey, a Queens Democrat, was seeking to reform. Her bill, first introduced in the 2006–2007 legislative session, followed in the footsteps of a historic reform in California. In the midst of the Catholic Church scandals, the California legislature passed a bill in 2002 that offered survivors of childhood sexual abuse a one-year "window" (2003) from the time the legislation was signed to file claims against their abusers. Victims still had to find the strength to fight and prove their cases, by no means an easy task given how long ago the abuse had occurred. In 2003, about 1,000 victims came forward (850 of them Catholic). This resulted in some apologies and financial settlements and, perhaps most important, it revealed the names of more than three hundred hitherto unknown perpetrators. (Governor Jerry Brown, a former Jesuit seminarian, vetoed a second bill that would have opened another one-year window, in 2013. It applied only to private institutions and Brown deemed it "simply too open-ended and unfair.") Since California's initial reform, nearly one-third of the states have dramatically extended or eliminated the civil statutes of limitations on childhood sexual abuse, while nearly three-fourths have eliminated at least some of the relevant criminal ones. New York State's laws, along with Georgia's, ranked among the most stringent in the nation.

If Markey's bill were to become law, underage victims would be given five additional years to report crimes after turning eighteen—so the statute of limitations' ticking clock wouldn't stop until they reached age twenty-eight. They would also be given a one-year window to file civil lawsuits if the statute of limitations had prevented them from doing so before.

Though the bill won the support of the State Assembly, it routinely failed to pass the State Senate, in large part because of the Catholic Church's strong opposition. Since the bill is retroactive, the church feared a tidal wave of complaints about past abuse. It said the legal costs of settling those cases could bankrupt it, or deplete funds that could be used to help the poor or devoted to other charitable work. Furthermore, the Markey bill would not apply to public schools or institutions—proof, they felt, that it was anti-Catholic legislation.

Given New York law, the survivors knew that the chances of taking Horace Mann to court were slim. But as the Harvard Club meeting approached, they mostly came to agree that legal assistance was vital.

If there was to be any recompense, or even an admission of guilt on the part of Horace Mann, the time to push for it was now, with all the leverage they could muster. Some wanted the satisfaction of having an institution in which they had placed their trust admit it had let them down. Some wanted emotional closure and hoped that a public forum on campus would help them heal while also creating an atmosphere where child sexual abuse would have a hard time flourishing in the future. Some simply wanted money for the pain and suffering they had endured through the years. Any of these endeavors would require legal help.

Unfortunately, "the whole process of picking the lawyers became a bit of a train wreck," Paul recalled.

"Most lawyers don't give a shit about this kind of stuff," said Paul Mones, the Oregon lawyer who has specialized in child sexual abuse cases for more than thirty years. "Abuse is not a big issue for lawyers; it's too emotionally draining and it's too much of an uphill battle. But there is a group of us in the country who do this kind of work and who feel it has the purpose of preventing sexual abuse in the future."

Before seeking counsel, the group settled on the idea that one lawyer should represent them all. I introduced Mones to several survivors and he and his sometime partner Michael Dowd, a New York attorney, quickly became the front-runners. They were considered two of the country's top experts in the field. They had represented numerous victims of abuse by Catholic priests and Catholic school employees, and had won settlements for clients in other cases, including one against the Boy Scouts of America. (Mones was an attorney in a landmark 2010 case that resulted in a nearly $20 million judgment against the BSA and led to the release of what came to be known as the "perversion files": thousands of documents, kept by the organization since the 1920s, that recounted allegations made against Scout leaders.)

In his first meeting with the group, Dowd presented his bona fides and fielded a lot of questions. One group member pointedly asked why Dowd had been suspended. It was a fair question, and he handled it calmly, saying he hadn't been found to have broken any law.

The exchange referred to 1986, when Dowd revealed that his company, which had a contract with New York City to collect overdue parking fines, had paid about $30,000 in kickbacks to Queens borough president Donald R. Manes in exchange for a lucrative parking ticket collection contract. Dowd, insisting that he'd been extorted by Manes, exposed the corruption to Jimmy Breslin, a columnist for the *Daily News*. When the scandal (which went far beyond Dowd's firm) exploded, Manes committed suicide. Dowd became the star witness for Rudolph Giuliani, the federal prosecutor investigating the case. Although Dowd was granted immunity, he was suspended from practicing law for five years for violating the state disciplinary code for lawyers.

"Many people wanted to hire him," said F., "mostly because he had done cases like this before and because he was a known quantity."

F. was one of the survivors who wanted to take a more maverick approach. Despite Dowd and Mones's impressive track record in handling these cases, some felt they needed a lawyer who could think outside the box. The statute of limitations was preventing so many decades-old abuse cases from coming to trial that some in the group felt they had to try something new.

At the time, both the school and the survivors were closely watching a remarkable case that was playing out in federal court. The Poly Prep case had begun when an alumnus, David Hiltbrand, accused the Brooklyn school's late football coach Phil Foglietta of abusing him—and further claimed that the school had ignored his accusations and those of many other men who'd been abused by the coach when they were boys. One of those former students was Jim Zimmerman, under whose name the suit, representing twelve plaintiffs, was filed. It was their contention that the school had ignored and covered up Foglietta's abuses. As a result, they said, their case concerned not only sexual abuse but also deceit.

In a bold and ultimately consequential legal argument, the Poly plaintiffs' lawyer Kevin Mulhearn argued that the suit should proceed because Poly officials had lied to students about when they first heard allegations of abuse. The gist of Mulhearn's argument was that the statute of limitations should not protect the school if it had dishonestly deprived victims of the kind of information that might have led them to come forward earlier. To advance his case, Mulhearn cited racketeering and fraud laws, and alleged violations of Title IX, a law that prohibits sexual abuse in schools.

As Mulhearn told Judge Frederic Block, the first accusation came shortly after Foglietta arrived at the school in 1966. William Jackson, then an eighth grader, told the school's athletic director, Harlow Parker, and headmaster, J. Folwell Scull, that the coach had abused him. Scull acted swiftly and decisively: he threatened to expel the boy, which became a pattern for each charge of abuse brought to the administration over the next twenty-five years. (Foglietta was forced to retire in 1991; he died in 1998.)

This, Mulhearn argued, was the beginning of a cover-up. Judge Block partially adopted Mulhearn's argument and made a crucial ruling: Poly could not use the state's statute of limitations to block the suit if school administrators had consistently lied about when they first heard of the allegations. Meanwhile, the *Daily News*'s Michael O'Keeffe consistently kept the case in the paper's front pages, writing dozens of articles about its legal and factual nuances. He called Poly Prep "a symbol of institutional indifference to sexual abuse in youth sports" and even compared Foglietta to Jerry Sandusky. Some of Foglietta's victims were as young as ten.

Until Block's ruling, all such cases had been considered (or not) in the shadow of *Zumpano v. Quinn*, a New York Court of Appeals decision that consolidated two sexual abuse actions. In May 2003, John Zumpano, a fifty-four-year-old man, brought a lawsuit accusing James Quinn, a prominent Roman Catholic priest in the Syracuse Roman Catholic Diocese, of sexually abusing him almost daily when he was a teenager. Zumpano's attorney, Frank Policelli, argued that the abuse had caused Zumpano such severe emotional and psychological damage that his client was in no position to pursue legal recourse or protect his own legal rights before the statute of limitations had expired. But the state Supreme Court justice Norman Siegel determined that the statute of limitations could not be extended and dismissed Zumpano's $150 million lawsuit. Although Siegel believed the suit had merit, he ruled he did not have the authority to extend the time allowed for Zumpano to file it. Too many years had passed. "As a trial judge, I cannot make the law, I can only follow the law that exists, and as I read it the law is clear," he said.

"*Zumpano* places an enormous burden on a typical sixteen-year-old kid who has just been sexually traumatized," Mulhearn said. "The young victim is expected to share their shame with an adult and in many cases go above their abuser's head or to the police in order to pursue justice. That's a tall order for any minor but almost unfathomable for someone who just had their world and confidence shaken, their sexuality called into question, and their trust in both teacher and school pulled from under them."

Another component of the *Zumpano* decision was even worse news for plaintiffs. In *Boyle v. Smith*, forty-two plaintiffs, represented by Dowd, contended that the statute of limitations should not protect the Diocese of Brooklyn, because it was aware that certain priests had sexually abused children and yet engaged in a pattern of concealment. The court disagreed: "It is not enough that . . . defendants were aware of the abuse and remained silent about it . . . A wrongdoer is not legally obliged to make a public confession, or to alert people who may have claims against it, to get the benefit of a statute of limitations."

The decision was a disaster for adult survivors of childhood sexual abuse in New York State. As Mulhearn explains, a plaintiff could overcome the statute of limitations only if he could "plead and prove that school administrators made affirmative misrepresentations to him (or otherwise engaged in overt acts of fraud and/or deception) *after* he was abused, and that in reliance on those misrepresentations (or overt misconduct) he refrained from filing a lawsuit against the school and its culpable administrators." In essence, it instructed churches and schools that if they remained silent it was far easier to escape legal accountability. If anyone was searching for a playbook on how to cover up sexual abuse, this would be it.

And yet Judge Block—who was known as something of a maverick—granted the Poly Prep plaintiffs some hope. Agreeing with Mulhearn's argument that Poly Prep had actively misrepresented Foglietta's "honorable nature," he scheduled an evidentiary hearing for February 2013 to determine whether the statute of limitations should be lifted.

Whether or not Mulhearn's advocacy would ultimately succeed, his unorthodox approach to the Poly case was making him a rising star among lawyers who handled sexual abuse cases. The child of a cop and a schoolteacher, he came to the role after a long journey.

I first met Mulhearn at Docks restaurant in Manhattan. Before we got down to discussing the similarities between the Poly and Horace Mann cases, we spent twenty minutes recalling the epic 1981 baseball game in which Poly's team beat the HM Lions—our only loss that season.

Mulhearn, who manned third that day for Poly, recalled that, early in the game, the HM catcher Bill Hughes had yelled at Inky, with tears streaming down his dirt-smudged cheeks, to pull our pitcher. I reminded him of my teammate Doug Gurian's massive blast over the left-field wall to tie the game in the bottom of the last inning.

I asked Mulhearn if he remembered the lanky lefty who, almost single-handedly, put an end to our perfect season.

"Remember him?" Mulhearn asked. "Dennis was my twin brother."

Dennis Mulhearn, Poly's left fielder, had a great season that day, as they say in baseball, ending the game with two homers, two doubles, and ten RBIs.

We recalled, as if it were yesterday, how the Poly center fielder

caught a sinking line drive to end the game as the tying run (me!)
rounded third base in vain. I stopped cold next to Kevin Mulhearn,
as he celebrated with his victorious Poly teammates. I've thought
about that game over the years—it was epic, even in the context of
that fabled season.

Thirty years later, life had thinned out Mulhearn's hair and added
about eighty pounds to his stocky frame. Kevin told me that Dennis
had drowned in 1993. The loss was devastating to him. "He drowned
after a prolonged battle with mental illness," he said. "He was diag-
nosed with schizophrenia and messianic delusion." On August 24,
1993, Dennis Mulhearn was near Boston Harbor when some kids
playing catch accidentally threw the ball into the water. "He jumped
in to get it and he couldn't swim. Sank like a rock." Kevin named his
son, who turned eight in October 2014, after his brother. "There was
a blanket of grief over me after Dennis died," he said. "That blanket
kind of slipped off of my shoulders when my kid was born. Now my
whole outlook is different. I used to get into these very dark blue
funks from the end of summer till Christmas. That doesn't happen
anymore. My son is playing soccer now, and I'm coaching the team.
Not that I know anything about soccer."

I informed him that Doug Gurian, our star pitcher who had hit the
game-tying blast in the bottom of the seventh, had perished in the
Towers on 9/11.

We raised our scotches and toasted both Dennis and Doug.

Like me at HM, Mulhearn did not exactly blend in at Poly Prep.
He liked to joke that "when everyone else was going to parties on
Friday nights, we were working as banquet waiters."

As Mulhearn and I sat across from each other that night, I asked
him, "How do two middle-class kids like you and me end up doing a
thing like this?"

"Once I heard the stories," Mulhearn said, "there was no going
back. That's why I have to fight so hard to get these cases heard. That
is, until they pass the Markey bill. I was a complete rookie when I got
involved in this [Poly] case, and I wound up putting my life and
career on the line. Now I'm committing myself to getting justice for

these guys. We are the very beginning of this thing. I think the dam is about to burst on these cases."

After our initial meeting, I introduced Mulhearn to the Survivors' Group. They were in a highly tense state as they debated which lawyers to choose. The few survivors who spoke with Mulhearn, including F., were impressed by both his knowledge of the law and his pugnacious spirit. Mulhearn pitched his services to the group over the phone, and after much discussion, the group asked Dowd, Mones, and Mulhearn if they would consider working together to represent all the survivors. All three had managed to reach significant settlements for past clients—adult victims of childhood sexual abuse who had accused private institutions of failing to safeguard them—and while money may not have been the only thing the survivors wanted, for many it was the most tangible. "I think there were a lot of plaintiffs who needed money," said one lawyer familiar with the case. "The only liability the school had was a negative alumni reaction."

Just as the three lawyers were deciding whether they would form a team, "Charlotte," one of the female claimants, informed the group that she had contacted Gloria Allred, an L.A. lawyer who bills herself as "a fearless advocate for justice and equality." Allred had made a career of high-profile cases often involving women's rights—and celebrities. She has been called a "longtime master of the press conference" and has made television appearances in the service of her clients. Targets of her suits have included Mötley Crüe's drummer Tommy Lee, Arnold Schwarzenegger, Herman Cain, and Anthony Weiner. Now she jumped at the chance to attach herself to yet another high-profile case. She had rented a room at the Palace hotel in midtown Manhattan and declared that she "would love to meet everybody."

Almost everyone who met with Allred and her co-counselors Nathan Goldberg and Mariann Wang came away with the conclusion that the team's professionalism and Allred's proven ability to attract media attention provided a powerful combination. The group assumed that Horace Mann was afraid of the press, and the addition of the high-profile counsel to the mix would turn that fear up to eleven.

Dozens of hours and thousands of heated emails were exchanged as the group zeroed in on representation. Some wanted the nuts-and-bolts approach of the feisty Mones-Dowd-Mulhearn team. "I wanted to go with Dowd. I really liked him," Xander, the Tek victim, said. "He was down-to-earth. And he seemed genuinely interested in helping us put our lives back together. And Mulhearn was a sharp cookie, a real out-of-the-box thinker. I thought we had a good shot at a RICO action against the school."

Others argued that Mulhearn had only just started the Poly case and was lucky to have gotten as far as he had. It was simply too early to tell at that point if Judge Block would allow the case to move forward. Many wanted the clout that Allred brought to the table and argued that media coverage was the only leverage they had with the school.

As these discussions were raging, Dowd met with representatives from Schulte Roth & Zabel, Horace Mann's law firm, to discuss moving forward. "One and done," was how Dowd categorized HM's general position, meaning the school wanted all claims to be dealt with swiftly and all at once. Dowd also reported that when he was pushed by Schulte Roth for a settlement number, he'd told the HM lawyers to think in terms of about $1 million per person. "Horace Mann hadn't said no" was how Dowd characterized their response.

The group erupted. "Who authorized you to negotiate on our behalf?" one of the survivors demanded. Others felt it was way too early in the game and an unbelievably naïve negotiating tactic to be the first to offer a number.

"Many of the survivors reacted angrily," Gene said. "I didn't have a problem with it, but some people thought it was unethical."

"I felt like he did a really stupid thing," F. said. "It's not so much that the number was inappropriate. It was premature and he had not consulted with the survivors. He wasn't even hired yet."

By then more than twenty of the survivors had signed with Allred and her team to be represented for the duration of any mediation process that might occur. Six others signed on with Mones, Dowd, and

Mulhearn. M., who claimed Somary had abused him hundreds of times, signed with Rosemarie Arnold, an attorney in New Jersey, where some of his abuse occurred and which has more lenient statute of limitations laws than New York. Several survivors still hadn't settled on representation.

The fast-approaching meeting at the Harvard Club was provoking a lot of anxiety. There the Survivors' Group would face school officials at last. Despite Friedman's request, the members would be bringing their attorneys as well. "There were endless discussions on what tone to take during the meetings," F. said. Almost all the survivors attended in person. Joseph Cumming participated via Skype from Germany. Before the meeting began, Allred asked that no one other than her clients be present while she addressed the HM side. Some of the survivors, who had grown accustomed to seeing themselves as one unit, were upset by her request. It was the first visible indication that the survivors had split into several groups.

In the Slocum Room of the Harvard Club, Tom Kelly and Steve Friedman sat at one end of a long wooden conference table. Allred, Goldberg, and Wang were at the other. Survivors and spouses and other supporters filled out the rest of the room.

Although she hadn't had time to collect all the facts, Allred (who would not speak on the record with me about the Horace Mann case) read a fifteen-minute opening statement that sounded much like a summation in court. She laid out all the ways the various students had been abused, and how Horace Mann had known about the abuse for decades. She also made the case for the school doing the right thing by the survivors.

When Allred was done, and the other lawyers and survivors entered, Steve Friedman opened with a proposal. "I'd like you to all consider asking your lawyers to go," he addressed the group. "Let's send home the lawyers and let's talk." Kelly amplified Friedman's suggestion to send the lawyers away by suggesting that their absence would elevate the conversation.

Paul was outraged. "How dare you sit here and make this big

pitch about let's all send home the lawyers?" he said. "We have been asking to talk for months. I personally only retained my lawyer twenty-four hours ago. Where have you guys been all summer? You've been busy meeting with your lawyers and now you are going to condescend to us as if we are naïfs led astray by our big bad lawyers? You didn't even have the decency to respond to us when we asked you all summer to meet with us? How dare you!"

Paul then turned his attention to Kelly and looked him in the eye.

"You were the one on the phone with us all this time. How dare you condescend to us!"

"They speak for me!" F. shouted across the table.

Once it was clear the lawyers were there to stay, Friedman continued. "This is not the Horace Mann I know," he said. "This is not our school."

"I think he was trying to sound conciliatory," F. later said. "But it got people really upset. It came off sounding like he was trying to disown what had happened. Like the present-day school bears no responsibility."

Friedman also used the phrase "one and done," the same expression Dowd had reported the school's lawyers using. His other demand was a total media blackout. "If any of this leaks to the media, we're done," Friedman threatened. "You'll see how fast I will shut down this entire process."

Allred grinned like the Cheshire Cat. "I don't know why, but I feel like that might have been directed at me," she said.

At one point Friedman was interrupted by Rebecca, the alumna who'd been abused by the English teacher Crawford Blagden. "You shouldn't have let them rape kids," she screamed. Mariann Wang, from Allred's team, quietly escorted her from the room. Based on a history of similar volatile outbursts, both in person and on conference calls, Rebecca was to spend a majority of her time separated from the rest of the survivors.

While Friedman had kept his remarks brief, Kelly went into yet another rambling monologue. When he repeated, once again, how important it was that nobody go to the media, F., who had felt silenced for decades, couldn't stand it any longer. "I can't promise you that," he yelled across the vast table.

Despite those moments of tension, it was agreed that the two sides would enter mediation to reach a settlement. Both sides also agreed to respect the media blackout. "Horace Mann made it clear they were not going to give out any money if there were stories coming out in the press," said one lawyer familiar with the case. "That was pivotal to them."

Although they'd forfeited the press leverage Allred seemed to offer, many of the survivors left the meeting with the sense that, after all these years, they had brought Horace Mann to the table and were on the road to reconciling decades of abuse and cover-up. Although that road would not be smooth, there was a general consensus that HM was taking the group and their lawyers with a seriousness that had, until that point, been nonexistent.

On the way out, Mulhearn commented to some of the survivors that Friedman had shown where his weakness was: clearly he was terrified of the media. The media *was* the message, and HM seemed to have removed that powerful weapon from the survivors' arsenal. Some of the victims began to wonder if agreeing to the media blackout, or signing with Allred at all, had been the smart move.

That night, a group of survivors went out for drinks to replay the day's fireworks and rehash the tumultuous events of the past few months. They were happy for the camaraderie and the miracle of the various websites that had brought them together to tell their stories and begin to heal. But there was also a nervousness in the air, and they girded themselves for the long, tough process that was about to unfold. Some of them got extremely drunk.

7

THE WILD CARD

I taught *Macbeth* to ninth-graders for years," the former teacher Joyce Fitzpatrick wrote to me (and the Processing Horace Mann community) days after the *Times* piece appeared. "When she's told that their house guest Duncan has been killed, Lady Macbeth is pretty inept in her first cover-up remark: 'Woe, alas! What, in our house?' I remember talking to classes about the powerful and ambitious caring more about image and reputation than about the king's death. And how a skillful actor would deliver this line so the audience would get that . . . Cover-ups undo Macbeth—half-truths, evasions, excuses, deflected blame, denial. Lady Macbeth goes mad with it all."

The mood on campus was tense. Camera crews circled, waiting to pounce on any teacher, administrator, or student who would defy the school's strict policy against speaking to the media. The current staff, most of whom had arrived well after the incidents of sexual abuse had occurred, wanted to get on with their jobs.

And many parents, who were typically spending $40,000 a year to educate their children, just wanted the entire matter to go away. Students who once wore the Horace Mann colors as a badge of honor now covered those same sweatshirts and hats as they strolled around the city. Others avoided telling peers where they went, to avoid snide comments from rivals about "the sexual abuse school."

Others felt that the story tarnished the school's name, especially as it showed little sensitivity to how the institution had changed over the years. "When your article came out people asked me, 'Do you worry?'" said Bret Parker (HM '86), who has two kids at the school. "No. If I had any inclination something was happening I would say something.

"The vast majority of people who I interact with, for them it was a thing that happened in the past," he continued. "It almost seems foreign and unbelievable because it's so contrary to how they see the school now. They've had to deal with publicity, but it doesn't seem relevant."

In the aftermath of the Harvard Club meeting, the board was between a rock and a hard place: The survivors were seeking damages and a comprehensive accounting of what had happened. How should the school respond? If they were too generous with the survivors, some trustees argued, it could put the school on the brink of financial ruin. If the full truth were to come out, with the board's authorization, the damage to the school's reputation and financial solvency could pose an existential danger. For a school like Horace Mann that relies so heavily on its reputation and its promise to top-notch parents that it will get their kids into Harvard, Yale, or Princeton (H.Y.P. in HM parlance), the PR damage would be too great. On the other hand, by taking a hard-line approach to negotiating monetary compensation with the victims, the board might also be seen as damaging the school's reputation.

However, once the board indicated at the initial meeting at the Harvard Club that it was willing to negotiate a mediated settlement with the survivors, the next question became: How much? There is an old adage in civil litigation that says defendants apologize with their checkbooks. "The apology is how many zeros are on the check," said Mulhearn. "A thousand dollars is a helluva lot less of an apology than a million dollars."

"Steve Friedman led the hard-line faction," said a person familiar with the board's deliberations. "He was effectively saying, 'Let's offer them as little as possible. If we offer them a lot, they'll come out of the woodwork. And nobody's going to sue us. We can pay them a pittance and get this out of the press. They'll go away.'"

After a lengthy debate among the board members, the Friedman faction won out. "As the Board of Trustees of a not-for-profit educational institution, it is clear that our primary fiduciary responsibilities and legal obligations are to the school today and to its 1,800 current students," Friedman wrote in an August 6, 2012, letter to the community. "We are charged with ensuring that our policies, procedures, and practices promote the safety, education, and well-being of our students; maintain the financial strength and integrity of our institution; and honor the intent of the commitments that have been made by our donors."

Although the "one-and-done" strategy may have been perceived by many as wildly insensitive to the need of the survivors and the wider community to heal, it made sense if looked at from a purely economic standpoint. It was better to pay the survivors, get the story out of the news, and shut the files in case the Markey bill ever passed.

And yet many in the community, including several wealthy and powerful trustees, believed that even on Friedman's terms, the board had badly misconstrued how to fulfill its fiduciary duty and overlooked one principal obligation: preserving the school's reputation. By failing to be up front about what had happened, the board had imposed upon the school a new reputation for obfuscation, if not denial. And that reputation was of paramount importance to, using Friedman's words, "the school today and to its 1,800 current students." No one wanted to bankrupt the school, as some defenders claimed, but it was clear that the school could have found a middle ground between resisting calls for transparency and significant restitution and destroying Horace Mann. The board seemed to overlook the deeper meaning of its fiduciary duty: its obligation to the future of the school and its future students.

•

As it became clear that the school would not support a full inquiry into what happened, concerned and outraged alumni began to talk among themselves. "Those early phone calls were pretty fractious," recalled Rob Boynton. "These were people I hadn't seen in years and we were not sure what we were doing. But it was clear to me that at some point the victims were going to get together and be represented by lawyers or someone else, and there would be mediation. The true victims needed to have a group that could say things they couldn't say. Leak things they couldn't leak. Be strident in ways they feel they couldn't. They needed the wild card and we had to be the wild card."

The Horace Mann Action Coalition—the group that picketed the HM parking lot—took on exactly this role. Spearheaded by Bill Hughes, Christina Propst (HM '87), and others, it would play a major part in the events to come.

Soon Rob Boynton joined the conversation. Boynton was one of the alumni I had called when I was first reporting for the *Times*. He mentioned Mark Wright but said that he did not want to talk about "Hannes," as he called him, being one of those who had been close to the maestro. His parents lived right down the street from him and he spent a lot of time at the Somary house, even going drinking with their son Stephen. "At the time you called, I didn't think anything had happened," he said later. "There were always all kinds of rumors about Hannes and boys, and Hannes and girls . . . But I never knew anything for sure; I didn't know anyone who'd had a direct experience with him. In high school all the good-looking boys are claiming they're getting laid and all the girls are having sex with everyone and you're not getting anything. So you assume all the rumors are false."

Whatever his assumptions, Boynton's mother (who was very active in the school) would not let him go on any of the "famed trips to Europe" with Somary. "She had heard things about them and did not want me to go," he recalled. "It was a point of contention because I was the president of the Glee Club; it was kind of what you did! She just put her foot down." His mother has since passed away and he says it wasn't sex but drinking that she had heard about on those field trips. "The thing that seems different now that I am a fifty-one-year-old and the father of an eleven-year-old and teaching twenty-year-olds [at NYU] is that there used to be a lot of boundary crossing," said Boynton. "The fact that we called them Hannes and Anne. That we would be at a party, drinking with your teacher—that was very exciting and felt very natural. For a sixteen-, seventeen-year-old you felt very adult."

After helping his friend J. come forward on Processing Horace Mann with his experience of being abused by Mark Wright, Boynton became one of the first to campaign for a more active stance; out of this shared impulse, the Horace Mann Action Committee was born. He recalled the political actions of his college years (divestment from South Africa, etc.) and said, "I was on the right side but didn't feel any passion about them. I felt really called, for the first time, to involve myself with this. My connection was deep and deeply rooted; I felt like I had something to offer in my skills as a mediator, and because of my understanding of how media works, and I felt I had a philosophical interest in this beyond, 'These people were treated terribly.'"

Peter Brooks (HM '66), a psychologist and management expert with twenty-five years of corporate experience, was one of the oldest graduates to take up the cause. He was not, when he first came to Processing Horace Mann, a Facebook kind of guy. His daughter had to prompt him to join.

Brooks and many like him had to square their experience of the school with a new and different reality: the icons who were shown to be predators, the safe zone that proved to be anything but. Letting go of that happy dream may have been the hardest part. "There is a great Le Carré quote from *Tinker, Tailor, Soldier, Spy*," Brooks said. "Smiley asks Toby, 'Did you ever buy a fake painting?' and Toby says, 'No, I sold a few.' Smiley says, 'The more you pay for it the less likely you are to question its authenticity.' I posted that on Processing Horace Mann. It was very competitive at the school; everyone valued that label. I remember junior, senior year the application process for colleges and the drama of 'who got in where.' I guess that was the point of it for some kids: what their parents had paid for their education. So twenty, thirty, forty years later you think, 'Did you buy a fake painting?' The question is, who's the rube? Is it the guy who made the fake painting, or the guy who bought it?"

The alumni who coalesced around acting rather than just talking about what was now commonly called "the Horace Mann scandal" threw themselves into the battle with the focus and abandon I had not witnessed since SAT season at the high school. As the survivors prepared for mediation, the newly minted HMAC took up the battle on other fronts, keeping the issue alive among alumni and the general public.

The beginning of HMAC, like that of many advocacy groups, was far from smooth. There were passionate debates about structure, constituencies, and how to best help the victims while not alienating the parents or incurring the wrath of HM's team of lawyers. Between busy careers and family lives, everyone was inventing "free time" they didn't really have for a high school that most hadn't thought much about since graduation.

And although their goals were similar, their approaches were wildly different. Josh Manheimer (HM '77), who acted as a point of contact for many alumni from the mid-1970s, was ready to throw caution to the wind and lob bombs at HM from day one. As a writer who makes his living creating direct response mail, he was a constant source of creative ideas: How about a billboard near the Horace Mann campus reminding visitors of the school's stonewalling? Or maybe a Google ad campaign targeting current parents, or anyone who searched for "Horace Mann School," for that matter? He even suggested renting an inflatable rat, like the ones unions use to pester management who hire nonunion workers, and placing it outside Steve Friedman's office at EOS Partners. (No one could find an inflatable stone wall.)

Bill Hughes was representative of another faction, one less interested in going to battle with the school and more inclined to support the survivors in their personal and legal battles as well as holding the school up to its stated values. "We are not on war footing yet," Hughes admonished the group—though the atmosphere felt increasingly like that of a war room.

But before there could be any reconciliation, there had to be truth. Although most of the survivors wanted an independent investigation, others simply wanted to mediate a settlement and move on with their lives. Representatives of the two groups spoke frequently in order to support each other without jeopardizing their own specific agendas.

In late July 2012, HMAC unveiled a website that documented the scandal. There was an in-depth time line detailing the dozens of acts of abuse that had occurred at Horace Mann beginning in the early 1960s, all the more shocking when laid out in a linear fashion. The launch of the website and the attendant publicity set off yet another round of shock and anger as more alumni across the world saw the names of their favorite teachers on the growing list of known abusers.

For both ethical and legal reasons, there were hours of discussions about the threshold of evidence needed to include a teacher's name on the list. HMAC's list began with published accounts. Although the coalition did not have the capacity to investigate each accusation, it would publish accounts only after ascertaining that they had been made at the time of the abuse. This would at least establish that the account was not a later invention. At times HMAC would also verify details with members of the Survivors' Group. They wanted to know if the account had been reported to anyone at HM. If so, some administrator or teacher would have written down and retained the account. Where were those accounts?

"The point of the exercise," Peter Brooks said, "was to see if there was a pattern. And there was. We learned of at least three sets of serial predators. Beginning in the '60s and continuing for decades were Somary, Berman, Lin, and Clinton. In the '70s there was Wright, Clark, Kops, and Terrence Archer. In the '80s it was Blagden, Klein, and a male and female coach.

"And in between, under an apparent umbrella of protection from Clark and Clinton, there were eight more."

When all the reports were in, there were credible claims against twenty-two teachers and administrators.

HMAC employed other tactics as well. In September 2012, to coincide with the start of the new school year, it organized a diploma return: alumni, unhappy with the school's response to the growing scandal, decided to mail their diplomas back to the school in the spirit of John Lennon returning his MBE to the queen of England to protest the U.K.'s supportive role in the Vietnam War. "The point was to take a stand while avoiding an on-campus confrontation with parents and being accused of messing with the kids," Brooks said. Some alumni sent a facsimile copy of their diploma provided by HMAC and others sent the originals. Some sent theirs and said "please hold until you decide to investigate." While it is difficult to determine the exact number of participants, the stunt got the group some press.

When it was clear that the school would not commission an independent investigation, HMAC attempted to raise $150,000 for the former judge Leslie Crocker Snyder to find out who knew what when. The group had selected Snyder, a thirty-five-year veteran of New York's criminal justice system, over several other prominent candidates. Snyder had twice run for Manhattan district attorney, once against her former boss Robert Morgenthau, under whom she had been the first woman to try felony and homicide cases as an assistant DA. She also founded and led the DA's Sex Crimes Prosecution Bureau, the first of its kind in the nation, and later coauthored the New York State Rape Shield Law, which limits a defendant's ability to cross-examine rape complainants about their past sexual behavior.

HMAC wasn't the only alumni group wanting to take action. In August 2012, two Horace Mann board members, Joe Rose (HM '77) and Regina Kulik Scully (HM '81), announced the formation of Hilltop Cares, a not-for-profit that would, among other activities, help survivors pay for therapeutic assistance.

Rose was an heir to one New York real estate dynasty (Rose Associates) and had married into another (the Georgetown Group). He was Horace Mann royalty. His father, Daniel, and his two uncles had all attended HM before making their fortunes. Daniel had funded the short video Kate Geis and I had made about Theo. The Roses had not only donated millions to the school, they had a building with their name on it.

Scully was another name to reckon with at the school. A PR professional, philanthropist, and film producer, she had, along with her brother Dominic, endowed several faculty chairs, including ones in English, foreign languages, and mathematics. For Scully, who was an executive producer of *The Invisible War*—an Academy Award–nominated film about the epidemic of rape in the military—the matter was deeply personal. *Boyhood Shadows*, a film she produced about the devastating effects sexual abuse had on male adult survivors, included the lifelong struggles of her brother Glenn, who was abused by a youth league swim coach.

As board members and prominent donors, Rose and Scully had both the money and the insider status to launch the initiative. Though the school did not affiliate with Hilltop Cares, it greeted the effort warmly. It was not controversial to applaud alumni who were coming together to support the victims; who could object to that?

In October 2012, Horace Mann refused to include a panel on allegations of abuse at its alumni reunion, which was held at the Conrad hotel in lower Manhattan. In response, HMAC set up a panel of its own across the street. It invited interested alumni to Poets House (a national archive of poetry, including books by the HM alumni Jack Kerouac and Anthony Hecht) to hear firsthand accounts of abuse suffered by some students.

"It's not anyone's intention to bombard, proselytize, harangue etc.," Brooks wrote in a letter to the community, "merely to credit the much-vaunted critical faculties we honed at Horace Mann to allow each to reach their own conclusions and their own peace."

More than seventy Horace Mann graduates gathered at Poets House. Boynton moderated the discussion, and several prominent members of the HM community, including Lawrence Golub and Joe Rose, were in the audience to listen to the survivors' testimonies. (Golub, a former board member, and Rose, a current one, made it clear that they were attending as private individuals and not as representatives of the current school.)

Christina Propst, one of HMAC's founders, stood and read a prepared statement from Alison Pollet (HM '86), a children's book author who lives in England. At the request of HMAC, Pollet contributed an account of being pursued and even harassed by Crawford Blagden. The intent was to corroborate the abuse that Rebecca said she suffered at the hands of the English teacher. Propst read the following to the assembled alumni:

> When I re-read the journal I kept for his class, I can see why he thought I was an option. Sex abusers tend to go for those they perceive as vulnerable. He encouraged us to experience the poetry personally, to write about our feelings and our lives. I did just that.
>
> After an entry about feeling agitated and lost in my house, while my father was hosting a poker game, he wrote: "If you get lonely among all those poker players, give me a call" and gave me his number. Next to a sad entry—even by angsty adolescent standards . . . he wrote in giant letters, all caps, down the margin of the page: "I LOVE YOU, ALISON POLLET."
>
> I can see now that, in some ways, he was giving me what I obviously wanted: affirmation, love. I know at the time that I appreciated his words. I could even appreciate them now— wildly inappropriate as they were—had he not wanted something in return.
>
> I shouldn't have accepted the invitation to his house. I knew there was something wrong with it. I was, to use my words from back then, "grossed out" by my teacher. I asked my brother, then in 9th grade, to wait with me on Riverside Drive

to be picked up. I remember feeling so bad about that—as if by allowing my little brother to see me get into the teacher's car, I'd sullied his innocence. He was just a kid. I think at the moment I needed to remind myself I was still one too.

Earlier in the trimester my teacher had given me pot—a giant rock of hash actually—so I'm going to guess we were probably stoned when he kissed me on the floor of his basement apartment. For those of you who have read the Processing Horace Mann forum, you've probably heard about his basement apartment—it's where a girl reported he raped her repeatedly. She was my brother's year.

There were a lot of phone calls after that, more proclamations of love. I have a letter, even. He started sitting with me in the cafeteria when I was with my friends, surprising me from behind with an embrace when I was standing in front of Mr. Singer's office. I was horrified. I was in over my head. But I also needed him to write my college recommendations. Some colleges required you get one from your faculty advisor; unfortunately, he was mine.

I don't recall how I finally rejected him. But I very clearly remember the late night call he made to my parents' house when he wept uncontrollably. I was as ill equipped to handle that as I'd been to handle any of it.

I know that there are alumni who wish the survivors of abuse at Horace Mann wouldn't make such a big deal about what happened. I understand exactly how they feel. Until June of this year, I'd hardly ever talked about what happened to me. I didn't share my story with the *Times*. That journal— with the folded-up letter inside it—has been in a box on a high shelf in my parents' house since 1986.

I now know my story matters: because it's connected to those of my fellow students and classmates. I would like to know how it came to be that there were so many predators teaching on one campus at one time. I would like to know how my teacher got his job. I recently heard he caused a scandal at the school he was at previous to Horace Mann by running off with a student. I'd like to know if that's true.

I'd like Horace Mann to hire an investigator who can answer these questions.

After all this time and all this silence, it seems like very little to ask.

The evening at Poets House was illuminating, healing, and exhausting. The next morning, on the drive back to his home in the Boston suburb of Randolph, Bill Hughes, who'd been in attendance, stopped by the HM campus. "I walked around the empty campus. It was a place I'd loved so dearly. Where I literally grew up. As I walked the grounds I remember thinking to myself, 'This is not my home.'"

HMAC, encouraged by the success of the Poets House format, hosted similar events for HM alumni in Boston, L.A., D.C., Chicago, and New York.

On December 26, 2012, the opposing sides in the Poly Prep case settled to the satisfaction of the majority of the plaintiffs. The agreement brought to an end the extended legal and public relations battle.

"After three and a half years my guys had battle fatigue," Mulhearn said. "I was out of money; ninety-five percent of my time was spent on this case."

At the time of the settlements, the court was on the brink of holding a hearing to discuss whether Poly's conduct was in fact so egregious that the statute of limitations should be waived. It is likely that Poly Prep settled at least in part because it wanted to avoid such a hearing and the possibly damaging revelations that would result.

Though they had originally sought $20 million in damages, the twelve Poly Prep survivors received roughly $800,000 each.

Horace Mann and the Survivors' Group finally came to terms on how the mediation process would take place. After months of haggling over who would be present and the parameters of the mediation itself, the date was set for the week of March 11, 2013. By mutual agreement between HM and the survivors, Commonwealth Mediation and Conciliation, a Massachusetts-based private dispute resolution firm, was chosen to broker the negotiation. Its goal was to bring about, as quickly as possible, a monetary settlement.

Paul Finn, Commonwealth's CEO, was a beefy lawyer with a thick Boston accent and a reputation as a no-nonsense mediator unafraid to do whatever it took to get both sides to reach an agreement. His firm, chosen from a pool of three, had heard thousands of cases, large and small, including the one against the Archdiocese of Boston, one brought by the victims of the Station nightclub fire in Rhode Island (in which a hundred people died), and the 2006 Big Dig ceiling collapse, which snarled Boston traffic for a year. Commonwealth's fees were to be split between the two sides.

The aim of mediation is a settlement both sides agree is fair—a bit of a unicorn in the world of civil justice. "The old adage is that [a good] settlement is when both sides are equally unhappy," said one lawyer familiar with the case. (Finn declined to speak to me for this book.) "The defendant pays more than he wants to and the plaintiff accepts less than he thinks he deserves. That's the ideal. I think mediation is a process that favors the defendant, not so much the plaintiff. The mediator is interested in getting the matter settled, period."

This is not a slam on Finn, who this attorney thinks did a good job in a difficult situation; it's just the nature of the mediator's role. "Mediators are driven to settle cases," the lawyer said.

As the months wore on and the Survivors' Group met with its various legal representatives, Paul became more and more involved with the group. He spent hours on the calls, often raising challenging questions such as whether to bring along lawyers when the group ultimately met with Horace Mann. He attended lengthy meetings with Kelly and tried to broker meetings between the board and the survivors.

On the eve of mediation, Paul and I sat parked outside my house and discussed the group's chance of getting a fair deal out of Horace Mann. He knew that some victims of child abuse by the Catholic Church had been compensated for surviving acts similar to the one he described to us in the woods long ago. In some cases, survivors had been compensated for times when fully clothed priests had rubbed up against them when they were fully clothed.

He said he was nervous about telling his story. Thinking that Paul had been hugged by Somary behind a closed door and had narrowly escaped an encounter with the maestro in a Connecticut hotel room, I flippantly suggested that he tell his "little Somary story, grab a check, and haul ass. Performance of a lifetime." It was a thoughtless thing to say, but given what we knew then about the prevalence and depth of the abuse, hugs behind a closed door and a walk in the rain to avoid Somary seemed almost trivial to me.

"What the fuck is wrong with you?" he snapped back with an intensity I had not expected.

"What? Are you—"

"You run around giving all this empathy to all these people," he continued. "And what does thirty-plus fucking years of friendship buy me? Anything? How do you know what happened to me?"

"I'm just . . . what?"

"Just get out of the car."

"Did something—"

"Just get out of the fucking car."

I stepped out of the car, stunned, and watched him pull away.

The next night Paul came over and we picked up the conversation where we'd left it. After decades of marital-style bickering, I could sense this was a big storm brewing.

I was slicing oranges to make him a glass of freshly squeezed juice as he sat on a barstool at the island in my kitchen. It was a familiar position, Paul bellied up to the bar, me pouring the drinks. We'd been positioned like that the day he walked into 17 Murray

Street, a bar in New York City owned by some of the Mets, and convinced me to go with him to Martha's Vineyard to figure out the rest of our lives. The same position when I served him warm beers and soggy peanuts at the VFW in Oak Bluffs when I decided to pursue writing and acting in Chicago and he music and therapy in Oakland. The same position, a few years after that, in a Chicago bar, when I introduced him to my future wife, Madeline.

He looked as though he'd barely scraped together any sleep since the night before. He was sluggish, his every move in slow motion.

"How do you know what happened to me?" he asked. "Did you ever even bother asking?"

"Yes, in fact, I did."

"When?"

"I asked you when we were sitting in my backyard," I said, gesturing out the window. "I kept pushing you to tell me if anything else happened with you and Somary. You don't remember that?"

"No." He shook his head. "I must have blocked it out."

"At least three times I asked you. And every time you said no."

"Well, then I lied." His voice was getting trapped in his throat. The words seemed to squeak out, like the sneaky air from a birthday balloon as you try tying the knot tight around your fingers. "I'll probably never tell you what happened."

I stopped cutting the orange and stared at him. He seemed weighed down by decades of tamping down dark secrets.

"Jesus Christ," I said, and set the knife and the orange on the cutting board. I walked around to where he was sitting and gave him a hug. We both started crying. We remained like that for about two or three minutes—just hugging and weeping.

"I'm so sorry," I said, apologizing for my flippancy and for all he was now telling—or not telling—me. "I'm so sorry."

I tried staying with him in the moment, but my mind was running like a racehorse. I wasn't just shaken and sickened and shocked and saddened. I was hurt. Paul had had more than thirty years to tell all—including the night around the campfire when Andrew first revealed that Wright had abused him; hundreds of hours spent hashing out every detail of our lives; my getting the assignment from the *Times*; his watching me chase down the deeds of Somary—the very man who had abused him. And still nothing. Silence.

I knew it wasn't about me, but a part of me was struggling not to take it personally. Aside from sadness, I felt betrayed, even a little angry. Why hadn't he told me? Did he think I would judge him? Did he think I would tell someone else? Why hadn't he told anyone? Why hadn't I asked? Why hadn't I pieced it together? What kind of friend was I? Was I so blind in every aspect of my life? Why didn't I know? Had I always known? Was I so naïve or obtuse to have bought the "Somary gave me long hugs" cover story for so long?

I asked Paul if his wife knew.

"I wasn't even planning on telling you."

I walked Paul to his motorcycle and hugged him once again before we said good night. As his taillights disappeared, I felt I needed no further evidence to disprove the notion that, as Friedman, Kelly, and the board kept insisting, "all this" was in the distant past.

If this lifelong friend, soul mate, and brother had managed not to tell me or his wife for all these years, I could only imagine the hundreds, thousands, and millions of people out there clamping shut these terrible memories. I stood stunned in my driveway for about half an hour thinking of all that pain, misery, and lost potential.

I trudged punch-drunk up to bed.

"Guess what Paul just told me."

"He's one of the victims?" Madeline asked.

I nodded in the dark. "I don't think I can take any more of this shit." Tears streaked my face and moistened my pillow.

8

MEDIATION

On March 10, 2013, the night before the mediation was to begin, a small group gathered at the Tribeca loft of one of the survivors. F., who had flown in from California, brought candy-filled piñatas with photos of different perpetrators pinned to them and hung them from the ceiling: Here was the face of Somary on a sparkly five-pointed star; there was Tek Lin hanging on a string. There was even a bright Mylar-covered Inky piñata that would have complemented one of his loud sweaters.

After a few drinks and some remarks about finally having their teachers where they wanted them, various members of the Survivors' Group took turns attacking the piñata with their particular abuser's face on it. "It was kind of a bizarre and wacky exercise," said one participant, who admitted to smashing the Somary piñata with gusto, "but I have to admit, a strangely satisfying one."

"What I really remember," said F., "is the sound of the baseball bat connecting."

After what became a primal frenzy, grown men swinging with abandon at the images of teachers who had harmed them long ago, there was a lot of candy lying on the floor. No one touched any of it. They swept it up and then headed to Midtown and their evening's ultimate destination: the cavernous basement ballroom of the Third

Church of Christ, Scientist, on Park Avenue. Gloria Allred's team had rented the space for "some casual downtime" prior to what was to be a two-week mediation process. There was no agenda other than for the survivors and lawyers to get to know one another. The dozen or so survivors, their attorneys, and some spouses were served elegant food out of chafing dishes by white-jacketed waiters. The relatively few people in the luxurious, dimly lit room only added to the clumsiness of the evening.

"It was like a cocktail party from hell," recalled one person. "It was a nice gesture, but it couldn't have possibly been more awkward. A buffet table, drinks. I wanted to have like eight drinks. I ended up talking stiffly with Gloria about her summer house in Malibu. It was pretty strange."

It had been mutually agreed upon that the mediation would take place at the spacious Manhattan offices of Horace Mann's legal counsel, Schulte Roth & Zabel, a respected white-shoe law firm that had handled, among many other transactions, the sale of Chrysler Financial to the TD Bank Group.

The next morning, March 11, two groups of survivors began assembling at the Schulte Roth offices. The larger group, representing twenty-five survivors, was represented by the Allred team. M., who said he was abused hundreds of times over three years by Johannes Somary, was represented by Rosemarie Arnold. All insisted the negotiation should not be just about money. They wanted Horace Mann to agree to an independent investigation and to campaign in favor of changing the statute of limitations laws.

As the survivors gathered, there was trepidation but also a sense of accomplishment.

"It was odd, I gotta admit," said one. "Here I was at the reception desk checking into a highbrow law office, and I was wondering what the receptionist was thinking. Did she know who I was?"

He and another survivor were led into a large, windowless conference room. A man in a suit, about ten years older than them, sat alone at the huge conference table that dominated the room. They didn't know whether he was a lawyer, a victim, or part of the mediation team—and clearly he was wondering the same thing about them. After saying hello and waiting a few awkward moments, the stranger finally asked, "So . . . what role do you two play in all this?"

"Um, just a couple of survivors chatting," one quipped.

"Oh, me too," said the older man, with visible relief. "I thought you guys were . . . like . . . lawyers."

On that first day, Horace Mann's counsel met with Mulhearn, Mones, and Dowd and argued that the attorneys, who represented six of the survivors, had no case. The school had no legal liability, they insisted. "For those unschooled in the nuances of the law, it was a compelling presentation," said one lawyer familiar with the case. "You looked at that narrow presentation and said, 'Gee, we really can't sue them.'" Yes, in the Poly Prep case, a judge had allowed the suit to go forward because of Mulhearn's argument that the school had committed fraud. But this was an anomaly, the Horace Mann lawyers insisted, not to be repeated. They had even written a statement on the whiteboard saying the decision had been an aberration (which must have been news to Mulhearn).

Whatever the merit of Schulte Roth's arguments, they proved effective. All six of Mulhearn, Mones, and Dowd's clients settled on the first day, with Kathy Howard receiving the largest payment. Though the suicide of Howard's son, Ben Balter, hung over the group like a shroud, it was the nature of the evidence that moved the school to be more generous with her: the letter Ben had written Horace Mann about Somary's abuse was a matter of public record, as was the school's failure to act on that letter.

Horace Mann then made a similar presentation to Allred and the lawyers on her team. After that, it was Allred's turn to meet with her clients. The atmosphere in the conference room where the survivors she represented were gathered rivaled the strangeness of the previous evening's hotel gathering.

It was as if the anxiety that people feel in a hospital waiting room were crossed with the exuberance you might experience at a high school reunion. Some survivors, separated by decades, were meeting one another for the first time; others hugged after not seeing each other since graduation.

Some had been abused hundreds of times over a period of years while others were made to feel uncomfortable after encounters that were sexual in nature. Some had gone to HM when it was still an all-boys school; others had attended the post-Inky coed version. Some had labored for decades under the impression they'd been an abuser's sole target while others had known that they had not been alone. Some had been referring to themselves as survivors for years while others would be sharing their stories for the first time. Some desperately needed the money while others were financially successful and just wanted to have their pain acknowledged in order to move on with their lives.

Whatever their differences, after decades of silence they had brought the mighty Horace Mann to the table. After nearly six months of crystallizing as a group, telling one another their stories, the moment of truth was at hand.

The chatting ceased the moment Allred, Wang, and Nathan Goldberg entered the conference room. They were accompanied by two men who looked like linebackers in suits—Paul Finn the CEO and Brian Mone the president of Commonwealth Mediation.

Allred entered the room wearing one of her signature bright red suits and opened the proceedings by saying that Horace Mann was afraid of the media her presence would generate and that the school wanted it all over very quickly. The facts seem to bear this out: the mediation was occurring only nine months after the publication of "Prep-School Predators." The feisty feminist attorney and her team appeared confident and ready for battle. Yes, she could showboat, and her reputation offended some—she once gave an anti-abortion state senator a chastity belt and then successfully sued him for libel when he complained that he had been "molested by a slick, butch lawyeress"—but she was a true advocate of victims' rights and had delivered in noncelebrity cases. ("Gloria's an effective advocate and people are afraid of her," said one of the other attorneys representing survivors. "Her media savvy had Horace Mann shaking in their boots for a while.") Back in her L.A. office was a framed letter from a girl whose godfather Allred had helped convict of molesting her. "Thank you for giving me my life back," the girl wrote.

When she finished, Finn seized the floor and introduced himself in a manner that left no mistake about who would be leading the next two weeks' proceedings.

"There was definitely a pissing contest between Allred and Finn," said one survivor. "These are two huge egos."

"How much money would I have to pay you to let me abuse your child?" Finn asked in his booming Boston accent, making eye contact with individuals in the room one by one. "What would it be worth to you?"

Of course there was no correct answer to this rhetorical flourish, but Finn was making a point. "Whatever money we get for you is *not* repayment," he continued. "No one can ever repay you for your pain. Or give you your childhood back. So you won't get what you deserve."

It was clear from the first moment that Finn was a charismatic, funny storyteller who joked, prodded, cursed like a sailor, and was willing to do whatever he had to do to get both sides to meet somewhere in the middle. As a lead arbitrator, Finn typically mediated between three hundred and four hundred cases per year, and he was an old hand at bashing down expectations.

"You guys have been through a rough ride," Finn told the group. "And maybe this will put some end to some of the interminable suffering."

Some felt that Finn's remarks were full of promise—emotional healing and cash compensation—while others thought his opening was a clear exercise in lowering expectations. "He never promised us anything," said one survivor. "If anything, he was trying to get us to come to terms with the important point that the whole notion of monetizing suffering was ridiculous."

But whatever financial expectations Finn had set up (or knocked down) with his remarks were soon muddied when the Allred team brought in John McCulloch, a financial professional. McCulloch explained that he specialized in helping plaintiffs figure out how to manage the money they received in a settlement, potentially structuring things to reduce the tax effect. It was like telling people what to expect when they win the lottery—or, as one of the survivors put it, "a clear message that significant money was going to change hands."

Next the Allred team brought in Louise Lipman, a licensed psychotherapist and a certified trainer, educator, and practitioner of psychodrama, sociometry, and group psychotherapy. Over the next two weeks, Lipman would help individual survivors prepare to tell their stories to the representatives from Horace Mann. She would show those who chose to work with her how to use descriptive detail and emotion and how to stress the long-term effects that the abuse had had on their lives. Her presence, by all accounts, was a huge comfort to the survivors.

Late that morning, once the game plan was understood, the group marched down to another large conference room on the floor below.

Allred enlisted the survivors to rearrange the tables and chairs so that they would sit facing the Horace Mann representatives. Her team had placed around the room large photographs of the victims at the time they were molested. It was strange for many of these adults to find themselves surrounded by pictures of themselves from those times.

When the room was properly arranged, the survivors found their seats. The group grew quiet as the Horace Mann contingent—Kelly, Friedman, and a crowd of lawyers from the school and its various insurance companies—entered and found their seats.

Rows of victims faced the HM people as if they were two football teams staring across the field prior to kickoff. There was no place to hide.

Finn stood and gave a brief overview of how the process was going to work before turning the floor over to the Allred team to make their case. Allred, Goldberg, and Wang took turns, using a PowerPoint presentation that featured harrowing quotes pulled from personal written testimonies and a time line of events. It also featured a schematic diagram of the HM campus, with a child's silhouette placed in the middle; the diagram was riddled with X's representing every known spot where sexual abuse had taken place. It included the head-master's house, the athletic building, buildings with names familiar to anyone who ever attended Horace Mann—Tillinghast, Pforzheimer, Prettyman—all were marked. In this condensed format, the Allred team impressively detailed the history of the sexual abuse that had occurred as far back as 1962 and as recently as 1996. By the end of the day, between the lawyers' summaries and the survivors' written testimonies, the extent of the accusations was stunning:

- It was common knowledge that a girl shouldn't get into a car, even with another student, with Joe Klein, the driver's ed teacher.
- Johannes Somary picked one special music student each year to lavish praise upon and then sexually abuse. He as-saulted student musicians in hotel rooms on Glee Club trips around the world, leaving many victims in his wake over his forty-plus-year tenure.
- Tek Lin, the beloved English teacher, school chaplain, and lover of flora, would invite students to his home and then ask them to spend the night in his bed.
- Mark Wright, the revered football coach and art teacher, performed numerous humiliating "physical exams" on his athletes. Wright had another student, Andrew, come by in-dividually to work on his art and abused him then.
- Robert Berman, the English teacher, created a cult of "Bermanites," changing the attire, vocabulary, and minds of select boys before subjecting them to all manner of sex-ual exploitation. He would assign boys extra homework, and if the student's work did not meet his standards, he would demand sex as punishment. Berman boasted to Steve Fife that many of his students had committed suicide.
- Berman spun Fife around and kissed him during a trip to Washington, D.C., in spring 1970. Fife began visiting

Berman's apartment near Columbia University, under the auspices of continuing a classical education by taking piano lessons with a former student of Berman's. Berman demanded Fife repay the debt by undressing and masturbating in front of him.

- Crawford Blagden, the English teacher, invited several of his students to get high in his home. He seduced, abused, belittled, beat, and ultimately raped a female student on the linoleum floor of his basement apartment.

- Terrence Archer, the brilliant and commanding biology teacher, mentored "Alvin," an inner-city student from the Manhattanville Projects in Harlem, before abusing him for years.

- An openly gay, much beloved art history teacher (unnamed publicly by his victim) had gotten F., a male student, drunk on an art history trip to Italy and had sex with him.

- The guidance department chair Bill Clinton collected information on victims, did nothing, and extorted sex from some of them.

- Inky Clark invited Jon Seiger, then fourteen, to the headmaster's Tudor mansion, where he and Kops gave him drinks before taking him out to a Manhattan club where older men purchased the sexual services of young men. After more drinks, Kops convinced two male prostitutes to come back to the headmaster's house for more drinks. The male prostitutes were instructed to "get things going" before Clark and Kops joined in. Inky and Kops abused Seiger all night. And Seiger was sexually abused by eight different Horace Mann teachers and administrators in the following months and went on to a life of drugs and prostitution.

In the middle of the litany, on the advice of her lawyers, Rebecca got up and quietly left the room. Rebecca's volatility had been triggered by the events of the past year; she had agreed when asked by her lawyers to absent herself in order to reduce the amount of information flooding her. She had been unstable before and during mediation, sometimes erupting at a fellow survivor who she felt had not endured the same level of suffering she had. "You think that's bad," she'd yelled at one Somary survivor during a meeting. "Try being raped on a linoleum floor and being beaten by a psycho! Crawford tried to throw me out of a car a few times!"

Wang spoke in specifics about the harm the children had suffered and how the abuse still affected them decades later. She invited those on the HM side to try to imagine how terrible it must have been for the children.

When the grisly details were finished, there were twenty-two perpetrators named.

Even more staggering than the number of predators roaming the sheltered halls of a single, tiny campus was that Allred's team demonstrated, beyond any reasonable doubt, that victims had repeatedly reported their abuse to both faculty and administrators. Ben Balter's 1993 letter to Headmaster Phil Foote, alerting him to Somary's behavior, was hardly the only accusation to be met with silence.

The lawyers' presentation also made it quite clear that some of the perpetrators were in collusion. When one of Tek Lin's victims reported his problem with Tek to Somary, Somary said he would take care of it—and Tek never bothered him again.

When Ron Klepper, who had already been abused by Wright, refused to leave the library with him, he was told by Kops that he had to go.

And after his evening of debauchery with Inky and Kops, Seiger was approached by Somary, who said, "I heard about the great time you had the other night with Mr. Clark and Mr. Kops. I'm glad you are getting to know them so well."

The Allred team's argument also shredded the notion that the current Horace Mann board and administration did not know about abuse before the publication of my article. Two Somary survivors, Ed Bowen and Joseph Cumming, had separately reported abuse to Tom Kelly in the spring of 2011, a full year before the *Times* story.

When the presentation was finally over, the room was shrouded in an exhausted silence. It was one thing to relive the trauma of your own abuse. It was quite another to hear a seemingly endless string of horrific abuse that spanned decades and to realize that if any of the adults in charge of the well-being of students had been doing their jobs and taken the accusations seriously, many of the subsequent acts might never have occurred.

"I literally went home and sat in a dark room for five hours after what I had heard," said one of the survivors, recalling the day's testimonies. "Sitting with all those grown-up kids and how they had never recovered, it was devastating. The psychic and emotional damages were staggering. The school was supposed to be about guiding people toward intelligent and fully realized adulthood. What happened instead was a complete perversion of the school's purpose."

The school's representatives showed little emotion through it all. Whether they had steeled themselves beforehand or were simply skeptical of some of the accusations, they sat clear-eyed during and after the presentation, occasionally taking notes.

After the Allred lawyers were finished, Steve Friedman, the HM board's chair, stood and read a brief prepared statement.

One survivor in attendance paraphrased Friedman's remarks as "'We understand that something bad happened.' But there was no acceptance of responsibility personally, institutionally, or otherwise. There was a lot of 'We want to do the right thing but we have responsibilities to the current student body and the current parents.'"

"He showed no emotion or compassion," another survivor said of Friedman's statement. "He didn't look anyone in the eye. He hedged around with all sorts of qualifying statements and legalese."

"He exudes an air of misery," said another.

The departure of the six represented by Mulhearn, Mones, and Dowd may have been jarring to some, but it made the battle lines clearer.

The survivors represented by Allred and the one survivor represented by Rosemarie Arnold were left to mediate a settlement with Horace Mann. The survivors and their lawyers walked upstairs to a third room, where they would be camped out for most of the next few weeks. The large conference room had a view of Manhattan and a huge table that could accommodate about thirty people. There was a nice buffet with chicken Caesar wraps, pasta salads, fruit platters, fresh baked goods, and hot coffee. They could have been there to discuss a merger or the dissolution of a company.

Before telling their stories to the HM team, those survivors who wanted to met with Lipman, the psychodramatist. Although Friedman, Kelly, and the HM lawyers had all been given written accounts of the abuse each survivor had suffered, Goldberg, Allred's law partner, wanted them to hear firsthand testimony most specifically about the long-term damage the abuse had had on their lives. He wanted the insurers and the school to see his clients not as faceless claimants but as human beings who had suffered.

Finn and Mone sat at the head of the large conference table. The survivor giving testimony sat on one side of the table between Allred, Wang, and Goldberg. Facing them on the other side of the table were Kelly, the Horace Mann lawyers, and a representative of the board assigned to hear that day's testimony. Friedman was present for the first day of testimony. The settlement committee, a small group of Horace Mann board members, sat in shifts; this process went on for the rest of the week.

By mutual agreement, the Horace Mann side was not allowed to ask any questions. This mediation rule was implemented by Finn in order to be respectful of the victims' vulnerability and to avoid the emotional outbreaks some questions might elicit. Everyone realized that it would be painful for the victims to feel like they were being cross-examined.

Despite the good intentions, the silence of the HM side had an unsettling effect. For some of those reliving their trauma, talking to "suits with legal pads taking notes" was a bizarre experience. Kelly, many felt, was the most emotionally present of the HM team.

"Kelly was really expressive and empathetic," recalled one survivor, "looking mad or sad at exactly the right moments."

Friedman, on the other hand, looked entirely impassive. "It was as if he had given himself the assignment to make his face look as neutral as possible," said one who testified. "There were no emotions, no looks of anger or empathy. Nothing. It's like he wasn't there or was bored or maybe even annoyed that he had to be there at all."

"It was like the only time they showed emotion or whispered to one another was when they felt there was a crack in your story that they might exploit," recalled another. "Here I was spilling my guts out about something that I'd spent the majority of my life keeping to myself, and these guys were assessing it like it was just another stock trade."

At times Finn would say, "How did that make you feel?" or "What was the long-term effect of that on your life?"

"I completely broke down when he did that," said one. "It was as if everything I'd been holding in for all those years just came pouring out. I was sobbing and I hated that loss of control. On the way out, [Finn] patted me on the back and apologetically told me, 'Sorry about that, pal. Had to do it. It was starting to feel a little dry. I wanted them to feel the emotions. Nice job.'"

One man who had been raped by Somary got so angry when telling his story that he had to be physically restrained and escorted from the room.

One by one, the survivors walked down the hallway to tell their stories.

When they came back to the survivors' conference room, they were met supportively by their fellows and, in some cases, spouses. When Andrew came back from his testimony, Paul put his arm around him. As Andrew collapsed in Paul's arms, Joseph Cumming, seated at the conference table, broke into tears. Other survivors rushed to his side for support.

It had been a particularly grueling few months for the minister. He had been a rock for others to lean on, a clearinghouse for other people's stories—and finally he had undergone a personal transformation as well, outing himself as a victim of sexual abuse. If his role had long been taking an emotional toll, it was now taking a financial one as well. His fanatical commitment to his work with the survivors made it difficult for him to continue his job as director of the Yale Center for Faith and Culture's Reconciliation Program, the interfaith group he'd established in 2005.

Giving personal testimony brought up a whole range of emotions for all those who spoke. For decades most had kept their stories to themselves, and then, as the Survivors' Group coalesced and defined itself, they shared their stories with one another. And now the moment of truth had come and gone. Many felt relief. Others felt a sense of regret and vulnerability. *I said too much. I didn't say enough. I shouldn't have cried. Should I have cried more?*

Friedman's and Kelly's every facial twitch was dissected with Talmudic specificity. Was Friedman's impassivity just a calculated negotiating tactic, or did he simply not give a shit? Would Kelly be able to stand up to Friedman and the board's other hard-liners, who effectively paid his half-million-dollars-plus-benefits salary?

After one survivor gave his testimony, Kelly approached him with a big grin on his face. "We'll do the right thing," he said. It was an expression that Kelly repeated, in one form or another, throughout the mediation process to many of those who testified.

By the end of the first week, the mood was hopeful. The survivors felt they were being taken seriously. Things seemed to be moving in the right direction. Everyone broke for the weekend with the sense that they had overcome their deepest fears and that Horace Mann, in its current form, would reverse decades of cover-up and obfuscation and help make the world right.

"The mood that whole first week was positive, I'd even say healing," said one survivor.

Gloria Allred and her team spent the remainder of Friday evening and Saturday conferring with each individual survivor to arrive at the monetary figure they would submit to the Horace Mann lawyers that Sunday. Many of the survivors were elated, if not surprised, at the high numbers they were asking of Horace Mann. Depending on the level and frequency of the abuse, some of the victims were seeking to be compensated several million dollars.

"That's when the wheels started coming off the track," one survivor said. "The figures that they asked for were astronomically high. I had coached myself early not to get too attached to a number, but I have to admit, I did walk around that weekend thinking my life was about to significantly change."

In fact, many of the victims spent the weekend feeling a few inches taller.

Monday morning was a waiting game as the Horace Mann lawyers met with the Allred and Finn teams to discuss the legal aspects of the case. If the school's representatives had been all ears the previous week, it was now their turn to do the talking. And when they did, lawyers from Schulte Roth reprised a paragraph they had added to the school's financial statements on June 30, 2012, two weeks after the scandal broke: "Articles have been published alleging that between the 1960's and mid 1990's certain students were sexually abused by former employees of the School," it read. "Subsequent to such articles being published, a number of former students of the School have retained counsel and have claimed that they were sexually abused while students at the School . . . The School retains its rights to assert that all such claims and actions are barred by the statute of limitations, and will defend any action vigorously if litigation commenced."

Schulte Roth essentially told the Allred team that its clients didn't have a legal leg to stand on—which many thought had been obvious all along. Why then did they bother to go through the painful mediation? "It was an elaborate floor show," was the opinion of one survivor (and probably more). The school's counteroffers, confidently reflecting that conviction, were extremely low. If Allred asked for $300,000, Horace Mann would counter with $10,000. If Allred's team asked for $800,000, HM came back with $50,000. If Allred's team asked for $1.2 million, $75,000 came back from HM.

At mid-morning, Allred, Wang, and Goldberg returned to the conference room to face their clients. The survivors found their A-team of lawyers looking shell-shocked. Finn and Mone, the mediators, didn't look a whole lot better. Everyone seemed stunned that Horace Mann had come in with such lowball counteroffers.

Finn spent most of the remainder of the mediation process shuttling back and forth between the Horace Mann cadre of lawyers and the survivors.

"All the offers were overlapping with one another," said one survivor. "Finn would go to HM, then go back to Allred, Goldberg, and John or Jane Doe to confer. It was back and forth like this three to five times with about twenty people or so."

Despite the back-and-forth, it was clear the mediators were not going to get Horace Mann to move very far from its original offers. And there was very little actual mediating to be done.

"[Finn and Mone] were under the impression that these cases had no merit and if there was a lawsuit, they would lose," said one lawyer familiar with the case. "They got some guys seventy-five thousand, one hundred thousand dollars—not enough to serve as restitution, but a lot better than nothing."

But those figures represented the high end for Allred's group. Most were offered a fraction of that. "The numbers were so low that they should have just walked," the lawyer continued. "If they asked for five hundred thousand or a million for a guy, [Horace Mann] came back with two thousand or five thousand. They should have said, 'Screw you, bye-bye, good luck.' And they would have come back to them and upped their offers. But when they came back and gave them another offer, that was the end of the game."

"Horace Mann believes they've taken the worst hit," Allred told her group, referring to my article and the ensuing storm. "They're not afraid anymore."

Wang explained that given the statute of limitations, she was not confident they could do any better if the cases went to court. "I've looked at all the precedents and all the judges we might draw, and I just don't think we have a case," she told her clients. "The only reason Horace Mann is giving us anything is because they want this behind them. These are only token amounts."

"We don't have to give you anything" was how Finn bluntly categorized HM's position.

There was a great deal of affection for Mariann Wang and Nathan Goldberg among the survivors (though at least one characterized Allred herself as "a clown"), but they had no cards to play. They had come this far on a bluff, and some of the survivors had managed to convince themselves that they had a chance at a large settlement.

Now they were devastated. After so many years, this was how Horace Mann was treating them? Horace Mann, a school with alumni and a board that boasted some of the world's richest hedge fund managers and heads of real estate dynasties, was counteroffering adult victims of childhood sexual abuse with pennies on the dollar? Each individual member of the group swiftly rejected the counteroffers. The only claims the school's lawyers seemed to take seriously were those that could be readily confirmed or that had such sensational media potential that it would be better to settle.

This was when people started talking about "retraumatization"— that the victims of sexual abuse and other trauma may relapse when human interactions, sometimes even innocuous ones, bring back the terror, rage, pain, helplessness, and loss of trust triggered by the initial act. The fact that Finn was running back and forth while the survivors had no access to HM may have aggravated those who craved more personal interaction and experience with the school.

Allred's team, trying to salvage something, suggested that there was strength in numbers and that perhaps they'd be in a better negotiating position if they bargained with Horace Mann as a unit and asked for a lump sum.

But the Survivors' Group, with very little discussion, quickly rejected the concept. It was one thing to negotiate one-on-one with the institution. It was quite another to negotiate with one another. "The reason we had gotten together as a group was because of the strength in numbers," one survivor said. "But I couldn't imagine the conversation [over] dividing up a lump sum. It would have gotten really competitive and awful. I mean, how do you decide who had it worse— someone who Tek slept with once should get x and then Jon Seiger who was passed around to eight different teachers gets a bigger number? What is the calculus by which you decide how someone is to be compensated?"

The mood changed from that of a high school cafeteria filled with camaraderie to that of a situation room roiled by anger and instability. The atmosphere was tense, filled with questions and theories.

"They were never afraid of the media," said one survivor. "They were only afraid of the *threat* of the media, and when we agreed to a media blackout we lost our leverage."

"Everyone quickly reverted to their most base selves," said another. "The lawyers among us started talking about disbarring and ethics. Others reverted to whining, screaming, telling jokes, shutting down, or retreating into their headphones. People were calling their mothers, their spouses, their therapists. It was awful."

Many of the survivors were stunned that the school seemed to be treating them like enemies.

Those more knowledgeable of the ups and downs of the mediation process were less stunned. "You are in a room of people who have all been sexually abused. It's a form of hell," recalled one. "Maybe they expected the initial offers to be less lowball than they were. I think it was partly the shock of the reality that this wasn't going to mean economic comfort for some of the survivors with less stable economic situations. But this is a standard in mediation. It is upsetting but not surprising."

By this point, Paul, like many of the other survivors, was furious. "The problem is that you conceded the moral high ground to them," he railed at both the Allred and Finn teams. "Last week it was all about ethics and morals and now you are telling us that it is just about business. You have allowed Horace Mann to define the terms of the discussion. By bifurcating the morals and ethics from the way we are treated in this process and saying 'this is just business,' you have already given everything away. But the business here *is* morality. The commodity here is our pain and suffering and HM's reputation; you have gutted the case."

As Paul spoke, the other survivors could see Finn seething.

"He'd probably seen lowball offers a thousand times," said one witness to this encounter. "But I think he might have been genuinely pissed at our lawyers for coming in so high."

"It's like all of a sudden we are in Vegas," Paul continued. "Are there no moral and spiritual values? The school feels no moral obligation to us?"

Finn reminded them of some things that Horace Mann had yet to say no to. Things like taking down all the signs with the names of perpetrators on them—something Horace Mann had already done and that Kelly openly bragged about. Outlandish demands like knocking down the headmaster's mansion, where Inky and Kops had raped Seiger. The mere suggestion drew applause from some of the survivors while others shrugged at the stupidity of the idea.

"You've already won," Finn insisted. "You guys should be proud. This is a great victory."

"Well, it doesn't feel like a victory," Gene interrupted. "I feel like a vagrant asking for a handout."

"You're missing the point, the big picture," Finn insisted. "Money is their way of showing their sense of responsibility. The issue was never on the table before. You are winning."

"Well, I don't feel like a winner," Gene persisted, his lower lip quivering.

"You people are so fucking busy being victims, you guys don't even realize that you've won!" Finn thundered, cutting Gene off as he launched into a profane tirade. "I'm tired of all this negativity. I'm out here night and day busting my ass for two weeks and you guys are acting like a bunch of fucking—"

"And you're getting paid handsomely for it," said G., reminding Finn of his hourly fee that was being split by both sides.

This was not Finn's first time at the rodeo. He'd seen it before: the lowball offer followed by despair followed by some negotiated settlement. After the outburst, Finn sidled up to Gene and sheepishly apologized, leading some to question if he had been engaged in a bit of theatrics when he blew up at the crowd.

"Say what you want, but the man knows what he's doing," one witness said of Finn. "He was like an actor and director at the same time."

Others began questioning whether Finn's Boston brawler shtick was sensitive enough for a case involving the traumatized survivors of sexual abuse.

"That may work and be appropriate in a union negotiations meeting or class action suit for a train accident, but saying 'fuck' and calling victims of sexual abuse 'pussies' was not sensitive or healing," said one survivor.

"Whatever his motivations, it led many of us to retreat," another said.

Mediations all share a certain emotional graph, and the heated exchange between Finn and the survivors was the peak. The survivors, whatever they felt about the moral weight of their claims, simply had no leverage.

You could take the offer or not, was the point Finn seemed to be making.

Whether he was playacting or simply insensitive, the tactic seemed to work. People began to negotiate their individual deals. Some, based on their dire financial situation or lack of stamina, negotiated faster than others.

Over the next few days, lawyers shuttled in and out of the conference room, one by one, calling their clients aside to report and negotiate.

Rosemarie Arnold, who represented M., was infuriated by the school's counteroffer. "They just wanted to settle with people who wanted bullshit—five to ten thousand dollars," she said of the mediation process. "My client had a serious claim. Somary had abused him hundreds of times and we could prove it. There were letters and a witness."

As the negotiations were in full force, Marc Fisher's *New Yorker* piece on Berman came out, giving the school another black eye. Some suggested this gave the victims more leverage because Horace Mann would need to generate some good news.

But HM held the line.

"It was exhausting. These guys were pros at haggling," one survivor said of the HM side. "This is what they do for a living, and they had all the time and skill and none of the emotional investment. It was fucking awful."

"Of course it was a negotiation," said another survivor, unhappy with what he viewed as the naïveté of some of his cohort. "We were the ones who'd hired the lawyers. And I think it's bullshit to suddenly say you were retraumatized because you didn't get what you wanted. But I know mine is a minority opinion."

"The only time I felt good in the entire mediation," said another, "was when Finn came back to me with a number, which was probably about in the middle of what most people were being offered, and I told him that I couldn't assess the number alone, because I would have to view it as part of the total settlement, which would have to include nonmonetary items. So I said that, essentially, I had no response for Horace Mann. This was essentially turning down their offer. 'Congratulations,' Finn said to me. 'You've just taken the first step towards not becoming a victim.' He was right in that it was the first time I'd felt in control of things for months. I then realized that the reason we were all so traumatized by the mediation was that HM was doing to us exactly what our abusers had done. They were depriving us of the ability to control our own fates. The simple act of saying no was hugely empowering."

While the lawyers and mediators were negotiating numbers, many of the survivors continued to push for an independent investigation and for getting Horace Mann to support changing New York's statute of limitations laws. But eventually they relented. "What was really infuriating was that Horace Mann said that they had 'no authority' to settle on any nonmonetary matters," one survivor said. "This was absurd, because it was obviously going to come up." He added, "The only way we were going to win that was if we all managed to stick together on it during the mediation. But people started peeling off one by one, as HM picked off the ones with the highest settlements. People who were already afraid were made to feel even more afraid, and the whole thing collapsed."

At one point, trying to break an impasse, Finn's mediation partner, Brian Mone, suggested that the victims settle on the monetary compensation and trust Horace Mann to conduct its own independent investigation. One survivor launched into a profanity-laden monologue worthy of Joe Pesci. "Who the fuck do you think you're dealing with here? Do you think I am an idiot? Why the fuck do you think we're here? Are you fucking thick? Do their own investigation? You guys might want to do a deal, grab some steaks, and get the fuck out of here, but don't insult my intelligence. Trust the Horace Mann School? Are you fucking kidding me?"

When Finn made it clear that HM would never agree to an independent investigation, he floated the idea that perhaps a report emanating from the private mediation itself could serve as an independent investigation. HM would have been thrilled to substitute the mediators' report for the independent report HMAC and others were calling for. It would have enabled the school to publicly say that an investigation had been done without it ever having to explore the culpability of some of its own faculty, administrators, and board members. After a brief deliberation, the survivors who had yet to settle decided it would be a bad idea for Finn to do this. "It was bullshit. We know what happened to us. We want to know who covered it up. Who knew what when?" one said. "It was another cynical move by HM."

Another running question was whether the survivors who settled would be able to tell their stories or would be forced to sign a nondisclosure agreement. "Some of us were worried that they would try to muzzle us all over again and that the silence would continue in perpetuity," said one.

Arnold, already angered by the tone and content of the proceedings, counseled her client to walk out of the mediation. That day she filed papers across the river in New Jersey, where Somary had taken M. on many occasions and where the statute of limitations laws for child sexual abuse were much less stringent than those in New York. Although New Jersey child abuse victims have only two years from the date the victim knew or should have known he or she was sexually abused to make a complaint, there is a catchall "tolling provision," or pause in the statute of limitations, that allows a case to be heard no matter how old the claims, for any reason a judge deems fair. In M.'s case, he had not known Somary had other victims until my article was published. He had lived his entire adult life under the assumption that the two were in love.

"When we didn't want to settle, [HM] acted like *they* were the victims," Arnold said. "They acted like they only had this limited pot of five million. The alumni are among some of the most powerful and richest people in the world. They were saying they didn't have to pay claims and only had five million to pay claims as the insurance companies were denying coverage. Not my problem."

In the midst of all this chaos, I met Jon Seiger at a pizzeria a few blocks from the Schulte Roth offices. Seiger, who claimed that eight teachers had abused him while he was a student at Horace Mann, was all too happy to take a break from the tense atmosphere of the mediation.

"I wanted to meet you here for a reason," he told me as we dug in to our slices.

This was the place where, he said, a few weeks after his evening with Clark and Kops at the headmaster's house, he'd run into one of the young male prostitutes they had rented for the occasion. Although Jon hadn't known it at the time, the east 50s of Manhattan were the pickup spot of choice for male prostitutes and their older clientele. The guy approached Seiger and apologized for forcing him to have sex with him and another hustler that night. He made it clear that Clark and Kops had paid them for their services, with the explicit instruction to use "any force necessary" to make sure it happened.

"He then told me how I could make a lot of money for having sex," Seiger said. "In some ways it was a good decision to get paid for having sex rather than just having it taken and used by my teachers."

Seiger told me his chance meeting at the pizzeria led to twelve years as a male prostitute and escort, both during his time as a student at HM and after. During that period he numbed himself with drugs and alcohol and eventually wound up posing for pornographic magazines. He also claims to have acted in more than thirty porn films.

Back in the Schulte Roth offices, as the mediation was winding down, Kelly was still talking to the group. "I know some of you feel shortchanged," he assured them as he walked around the conference room. "Don't worry, we will get you therapy and make you whole through Hilltop Cares," referring to the charity that proposed to subsidize therapy for survivors. But no one knew if the nonprofit was a real organization or merely another Kekst-inspired spin. Other than the early press (*The New York Times* announced the creation of the Hilltop Cares Foundation in August 2012), there had been little follow-up. Hilltop Cares had become a bit of a joke among some of the survivors, who cynically wondered "if Hilltop still cared."

When the two weeks of mediation were over, twenty-one of the twenty-five survivors represented by the Allred team had settled. Most did so for a fraction of what their lawyers had originally asked for. After decades of waiting for Horace Mann to do the right thing, few were willing to wait any longer. Most settled out of fatigue and the desire to move on with their lives. Others, given the current statute of limitations laws, figured this was the best they would do.

The school's total payout was estimated at between $4 million and $5 million. In comparison, the Poly Prep survivors each got roughly $800,000. Penn State paid an aggregate total of $59.7 million to settle with twenty-six of the victims in the Jerry Sandusky child abuse scandal. For the fiscal year 2013, which included the mediation, Horace Mann's lawyers received upwards of $2 million in legal fees.

9

BLOWBACK

Horace Mann had almost put the survivors' claims behind it—but not entirely. There were a few holdouts, including Joseph Cumming, G., and F.: they would not settle until Horace Mann agreed to cooperate with the independent investigation that HMAC was trying to get started. Those who did settle were often unhappy about how the mediation had gone.

"It was never about the money for many of us," one survivor said. "Horace Mann made it about that. I had to sign an NDA about the money and the specifics of the mediation. They recognized that they came off like bastards. I don't know what they got out of treating us like that. The school dealt with us like we were cafeteria workers who wouldn't take a contract."

Others felt the fellowship of sufferers almost made the entire ordeal worthwhile. "If there was anything positive about the mediation it was that I got a pretty good feeling about so many of the people in the room," said another. "I settled at around fifteen percent of what my lawyers wanted. Horace Mann originally countered with three percent. I'm very upset with the lawyers. They ill prepared us. They can say they were surprised, but they were not supposed to be surprised. That's not their job to be surprised."

"I did not enter mediation looking for a magic moment and was surprised that others had," countered another survivor. "Mediation wasn't about that. It was all about the marketplace. People didn't understand that. People were looking for Mother to make it better but Mommy didn't care. Mother is part of the problem."

On April 22, 2013, Allred, flanked by five of her clients, held a press conference at the Omni Berkshire Place hotel in New York City. The goal was to gain some attention and to publicly ask the school to support an independent investigation.

Already angered by the Allred team's adherence to the media blackout during mediation, Boynton let some of his friends know exactly how badly he thought their lawyers had miscalculated the situation. He was also infuriated that, by his account, Allred had, in a telephone conversation, promised to coordinate the press conference with the Horace Mann Action Coalition and had failed to do so.

Sensing that the situation was spinning out of control, Allred's co-counsel Wang sent Boynton an email the next day, insisting that he had misunderstood the original phone conversation with Allred. She said she understood that many of their clients were unhappy with the way mediation had gone, but urged him to be cautious in his public pronouncements and, in her phrase, to "keep our eyes on the prize and pressuring HM to do the right thing" rather than disparage the lawyers.

Boynton, who'd held his tongue for months, sent Wang a blistering response:

> We all knew from the start that this case wasn't going to have a "happy" ending. People's lives were ruined and no amount of money (or apologies or investigations) will make them whole. Let's be straight about this: neither I nor anyone else at HMAC bear any ill will against you. We have supported, and will continue to support, your efforts at every turn . . .
>
> I think it was a disaster that you allowed, and enforced, Friedman's gag order last fall. That was the moment you lost most of your leverage. The BOT knew full well that you'd never bring a real case, both because of the statute of limita-

tions, and because that is simply not your m.o. Their goal was to shut down the story, and they succeeded.

I suspect things might have turned out differently had you held Monday's press conference in September. As it is, I believe HM played you, buying your silence with intimations of a multimillion-dollar windfall, which they never intended to pay. Instead, they strung you along for months and made a low-ball "take it or leave it" offer at the last second. They knew you had no fallback strategy, and that their monetary offers (no matter how small) would divide your clients, playing those who were destitute against those who weren't.

It dismays me to read that you are still, at this very late date, counting on the BOT to do "the right thing." My sources tell me they'll issue an apology. And, at some point in the future, they'll phase out all the emeritus trustees, so it doesn't look like Hess and Katz are being singled out. As for an investigation, I very much doubt they will do more than agree "in principle" to conduct one "at some point in the future." And I don't believe the incriminating "documents" you insist only HM can produce are still there, if they ever existed in the first place. In addition, I think you are making a mistake by leading the public to believe that a successful investigation requires HM's cooperation. Did Amos Kamil or Marc Fisher have subpoena power? Have all the lawyers, investigators, police and school administrators uncovered a shred of new information? We've already been approached by a number of credible people who say they have information. "I kept waiting for someone to ask me," one woman told me.

Meanwhile, HMAC continued to press the school to support the investigation. "Our goal is to produce a report that will summarize everything that occurred, explain the conditions that allowed abuse to flourish, and make recommendations that apply to independent schools anywhere," read one of the group's press releases. "An independent investigation is properly the responsibility of the school itself.

Because Horace Mann refuses to do either, it falls to the Horace Mann community to hold the school accountable."

That same week, Robert T. Johnson, the Bronx district attorney, issued his report. The investigation revealed "a systemic pattern of alleged abuse" beyond what the media had reported a year ago. "The reported abuse ranges from what may be characterized as inappropriate behavior to child endangerment, actual instances of sexual contact, sexual intercourse and criminal sexual acts."

The report said that the DA's office received direct information regarding at least twelve abusers. The majority of the abuse reported was said to have occurred in the 1970s, but additional instances were reported from the 1980s and 1990s. "To date, all instances of reported sexual abuse occurring at Horace Mann between 1962 and 1996 are beyond New York State's Criminal Statute of Limitations," the statement read. There was no legal "recourse for a prosecution of any act of past sexual abuse at Horace Mann which has currently been reported."

The DA's report did not address the school's culpability in allowing the misconduct to continue and remain undiscovered for more than three decades. But it did note that "throughout the almost four decade period of sexual abuse at Horace Mann, there were instances of abuse coming to the attention of school officials without law enforcement being notified." There were at least twenty instances of sexual abuse brought to the attention of Horace Mann teachers, administrators, and board members. The report made it clear that the District Attorney's Office judged inadequate Horace Mann's September 2012 policy on reporting sexual abuse by employees. The office felt that Horace Mann's policy needed to be "amended to highlight the importance of immediate notification to law enforcement."

The DA's findings also shed light on New York State laws by which private school officials are mandated only to report sexual abuse by parents and guardians but not by school employees. In other words, if a teacher observes that a child has a bruise from home, the teacher is required to call child welfare services. But if the teacher suspects another teacher of sexually abusing a child, there is no mandated reporting. Hypothetically, if they were to call a state agency to accuse another teacher of abuse, the agency would regard this as a report filed by a nonguardian, and the teacher would be encouraged (but not required) to call 911 instead. This protects teachers and administrators who may have known about the abuse but done nothing. Public school teachers, by contrast, are required to report all credible claims of abuse. Kids in public schools are better protected than their peers in private ones.

Two months after the mediation ended, Horace Mann invited classes to reunions. The class of 1958's fifty-fifth reunion invitation asked guests to join Tom Kelly, as well as Richard Traum and Michael Hess, both members of the reunion committee, for brunch at Mr. Kelly's home and for cocktails at the Waldorf-Astoria.

After survivors and others vociferously objected to the appearance of Hess's name on the invitation, Hess was removed from a list of trustees emeriti on the school's website. When asked about the incident, Hess said his name never appeared on the invitation. When he was sent a link to a front-page *Riverdale Press* article with his name clearly appearing in a photo of the invitation, he explained that he must have been appointed to the reunion committee at some point but insisted that he had nothing to do with planning the event. "I don't know how my name got on that invitation," he said. A few weeks later, a letter to the HM community from Steve Friedman, the board's chair, and Headmaster Tom Kelly announced a curious plan that made it clear Horace Mann would use any means necessary to make sure the entire matter was in its rearview mirror. The letter concluded:

Finally, the Board of Trustees has accepted the proposal of Commonwealth Mediation that Commonwealth Mediation prepare an independent summary of the reported abuses, without identifying the survivors. The mediators involved have heard from thirty-one alumni/ae who described in painful detail the inexcusable conduct of their teachers and administrators that occurred between seventeen and fifty-one years

ago. Given the passage of time, most of the abusers are either
dead or mentally infirm; the remainder, we understand, are
unwilling to respond to the allegations, and the School does
not have the authority to compel these individuals to do so. It
is these reports heard by the mediators—shared privately
and in person by survivors—that provide us the greatest in-
sight into what happened. The Board of Trustees and Head
of School have agreed to make the summary report available
as soon as practicable.

Horace Mann was offering to publish the accounts of the abuse
given privately in the mediation—with the names redacted. In fact,
neither the survivors nor the mediator had agreed to such a plan. During the mediation, Commonwealth had briefly proposed an independent investigation, not a summary of accounts that would ignore the
role of the school. In the letter, HM apologized for the harm done by
abusers but made no mention of the fact that its leaders allowed, enabled, or in some cases participated in the abuse.

The letter also noted that a survivor would be appointed to the
Head of School Committee, a subcommittee of parents and alumni
with direct access to Kelly. On the surface, the appointment appeared
to be a step in the right direction, but according to a current parent,
the committee "does cocktails and shakes hands" but has no real
power. The demand that the school name a survivor to the Board of
Trustees went unmentioned.

Within a matter of days, Allred and Wang responded in writing
to Horace Mann's statement.

The "painful detail" referenced by Horace Mann were victim
impact statements made by our clients at the mediation. These
statements were enormously difficult and gut-wrenching.
They took a high emotional toll on each of our clients, many
of whom revealed facts that they had kept hidden for decades,
even from people who are closest to them. Our clients made
those statements in reliance upon express written and oral

representations that everyone involved in the mediation process would keep these statements and the facts presented in them confidential. That is not to say that our clients do not want transparency or do not want the school or an investigator to hear of their abuses. To the contrary, they want the facts and details of the abuse to be absorbed and analyzed in a full independent process that includes an examination of school records and interviews of not only abusers but of school board members, administrators and teachers who observed and/or knew of the abuse and either took no action or actively took steps to ensure that the abuses stay hidden.

Furthermore, Allred and Wang wrote, "we contacted Mr. Finn to find out whether or not Horace Mann" was correct to announce that "Commonwealth Mediation, his firm, had agreed to prepare 'an independent summary of the reported abuses,' that would be based upon what had been 'heard by the mediators—shared privately and in person by survivors' at the mediation. In response to our inquiry Mr. Finn wrote to us on May 27th stating: 'We have not been hired to do anything.'"

In the same letter that promised a Commonwealth Mediation report, Friedman and Kelly referred to Horace Mann as our "nourishing mother" (translating "alma mater" from Latin) and stated that the school "provides the resources and guidance we need to flourish academically, socially, physically and emotionally. We also count on her to care for us in times of personal need, institutional tragedy or crisis."

The sum of resources on the section of Horace Mann's website titled Child Abuse Resources, as of this writing, consists of seven letters written by the administration and a link to the Family Handbook. No counseling, no assistance, just contact information for reporting abuse to Headmaster Tom Kelly.

10

STRANGE AFTERMATH

Horace Mann has failed the survivors. But was there a better way?

Soon after "Prep-School Predators" came out, I received a mysterious email from someone calling himself Marcel Marceau, after the world-famous French mime. After several conversations, "Marcel" was comfortable enough to reveal himself to me as Whit Sheppard, a man roughly my age who had graduated from Deerfield Academy in 1983.

In 2010, Sheppard, a freelance writer, was commissioned to write the official 125-year history of the Horace Mann School. The book was to be your standard "authorized biography" of an elite school—the type of glorified puff piece many institutions hand out to wealthy donors and display on coffee tables at the admissions office in order to showcase their rich and storied history. Sheppard was a few months away from handing in his manuscript when my story hit the Internet. "I found myself in the unenviable position of having to finish work on it knowing what I now knew," he said.

Sheppard's difficulty went beyond the professional challenge of reconciling Horace Mann's "official" history with the revelations that kept pouring forth. The issue of sexual abuse at an elite prep school was a deeply personal one for him—and something he had chosen to keep mostly silent about for nearly three decades. Although he had approached Deerfield's former headmaster Eric Widmer back in 2004, with a vague story of how he was molested by an unnamed faculty member, both Sheppard and Widmer tacitly agreed at the time to "let bygones be bygones."

Now Sheppard felt he could no longer contain the dissonance between knowing what the world knew about Horace Mann and what the world did *not* know about Deerfield. "When I read your article," he told me, "I knew I would have to pursue this in order to move on with my life. Every private school—like Deerfield and Horace Mann—lives on its reputation. They have these lofty stated values about building character. Deerfield's motto is 'Be worthy of your heritage.' I have deep clarity about my own values. I wanted to find out if it was just rhetoric or would Deerfield actually live up to its credo."

Sheppard sat down and composed an email to Deerfield's current head of school, Dr. Margarita Curtis. It took only twenty minutes to write but had been incubating for decades. "I am a truth seeker and a truth teller," Sheppard told me. "I wanted the letter to be conciliatory. I don't have hatred. I looked it over and realized I was ready. I sent it."

"I have not ever named the teacher, coach and dorm master who molested me," Sheppard wrote Dr. Curtis. "But when I see the photos of returning alums at reunions being led in joyous song by the much-beloved 'Czar,' Peter Hindle, the same man who molested me as a Deerfield student living on his corridor, I feel a measure of sadness and chagrin." (Hindle, almost eighty now, is no longer associated with the school.)

Dr. Curtis and the Deerfield board took Sheppard's claims very seriously. Almost immediately Deerfield offered a public apology. A few months later, in August, Dr. Curtis flew down to Virginia to visit Sheppard and hear his story firsthand.

"They bent over backwards not to piss me off or do more harm," he said.

Deerfield hired Debevoise & Plimpton, a New York–based international law firm widely regarded as one of the most prestigious in the nation, to conduct an independent investigation to find out if there were other adult victims of Hindle.

In March 2013, Deerfield released a five-page report of the investigation's findings, saying that it had "confirmed that sexual conduct by Peter Hindle occurred with the student who came forward and there is evidence that such conduct occurred with at least one other student." The report acknowledged that prior administrations could have done more to investigate allegations of wrongdoing by Hindle, including after Sheppard's 2004 vague letter of allegation to the school. The investigation also uncovered two victims of another longtime teacher, named Bryce Lambert. (Lambert died in 2007.)

Although he was pleased that the school undertook the investigation, Sheppard was surprised that it had turned up so few victims of Hindle. "I think it's highly unlikely that this pedophile teacher only molested that few students over a forty-four-year period," he said. "I'm sure that there are many more out there."

All in all, Sheppard felt that Deerfield's handling of his case had been respectful and centered on his healing. "It has been very helpful in helping me to move past it," he said. "I feel like they were smart enough to learn from other institutions that went before them. They took me seriously. They were interested in knowing more. So far they have done all the right things."

Sheppard's journey from the shadows culminated in a front-page article in *The Boston Globe Magazine* on July 21, 2013. Using his own name, he told his story publicly for the first time. "I've decided to reveal my identity in the hopes of lessening the stigma associated with being a survivor of sexual abuse and encouraging others on their own path of healing," he wrote. "Nothing about this process has been easy, but it has given me a renewed sense of integrity and self-respect. It was the right thing to do, and I'm glad I did it."

After the article appeared online, Sheppard received a note of congratulations from Tom Kelly, with whom he had worked closely on Horace Mann's official history.

The summer of 2013 was long and sad for many of those involved with the scandal. Those survivors who had settled in mediation returned to their lives with varying levels of satisfaction while many others were questioning what to do next.

Gene was one of those happy to have put the matter behind them. "I felt like I'd stood up to Horace Mann," he said. "Like I got some of my humanity back." Perhaps this was what closure looked like.

Andrew was content to go back to his family and work on the West Coast and not think about Mark Wright, the mediation, or anything having to do with Horace Mann.

Jon Seiger fell into a depression and didn't return calls or emails for months.

Kevin Mulhearn was infuriated by the way the mediation played out. "They got away with soul murder," he said of Horace Mann, "all because of an arcane statute of limitations law. It's just a misguided law and actually gives institutions a playbook for dealing with sexual abuse. It incentivizes them to conceal it and then run out the clock on the statute of limitations." For six weeks Mulhearn holed up in his home office in Orangeburg, New York, and banged out the manuscript for a book aimed at trial lawyers and judges titled *An Antidote for Injustice: A New Paradigm for Winning "Old" Sexual Abuse Cases Against Complicit Private Schools*.

M.'s lawsuit was grinding its way through the New Jersey court system. Horace Mann's lawyers tried dismissing the claim by arguing that, as a New York entity, the school had no legal business in New Jersey. Some former teachers, like Joyce Fitzpatrick and Bruce Weber, continued to express outrage at the school's handling of the situation. In April 2013, Weber wrote an email to Kelly and Friedman:

> Gentlemen, my name is Bruce Weber. I write for *The New York Times*, but from 1978–81, I taught English at Horace Mann. I knew Tek Lin, Robert Berman, Johannes Somary, Mark Wright, R. Inslee Clark and Stan Kops; I worked alongside them. That these men, and perhaps others, abused their authority and took sexual advantage of the children in their care is, of course, repugnant and reprehensible. That they

went about their vile business undetected by their colleagues is remarkable—thinking back to 35 years ago, I find it unbelievable. But that they hid their deeds so successfully is testimony to their knowledge of their own shame and culpability, and the fact is that their behavior was so insidious as to be unimaginable to us—and so we never imagined it. Now, however, we know: They were true villains, engaged in villainy. They had real victims who suffered real consequences, and as we now also know, when some of them sought help and relief, they were again ill-served by school authorities.

That Horace Mann . . . has not undertaken to cleanse its reputation by conducting a full investigation of the crimes and of the subsequent actions by those in power to minimize them—these are also institutional sins. With this letter, I add my voice to those who have urged the school to begin making restitution to those young people it failed by issuing an apology and by vowing to report fully on the history of abuse at the school. Absent these steps, Horace Mann, a great name in education, will be irrevocably bound to other names: Tek Lin, Robert Berman, Johannes Somary, Mark Wright, R. Inslee Clark and Stan Kops.

Soon after, in an email with the subject line "Time to go, fellas," Fitzpatrick wrote Kelly:

I taught English at Horace Mann, alongside child abusers.

The current Administration and Board are indistinguishable to me now from their counterparts in my era who knew the worst and said nothing. Recent remarks about privacy and so forth, while a full investigation is avoided on bogus grounds, are unconvincing, to say the least, and harm the school to which you, ostensibly, proclaim such devotion.

You have become the problem and the stone face of a school seen as indifferent to pain and crime. Lip service is insufficient. For the good of the school, go. Or reverse course, fire your ineffectual p.r. team, and do the right thing.

Ego or honor, gentlemen? Pick one. Every book I ever taught at Horace Mann explored that conflict and its consequences. Hear that knocking at yon gate? That's Antigone, demanding to be let in.

No one in my classes ever wanted to grow up to be Creon.

Go. Or fix it properly.

If Allred and her team had adhered to the media blackout, Boynton, Brooks, and HMAC were hard at work trying to keep the issue alive in the media.

And with each new article, Tom Kelly was more embattled. When the *Daily News* and *The Riverdale Press* wrote articles about the removal of Michael Hess's name from the list of trustees emeriti on the school's website, he received an outraged letter from Daniel Lund (HM '58), a retired arbitration attorney, decrying "the shabby treatment" of his classmate and friend Hess. "I suspect if you look out of the window of your office, half of the buildings you see on campus would not be there if it were not for Mike's dedicated service over years to the school," wrote Lund. "I know that you are not responsible for the recent articles . . . with the recitation of hearsay and smears that do honor to the tradition of McCarthyism in our political discourse. But I do think that you have some responsibility for the cowardly act of removing Mike from the list which could only encourage this slanderous discourse."

The community engaged with Processing Horace Mann reacted to each new story as if it were an aftershock of an earthquake—but by then they had become entrenched in their firmly held positions, which could best be boiled down to "independent investigation" versus "this is all in the past." After HM sent out an invitation to an upcoming alumni event with the mention of a barbecue at Clark Field, Processing Horace Mann erupted once again. Had the school learned nothing? Was it all just spin? How, after all we'd been through, could a mistake like this be allowed to happen?

"I often feel like tearing the school down brick by brick and leaving a gravestone in its place, yet it was a part of my life," wrote Gene. "The crux is this, HM never has admitted it had any knowledge of decades of abuse even after our now knowing there were 25 reports including my own to the Chairman of the Board . . . If HM were able to take responsibility for its role, not just partial financial responsibility (believe me the settlements could not come close to the losses we experienced) that would help. Until then, there will be continued, unrelenting anger and HM will be seen as a bully, self-protective above all, and, as an organization, inhumane to its own."

The exchanges took on a tiresome familiarity and the civility and decorum that had characterized the site in its infancy had devolved into shouting matches and the posting of one-sided screeds. Reading them became depressing. Charles Balter, Ben's surviving brother, and James Haft (HM '79), whose children now attended Horace Mann, engaged in especially heated exchanges. Haft took the unpopular position that the school's current needs should take priority.

At one point, he even suggested that Balter was overly obsessed with Hess, the man who had told his mother to drop her pursuit of justice for Ben. Balter shot back:

> The institution you represent did irreparable harm to my brother, my mother, my father, and so many countless others. You are simply in no position to be counseling victims or their family members in any way, shape, or form. That you continue to do so at this date is heartless and reprehensible. It is quite clear you have never read anything about the effects of sexual abuse. The institution you represent is the perpetrator. The perpetrator has no right to be counseling the victim on anything . . . You don't care at all about the victims, because in your minds, you're the victims, and the only crime is that all of this became public. Otherwise, Michael Hess and all the other scum for whom you advocate would still be sauntering through their lives, and nobody would know the better . . . If you want to help, have Horace Mann fork over $110/week to me to pay for my therapy costs for having to deal with this BS situation and these BS people. Or, get Michael Hess to call me and apologize. Those are the only things you can do that would

be remotely helpful. Anything else will simply further reveal your selfishness and narcissism.

The posts went back and forth like this for months, with contributions slowing to a trickle; PHM began to feel like a battlefield of ghosts.

Michael Hess was not an abuser, but thanks to his powerful connections—he was a former counsel of the City of New York and a former partner with Giuliani Partners—he symbolized for many the powerful elite at Horace Mann who were determined to ignore the injustices that had occurred at the school, and the school's culpability.

Whether such anger was justified or was what Paul called "outrage inflation," one thing was crystal clear: after two years, the situation seemed only to be getting worse. There was a part of me that felt guilty about opening Pandora's box. Although I was certainly not the cause of the reinjury, I did, at times, question what good all this was doing. Whatever had happened since my article—the denial; the revelations; the forming of Processing Horace Mann, the Survivors' Group, and HMAC; the mediation; the constant media attention—there was little sense of closure. When I embarked on my interviews I told one friend, who asked not to be named, that I felt I'd stuck my finger into a light socket. He shook his head. "Nuclear power plant," he said. The ongoing conflagration, with its flying accusations and raw emotions, was yet another reminder of why people keep silent for so many years.

On August 16, 2013, a Horace Mann representative went on the record saying the matter was closed, telling New York CBS 2's Amy Dardashtian that "the school has no plans for further review of dozens of allegations of sexual abuse levied at former teachers."

"It's a slap in the face," Ron Klepper told the reporter. "I think they believe that people have short-term memory and that they could just sweep us under the blanket."

Joseph Cumming issued the following statement in response: "I am shocked that Horace Mann would say that this matter is now closed. It is not closed for the victims. We still live every day with the memories of what more than 20 teachers did to us."

The Horace Mann Action Committee remained as determined as ever to hold the school's feet to the fire. It had been a full year since the Alumni Council passed a resolution urging the board to undertake an independent investigation. And again, the board had not responded. HMAC decided that if the school wasn't going to pay for an independent investigation, it would take matters into its own hands.

"It falls to us to do what Horace Mann should have done decades ago," Peter Brooks said when he sat on a Stop the Abuse panel in Framingham, Massachusetts. "Which was not only to find out the details of what happened to the victims but how it was allowed to go on for so long."

Despite all the wealth of the alumni, HMAC was having trouble raising the money to fund Judge Snyder's independent investigation. They engaged RocketHub, a crowdfunding platform, to raise $150,000 for Snyder and her team to continue. While the investigation lurched forward, the school had not budged on its refusal to cooperate.

"My attention and efforts, appropriately so, are focused on the matters before HM, not the HMAC," Tom Kelly told *The Horace Mann Record*. "Having cooperated fully with the extensive review conducted by both the Bronx DA's Office and the NYPD, the School will not be conducting an additional investigation . . . The school will not participate in an independent investigation. An investigation would ruin the school's finances, and without evidence, would only be slanderous."

Others laid the blame for not cooperating with the independent investigation solely at the feet of Steve Friedman. "He has been the single most intimidating force on everybody they tried to speak with," said one person familiar with the efforts of Snyder and her team. "They wouldn't even speak to them off the record. He has people scared shitless. One woman who had been on the Board of Trustees knew a lot, and what I got from her was that Friedman told her everyone would be sued if they spoke, said anything publicly . . . He implied to some parents it might hurt their kids; they wanted to get into the best schools, didn't they? The level of intimidation both overt and implicit has been just shocking."

•

In mid-September, it seemed something was shifting. Bill Hughes, today the head of strategy at an education technology company, wrote on PHM, "Vilifying the wealthy because they are wealthy is problematic for me. HM is full of the children of privilege, but does that mean then that all of our friends (if we ourselves are not of that class) are evil? If so, it belies the kinship we say we have as alumni of HM."

Hughes noted the different constituencies with their varying goals: support for survivors, litigation against the school, an independent investigation, regime change, more compensation for victims and their families, and the restoration of Horace Mann's good name and reputation as a place that lives up to its motto and deserves its alumni support. He wrote:

> From the days when I helped get HMAC started, I have been troubled by one key missing ingredient in moving beyond "processing" HM: what's the transcendent goal? . . . For my part, the vitriol, name-calling and plain negative energy that goes into some of our discussions is something I cannot afford to participate in, for my own mental health . . . Personally, I am less interested in digging into the muck of the human experience on a FB group. I'd rather do that face to face, person to person, like I do in my daily life.
>
> I am looking for opportunities to frame a more productive and broader narrative to describe the journey we could be on—together. That may not be enough for some, and I understand that. But I will challenge those that cannot wait for or work for a coalescing of concerns (which means you MUST "sand down" the rough edges of your own positions) with the following questions:
>
> 1. What affirmative thing are you fighting for? Or is it just to cut the bad weeds? If it's the latter, are you sure you have hold of the root? Otherwise, they'll just grow back.
> 2. What makes you different? I empathize with many of the characterizations of distortions of wealth and power that were mentioned at the start of this post, but when one takes a stance of revenge, one often must

start acting like the opposition. When we character assassinate our former classmates, isn't that abuse, too, or are they not deserving of your grace, also?

Hughes and I had dinner in Manhattan a few days after this post. I reminded him of the second time we spoke during the course of my reporting. "Bill, you told me then that because of my name, I was part of a prophetic tradition and that part of that tradition is giving people hope. I took that comment seriously and have been asking people, 'Who has handled a situation like this well?'"

"I don't know, Mouse," he said. "But I thought we were better than this."

That same night, Rob Boynton, Peter Brooks, and Kate Geis of HMAC made their way to the HM campus to meet with Justin Lerer, who was acting as a liaison with the Board of Trustees, and representatives of the Alumni Council. They were joined by G., the victim of Mark Wright who'd been the first to corroborate Andrew's account of his abuse.

Brooks had worked long and hard to secure this meeting in an attempt to put a human face on HMAC and show the board that they were simply concerned alumni and not some lunatic fringe hell-bent on the school's destruction. Lerer opened the proceedings by welcoming "fellow alumni." Boynton then set out to underscore what the group hoped to achieve through an independent investigation and emphasized what they were *not* seeking (lawsuits, financial profit, more negative publicity, etc.).

The two groups spoke together for more than three hours with pretty much everything on the table. It was a pleasant enough meeting and all agreed to meet again.

"I think it went well," Geis reported to Christina Propst in Houston. "It felt like a door was opened and will remain open now. They saw that there were no 'knives and pitchforks' but some diligent alums who also want what is best for the school. Overall I was surprised that many were not as knowledgeable about the history of the abuse [as we were]."

On PHM, alumni who were also parents of current students continued to express their conflicted feelings. "I have two sons at HM," wrote Marjorie Greenspan Kaufman (HM '78). "Both boys have participated in animated conversations at home about the past abuse at HM. Today the grandson of Mahatma Gandhi visited with the Middle School kids. Matthew, my 7th grader, reported to me that, following Gandhi's visit, his history teacher stated that 'following much disruption, now there is peace at Horace Mann too.' To my great pride, Matthew raised his hand and said, 'How can you say that when there is considerable unease about the Board of Trustees' refusal to cooperate with an independent investigation?' (seriously, those were his words exactly). Bravo, Matthew Kaufman. I am proud that you are my son. *Magna est veritas et praevalat.*"

In the back-and-forth that followed her story, Kaufman addressed the issue of parents who wanted the whole thing to go away: "I beg that you all pause a moment to consider the quandary we face. We spend hard-earned money to send our kids to HM and feel they are getting an excellent education. We are a community of families and friends. No-one wants to compromise our kids' experience at HM. HOWEVER, in the name of human decency and for a host of moral and ethical reasons, many of us are sickened by the Board's behavior."

As the school became more determined to put the scandal behind it, HMAC was busy seeding stories in the press. The *New York Post* reported that nine wealthy board members had left the board, at least some in protest of the school's obdurate stance. They included the financier Jamshid Ehsani; the attorney Deborah Cogut, whose husband founded Pegasus Capital; Beth Kobliner Shaw, wife of hedge funder David Shaw; and David Schuchman, who manages the computer pioneer Michael Dell's fortune. These individuals alone had a net worth in the billions.

Cogut departed, but not without a fight to reveal the wrongs committed by the board. She told the *Post* she'd asked to be relieved of the confidentiality agreement she'd signed when she joined the board twelve years before, but the request was denied by the chairman.

In response to the trustees' departure, the school issued a report claiming that Horace Mann had a record-breaking year of fund-raising. While it was true that total contributions were up, the donor base had shrunk by 350 alumni. Clearly, a few wealthy donors and current parents were making up the difference. "The school's past affected fund-raising," the director of development, Melissa Parento (HM '90), said in *The Horace Mann Record.*

In the fall of 2013, after months of holding out for an independent investigation, both G. and Joseph Cumming finally settled with Horace Mann. "I signed my HM settlement yesterday and put in mail to counsel," G. wrote to fellow survivors. "While it was good to be a hold-out, eventually I came to question the utility for me and my cash-strapped family. For what it's worth, my personal calculus [is the] desire for a little more emotional closure . . . and . . . the growing realization that trying to enter into a direct moral discourse with HM's current leadership has been a waste of time and effort."

"My wife and children wanted me to [sue]," Joseph told me. "That was the main reason. I never wanted or intended to. But as long as I had not settled I felt that when I called for an independent investigation they could say I was just fishing for evidence. Now that I've settled I feel like I have the moral high ground in lobbying for the Markey bill, as I clearly have no financial interest for myself. I did what I did and it's over. I'm not agonizing over it anymore. Was it the right decision on balance? I don't know. But the money was so insultingly low it wasn't the issue. If they had given me a million bucks, in some way the apology would feel like a real apology. It felt like another insult."

On Saturday, September 28, 2013, alumni from the classes of 1963, 1968, 1973, 1978, 1983, 1988, 1993, 1998, 2003, and 2008 gathered at the Conrad hotel in Battery Park City for dinners and cocktail parties. "I've been to almost all my HM reunions before this one and I loved them," said F., a survivor then living in California. "At HM I was an insider and well loved, and returning to that environment always pumped me up. At this one, I felt very small and afraid and very much an outsider. It was harder than I thought it would be."

The evening took a bizarre turn when Kelly introduced Gary

Marcus (HM '68). Marcus, now an entrepreneur based in Eugene, Oregon, had been expelled from Horace Mann for reasons that Kelly called "arrogant and ignorant" on the part of the school. In an attempt to make amends, Kelly handed Marcus an honorary degree and the microphone.

The gathered alumni listened spellbound as Marcus explained that, as a seventeen-year-old student, he had had sex with his exchange family's mother in Japan. Marcus left Japan in the middle of the exchange program, and the loss of face caused the Japanese entity to break off relations with HM. The school was angry with Marcus for leaving but, out of loyalty to the woman, Marcus refused to explain why he'd departed the program and was then expelled from the school.

Marcus went on to say that he had been involuntarily committed to a *One Flew Over the Cuckoo's Nest*–style mental asylum, where he said he was brutally held prisoner. When he tried to escape, he was dragged back, beaten, drugged, and locked up. After more than a year, Marcus figured out a way to call his family friend Roy Cohn (HM '42), the lawyer best known for prosecuting the Rosenbergs for treason, assisting Senator Joe McCarthy in his Communist witch hunt, leaving government in disgrace, and then serving as defense attorney to several New York Mafia bosses. Marcus said that after Cohn managed to get him released, he headed out to Oregon, where he unsuccessfully tried to work with Ken Kesey. After spending a few years farming, Marcus got his GED, went on to college and graduate school, and enjoyed a successful career as a businessman and now as a philanthropist.

The gathered alumni sat shell-shocked by the story. Marcus then launched into effusive and maudlin praise for Horace Mann and Kelly. He promised to dedicate the rest of his life to trying to bring the Horace Mann style of education to poor people everywhere. As he heaped praise on Kelly ("a genius, a world leader in education, a philosopher king"), Michael Deutsch (HM '73) audibly muttered, "We get the point, move on."

Marcus then handed Kelly a check for $10,000 (which was, in fact, the point) and encouraged those gathered to do the same.

Eric Siegel (HM '73) wasn't satisfied. He wrote on PHM:

After the story is finished we all realized there is something off about it. The guy did something incredibly stupid, arguably worthy of expulsion, HM actually did nothing wrong . . . If he could call Roy Cohn after a year, why didn't he call him after a day? . . . And his completely uncritical praise of Kelly and the school combined with a flat out fundraising pitch makes the whole thing seem like clunky theater staged by Kelly in the naive assumption that this story will change people's opinions about the school. I felt like I needed to wash my hands and have a drink. So we all drank a bit more, agreed that we were incredibly special, and went home.

11

WHAT DOES JUSTICE LOOK LIKE?

On November 21, 2012, NBC aired an episode of the police procedural *Law & Order: Special Victims Unit* called "Lessons Learned," about "Manor Hill Academy," a private school on a vast expanse up in Riverdale, New York.

The episode guest-starred Buck Henry and Elliott Gould as former Manor Hill teachers accused of abusing students, and Charles Grodin as Manor Hill's steely-eyed chief director, Brett Forrester. The school, led by Forrester, adamantly denies the abuse claims and refuses to offer an apology, which it sees as an admission of guilt. When Forrester learns that his own son is one of the victims, he has the kind of epiphany dictated by the unforgiving format of the TV hourly. He convenes a meeting of the entire community (including the SVU detectives who have been pursuing the case) and, while making an official statement, breaks down and admits to the legacy of sexual abuse that had been kept for years within the walls of the prestigious academy to which he has devoted so much of his time and money. Forrester then vows to help the victims and to launch a full investigation.

I felt bludgeoned into silence. Not only because the producers of *Law & Order* had taken the fruits of our labor and not bothered calling (much less paying) us but also because of the message I felt the

episode was sending. By virtue of Forrester's apology, millions of view-
ers would walk away thinking that Horace Mann had indeed done
right by the victims and the larger community. That there had been a
catharsis and justice had been served. Roll credits.

As I shut off the TV, my fifteen-year-old daughter Maia set me
straight. "It's perfect," she said. "A crappy TV show is teaching Horace Mann about values."

Like some of the survivors and their allies and advocates in
HMAC, I felt stuck in a spin cycle—angry at Horace Mann for not
acting more forthrightly, hopeful when I allowed myself to consider
another scenario (even if it was presented in the alternate reality of
TV drama), and then angry all over again. I began looking at how
such crises were playing out in other institutions, particularly other
schools. I wanted to know: What does justice or healing look like?
Could it be found in court?

On October 27, 2013, I made my way to Courtroom 12B on 500 Pearl
Street in lower Manhattan to hear oral arguments in a sexual abuse
lawsuit. The suit had been filed by thirty-four former Yeshiva University prep school students against the Washington Heights institution.
The suit sought to hold Y.U., a Modern Orthodox Jewish school that
comprises both a high school and a university, responsible for hundreds of acts of abuse by two former rabbis and an alumnus employed
by the school, starting in the 1960s. The victims, some now in their
sixties, were being represented by Kevin Mulhearn, who'd had such
success with the Poly Prep case.

I sat in the gallery with about sixty people, many of them victims
and family members of George Finkelstein and Macy Gordon, the
two rabbis who had worked at Yeshiva University High School for
about twenty-five years. Here Judge John Koeltl of the United States
District Court for the Southern District of New York was to hear oral
arguments over whether to sustain Y.U.'s motion to dismiss the case
on grounds that the statute of limitations had run out. Some of the
men in the gallery, mainly in their forties and fifties, wore yarmulkes.

At least one former student had flown to New York from Florida for the two hours of oral arguments.

Mordechai Twersky, whom I'd met the year before in a café on swanky Emek Refaim, the main street of the German Colony in Jerusalem, where he lives, said he found the strength to come forward in part because he'd read "Prep-School Predators." When Twersky, who comes from a long line of respected and prestigious rabbis, spoke out, he was swiftly joined by nearly two dozen other former students who had kept their secrets to themselves. I introduced Twersky to Mulhearn, who soon found himself representing all thirty-four former students who said they were abused by Finkelstein and Gordon. The former students filed a suit that alleged a "massive cover-up of the sexual abuse of [high school] students . . . facilitated, for several decades, by various prominent Y.U. and [high school] administrators, trustees, directors, and other faculty members." In June 2013, Y.U.'s longtime president, Rabbi Norman Lamm, resigned as chancellor, admitting to responding inadequately to the charges at the time. In an extraordinary mea culpa that was emailed to faculty, students, and alumni, Lamm wrote, "I acted in a way that I thought was correct, but which now seems ill conceived. And when that happens—one must do *teshuva*," the Hebrew word for repentance.

Mulhearn was determined he would never let another institution off as easily as Horace Mann. He slapped Yeshiva with a $680 million lawsuit—$20 million per victim. "I'm gonna get my [Y.U.] guys what they deserve," he said. "But more than that, I'm going to get them their day in court."

Once again, New York's stringent statute of limitations laws formed the bulk of the defense's argument for dismissing the case. "There is no debate that the abuse each plaintiff endured, if true, is unacceptable," the Y.U. attorneys stated in a court filing. But "the law strikes a balance between the rights [the plaintiffs] could have exercised long ago, and the defendants' competing rights to a fair opportunity to present evidence in their defense. The passage of time, fading of memories and passing of witnesses deprives defendants [of] a fair opportunity to defend themselves against plaintiffs who sat on their claims."

When the defense attorney Karen Bitar presented Y.U.'s argument, Judge Koeltl interrupted on several occasions. He stressed that in the Poly case the school falsely told at least one student that it had investigated claims against the staff member and found them to be false. In the Y.U. case, as in the Poly case, there were also instances where victims alleged they *had* made timely complaints to the school. Bitar argued that nothing had prevented the nine students who had reported abusive incidents to Y.U. within the period of the statute of limitations from filing a civil suit.

When Mulhearn stood up, he knew that this was his shot to prove that the Poly case had not been a fluke. He would get to test-drive some of the new arguments he'd developed since the HM mediation. Dressed in a dark blue suit, his rumpled white shirt hanging out of his pants, Mulhearn addressed Judge Koeltl. Without the use of the microphone, Mulhearn filled the courtroom with his passionate machine-gun Brooklyn-style staccato. He began by chastising the defense's characterization of what Finkelstein did to his clients as wrestling. What "Mr. Finkelstein"—Mulhearn made a point never to refer to either Finkelstein or Gordon as rabbi, an appellation he felt neither man deserved—did behind closed doors, for decades, was to forcibly pin these "defenseless boys" to the floor, "where they couldn't move, and proceed to hump them in the backside with an erect penis until he achieved climax." Finkelstein then ordered the students not to tell their parents, Mulhearn said. "Nothing was done about Mr. Finkelstein until 1995, when he was finally, quietly fired," he added. Calling it "wrestling" made light of the seriousness of the crimes. In the gallery, several men vigorously nodded their heads. Others groaned.

Mulhearn went on to argue that the statute of limitations did not apply in this case because Y.U. fraudulently covered up the abuse. It also misrepresented the safety of the school in its marketing materials, including yearbooks, pamphlets, and advertisements.

To illustrate how difficult it had been for his clients to understand the extent of the cover-up, Mulhearn gave an example of the Y.U. victim John Doe XX, who had been abused between 1983 and 1986. Mulhearn said his client had no way of knowing that three students had reported Finkelstein for inappropriate sexual behavior to Rabbi Norman Lamm, Y.U.'s president, between 1983 and 1985. Further, in 1985, Y.U. named Finkelstein "educator of the year," and in 1988 it promoted him to principal. Mulhearn argued that by the time John Doe XX reached the statute of limitations, in 1989, he believed Y.U. saw Finkelstein as an "exemplary educator."

"It wasn't that he was being lauded as a good teacher but *the* teacher of the year," Mulhearn said.

Mulhearn contended that because Y.U. ignored student complaints and maintained that Finkelstein and Gordon were men of good character—even after the school was warned of abuses—the students could not recognize that they had a chance of bringing a successful claim. This, Mulhearn insisted, nullified the statute of limitations. The clock should only start ticking from the moment Twersky and the other survivors came forward.

The pain on the faces of the men in the audience was unmistakable. Whatever the legal issues were, it was clear that the process of seeking justice was brutal on the survivors. It certainly didn't look like healing.

Watching Mulhearn do this daring legal high-wire act just to have the case heard was painful. His argument only confirmed my belief that the arcane statute of limitations on child sexual abuse cases was misguided.

A few months after oral arguments, I happened to be interviewing Mulhearn on the phone when he received the news that Judge Koeltl had dismissed the Y.U. case due to the statute of limitations.

"You are talking to one angry man right now. I gotta talk to my guys," Mulhearn said before hanging up. Mulhearn appealed Koeltl's decision. A few months later, a three-judge federal appeals court panel upheld the decision, ruling that the Yeshiva students waited decades too long to file their claims.

"A crime against humanity," Mulhearn texted me when he learned of the panel's decision. "But it's not over by a long shot."

•

I wondered if justice looked any different in New Jersey, where the statute of limitations was more forgiving. M., whom Johannes Somary had abused hundreds of times, was trying to have his case heard. The school maintained that it had no offices in New Jersey and that anything that occurred there was extracurricular and therefore not its responsibility. According to court documents, HM said that Somary "was acting outside the scope of his employment when he allegedly sexually abused plaintiff, a student. Mister Somary was clearly not employed by Horace Mann to perform such actions and the allegations all stem from sexual acts that occurred outside the 'time and space limits' of Mr. Somary's employment."

Rendered in such legal language, M.'s saga seems all the more poignant—and the school's defense unwittingly damning. "In opposition, plaintiff alleges that Mr. Somary abused him on at least two occasions at school-sponsored events," the court wrote. "The first act of sexual abuse at a school-sponsored event took place on the way to a Glee Club concert held at Dwight-Englewood High School in Englewood, New Jersey, where Mr. Somary's supervisor, Inslee Clark, was present . . . Plaintiff alleges that Mr. Somary sexually abused plaintiff in the bathroom of Dwight-Englewood High School at the Glee Club concert and in Mr. Somary's car on the way to the same concert."

The second time was at a concert at Princeton High School—an outing Inky also attended. M.'s suit asked the court to accept that the school knew of Somary's propensities "and failed to exercise appropriate supervision over him." These field trips were essential to the HM experience and, "importantly, Horace Mann benefited financially from sending Mr. Somary and the Glee Club members to New Jersey and receiving shared revenues from the sale of tickets for the Glee Club concerts."

To the surprise of many—including even M.'s attorney, Rosemarie Arnold—the court found in favor of the plaintiff, saying he had "successfully demonstrated the requisite 'minimum contacts' that would substantiate the exercise of specific personal jurisdiction." Further, the presence of Inky, at an event the school profited from, no less, was judged harshly. "The Supreme Court has imposed a duty upon employers with *in loco parentis* responsibilities to exercise reasonable care in the supervision of employees." The court ruled that M. had "set forward sufficient facts to maintain a claim for negligent supervision in New Jersey." While the crucial question of whether New Jersey or New York law would ultimately apply was left unsettled, the judge refused the school's motion to dismiss M.'s complaint.

"The main issue in our case is the fact that Horace Mann knew that Somary was a sexual predator before my client even went to the school," Arnold told *The Riverdale Press*, "and rather than deal with it, not only did they sweep it under the rug, they tried to cover it up."

Arnold was asking Horace Mann for $15 million. "I don't need the money and neither does my client," Arnold said. "We want the truth exposed." Although Arnold said she knew M. wouldn't get the full $15 million, she told me she had "no intention of settling for a lot less than that. And neither does my client. But even if he did, he can't get his life back. He's a fifty-seven-year-old heroin addict. What justice is there for him? There's no justice for any of them."

M.'s case settled in March 2015.

A week earlier, Steve Friedman sent a letter to the community, announcing that he would be stepping away from Horace Mann's board, after serving nine years as chairman and sixteen in total. "It has been exhilarating and at times challenging," Friedman wrote, making no reference to the abuse scandal or the painful mediation process.

He did, however, mention the scandal when he spoke with *The Horace Mann Record* about his resignation. "Trying to get a resolution to the best of our ability and to be as fair as possible to the number of people that we had to deal with was very hard," he said. "We did it methodically, slowly, but it took an enormous amount of time."

"Friedman strived to balance addressing the needs of current students and faculty while working to heal relationships with former alumni who had suffered sexual abuse as students and later reported their accounts to the school," the paper reported.

Not surprisingly, some members of the community took issue with the *Record*'s conclusions. "That's pretending there weren't dozens and dozens of timely reports that were completely ignored over the years," Peter Brooks told the *Daily News*. "A lot of alumni are happy to see Steve Friedman go," one anonymous alumnus told the *New York Post*. "Penn State did the right thing with an investigation. Horace Mann should have done the same; it is the only way to make sure there is closure and it never happens again." The scandal and the lack of an investigation had resulted in a slowdown in fund-raising and in applications for the school, the source said, adding, "It is a black eye that never got treated."

Michael Colacino (HM '75), a longtime board member and president of the commercial real estate firm Savills Studley, was named Friedman's successor.

"While I'd like to think Friedman's resignation will lead to reform, I note that Colacino was cited in a 2013 *Daily News* piece as the other leader of the 'hard-line' faction of the board," F. wrote me. "No reason to make an enemy of him off the bat—but probably no reason to expect a major shift. Looks like he was hand-picked."

Despite F.'s skepticism, the Survivors' Group wrote another collective letter inviting Colacino to meet with them to chart a course forward.

If M.'s case in New Jersey tested the value of civil actions, Virginia showed what the criminal justice system could do in similar cases. "Horace Mann on the Potomac" was *The Daily Beast*'s headline about a sexual abuse scandal at the Potomac School in McLean, Virginia. Our "nurturing mother" had become national shorthand for sexual abuse in an educational setting.

For close to thirty years, Christopher Kloman taught geography and math, and was an administrator at Potomac, a private school whose stature in D.C. is analogous to that of HM in New York. Kloman was well regarded and well liked and, like many "successful" child abusers, used his position and popularity to groom young girls. When high-ranking school officials became aware of the allegations at the time, *The Daily Beast* reported, they directed Kloman to attend counseling.

Although the Potomac case had some similarities to Horace Mann's, there were some glaring differences. Unlike at Horace Mann, Potomac's board and administration stressed transparency and attempted to keep alumni informed about developments. The school urged former students to come forward with any information.

The other major difference was that Virginia state law allows criminal cases to be brought against sexual abusers regardless of when the events occurred. Five women, represented by Gloria Allred, brought criminal charges against Kloman. Although some of the survivors, like their counterparts at Horace Mann, were still demanding a public apology and answers as to who knew what when, they could rest assured that Kloman would not be preying on young girls anymore. In October 2013, Kloman, then seventy-four, was sentenced to forty-three years in prison.

After the sentencing, Potomac's board authorized the law firm of Debevoise & Plimpton to investigate Kloman's years at the school. In addition to the five victims whose testimony led to the criminal conviction, the investigation found "strong evidence" that Kloman had sexually abused twenty-six former students in addition to the other five. The report also revealed that various school heads, administrators, teachers, and board chairs were told directly or indirectly about particular allegations, which ranged from touching to rape.

Kloman's conviction was a notable victory for the survivors. But was a courtroom, even one in a state with less conservative statute of limitations laws than New York, the only place to seek justice? Monetary compensation was an acknowledgment that terrible wrongs had been committed. Such settlements had aided certain survivors, allowing them to feel heard, if not whole, and helping them to feel that their lives were back on track. But as Paul Finn had rhetorically asked at the opening of the HM mediation, "How much money would I have to pay you to let me abuse your child?" Could any sum answer a lifetime of hurt?

Was money or prison the best we could do? Was there no other

way for an institution to give adult victims what they needed at the
same time as it preserved the name and the integrity of the institution itself?

On November 19, 2013, Peter Brooks and I spoke on a panel at a
Prevention Summit in Framingham, Massachusetts. Brooks presented
the many ways Horace Mann failed in the past while my comments
focused on the school's current failures. But what made the greatest
impression was the story told by our fellow panelist Dr. Charles Conroy,
the executive director of the Franklin Perkins School in Lancaster,
Massachusetts. Perkins, founded in 1896, enjoyed a sterling reputation
for serving children and young adults who have behavioral disorders
or are cognitively delayed.

Conroy was the executive director in October 1995 when he was
approached by two former students, then ages twenty-nine and thirty,
who reported abuse they had suffered between the ages of fifteen and
seventeen. The accused—four former school counselors—had sexually abused them and possibly as many as twelve other students between 1977 and 1981.

The two former students approached Perkins in much the same
way that Gene and Steve Fife had approached Horace Mann many
years after their abuse by Berman. But the similarities ended there.

Conroy, with advice from the school's lawyer, Eric MacLeish, immediately treated the allegations as true. Building on Perkins's
stellar reputation for helping people, Conroy and MacLeish were determined to assist any victims who came forward. "We decided to
listen to people. Not circle the wagons," Conroy said. "Our job was to
assist victims. Not make things worse. It's very clear that victims
want two things: someone to believe them and an authority figure
from the school to tell them sorry." The stance enabled Conroy to
focus not on the legal implications of the allegations but on caring for
the victims.

Conroy quickly deemed the claims credible. Even though both
victims had learning disabilities ("what today might be labeled

ADHD"), he was impressed by their excellent and detailed recognition of events that had occurred ten to fifteen years earlier. The victims, who had been in and out of psychiatric hospitals and in therapy since graduating from Perkins, both told Conroy they were not coming forward in order to file lawsuits. Rather, they'd decided to come forward to achieve a sense of closure and to help prevent similar abuse in the future.

After hearing the victims' accounts, Conroy contacted local law enforcement officials, the state's attorney general's office, and several Massachusetts state agencies, including the Department of Social Services and the Office for Children. Both said they could not investigate the charges because their agencies did not exist when the abuse occurred.

Despite the fact that one of the abusers was dead and three had moved out of the state, Conroy and the school's Board of Trustees "felt a moral obligation to make sure that these men no longer work with children. We contracted with two professionals—a doctor and a psychologist—and we gave victims coming forward the option to speak with them as opposed to someone from the administration. Ultimately ten victims came forward, but we know there were more. One of the sick things is that the staff had allowed the older kids who they had abused to abuse the younger kids. This was their way of keeping the silence. There were many, many more victims. Much bigger. It went on for twenty-five years."

Conroy reached out to his community by sending letters to the parents of children at Perkins. He then continued with his own investigation. "We hired a skip tracer, a professional the IRS uses to track down anyone with a Social Security number, to find the perpetrators." Even though the incidents had happened fifteen years earlier, they were able to find all but one of the abusers. The school then hired a private investigator to locate the last one. "We wanted to alert the authorities wherever they were living," Conroy told me.

Conroy then did something that, by his own admission, was quite risky. He invited about thirty prominent residents of Lancaster and Clinton, where Perkins is located, to brainstorm how to best handle the situation. "At the time I took a huge gamble," he said. "In hindsight it turned out to be brilliant. Business leaders, state reps, even some press. I wanted to know what they thought we should do about this."

Despite safety measures like background checks and staff and student training, no system is infallible. So Conroy implemented a new policy that launched an internal investigation each time a staff member or a student reported an instance of sexual or physical abuse. In the years since Conroy took the helm at Perkins, the school had conducted five investigations into possible physical abuse and one case of sexual abuse.

"It's very painful and devastating," Conroy said. "But the fact of the matter is it is how you handle a crisis like this. Putting the information out there and letting people know it's out there is a lot better than sweeping it under the rug. We ended up paying about fifty-five hundred dollars in therapy costs for one victim who didn't have insurance."

"It was very hard," one of the victims told Conroy at the time, "because I was so young. I feel a lot better now."

"I feel a lot happier now," the other victim told him. No lawsuits were filed, because Massachusetts's statute of limitations had run out on both criminal and civil cases.

"It's nice that we didn't get sued," Conroy said. "But it was part of our moral and ethical obligation to go far beyond that. We are in the business of taking care of vulnerable people. The board felt very strongly about it. I am absolutely convinced that how you handle it says everything about your future. If you sidestep, downplay, or in any way demean the people, you are in big trouble. And if you buy into the notion that these people are looking for money—you're finished."

In August 2013, Horace Mann sued several divisions of AIG after the insurance company refused to reimburse it for more than $1 million of the damages the school had paid out. According to stories in the *Daily News* and elsewhere, Horace Mann claimed that the insur-

ance giant failed to promptly notify the school that it was denying coverage and had wrongfully neglected to defend and compensate the
school. The suit noted that Horace Mann had contacted the insurer
several times about two claimants who fell under its policies, but six
months had passed until a denial notice was received. This passage
of time, the school's lawyers argued, violated an insurance law obli-
gating companies to issue responses as soon as possible.

AIG countered that the school's "chosen strategy was to preserve
its reputation by quickly settling all purported claims regardless of
viability and then foisting responsibility for payment onto its insurers." Given the current statute of limitations on child sexual abuse,
AIG argued that the claims were not "legally viable and should have
been vigorously defended rather than settled."

When the case came to pretrial oral hearings, the State Supreme
Court justice Charles E. Ramos made it clear that the school was
unlikely to win its case. "They've got some good defenses here," Ramos
said, nodding in the direction of the insurer's lawyers. Ramos, himself a Horace Mann alumnus, took the case despite a defense motion
requesting that he recuse himself.

Ramos asked Horace Mann's lawyer, Howard Epstein, if HM
trustees knew about Ben Balter's 1993 letter telling administrators
about being abused by Johannes Somary.

"There was no evidence of that," Epstein said.

"There was a meeting with trustees," Ramos said as he leafed
through the case file.

"Well, some trustees," Epstein admitted.

"One will do," the judge replied, noting that Horace Mann had
been obligated to tell its insurance company of the reported abuse
when trustees learned about Balter's letter.

Ramos encouraged the two parties to reach a settlement.

Early on this journey, as the story of the abuses grew in scope and as
evidence that the school had acted negligently seemed to be growing
too, I had higher hopes for Horace Mann. I thought the school would

take a leadership position and come clean about its mistakes. I had also fantasized that wealthy alumni might fund an independent on-campus institute to study the prevention of child abuse in schools and other youth-serving institutions, such as camps. Such an institute might be a part of the daily life of the students and would sponsor research, host symposia, offer classes, and give HM a means to heal and to project itself as the educational leader so many of us thought it had been and still could be.

In a way, I suppose, I was still seeing Horace Mann through the lens of a teenager—as the all-knowing and powerful Oz. And part of growing up was realizing that those who were supposed to take care of us had let us down.

Early in this story, I was working under the impression that all the teachers knew. I assumed that the open secrets floating around the cafeteria were shared widely in the teachers' cafeteria. And, in some cases, that was true. Anne Mackay, a theater teacher, told me it was well known that Somary would choose one special student a year. They even joked about it.

Even if all the teachers didn't know (and how could they know the full extent of it all?), I was angry at the adults in the building. Yes, it was a different time, but that argument took it only so far. The teachers knew what they were doing was wrong. Otherwise, as Joyce Fitzpatrick pointed out in her open letter, they would have done what they did more openly.

"It's very hard to rat out a colleague," one former teacher told me when I asked him why, if there were rampant rumors about the driver's ed teacher Joe Klein, he hadn't done anything about it. "It is very hard to accuse someone of something that you're not sure one hundred percent that they did." This same teacher was later named as a perpetrator.

In December 2013, Marjorie Greenspan Kaufman agreed to become the chair of Hilltop Cares, the foundation started by HM alumni to help survivors. In many ways Kaufman was a perfect choice. As a managing director for Golden Seeds, a venture capital and private equity firm based in New York City, she had both business experience and gravitas. As a parent of two boys currently at HM, she had no desire to see the school of today weakened by events of the past. But there was no mistake as to where she stood on the question of the school's responsibility. If Clark, she wrote on Processing Horace Mann,

> was himself a sickening sexual predator of young boys and aware of, or complicit in, illegal, unethical and immoral activities of many other teachers, shouldn't the Board of Trustees at that time be held accountable for gross failure to supervise and breach of their fiduciary responsibilities? The trail starts and ends at the top of the governance structure. Who, if anyone, on the Board knew the truth about Clark before his hiring or during his tenure and chose to remain silent? Given Clark's stature at Horace Mann, these horrifying accounts of molestation now appear to have been an institution-wide problem, not simply the sordid, isolated acts of a few teachers. Perhaps we cannot fault other teachers at that time for not speaking out or taking action, given that their boss was a fiend.

At the same time, Kaufman chided others in the forum for ignoring "that the school today is filled with terrific kids of many ethnicities; dedicated, caring teachers and thoughtful administrators who are all innocent bystanders to the truly evil stories being revealed now. There is no point in hurting all of them to repay the crimes of past generations." She also openly praised Kelly's efforts to sensitize current children and teachers to the nuances of predatory and inappropriate behavior.

"They have a New York regulatory agency that comes in and does trainings with the kids," said Holly Thomas, who has one kid in the school. "In sixth and in ninth grade. They speak to all of them as a group and as individuals. At this point the kids are like, 'Here we go again.' It's so open and out there. They think, 'Wow, why are we still talking about this?'

"If there were any questions about a teacher's behavior," she continued, "they are gone in a minute. Even in the middle of the year. A real zero tolerance [policy]. Horace Mann is almost hyperaware."

Some parents believe the hypervigilance has gone too far. "One thing that I think is unfortunate: all this has made the line between student and teacher much greater," said Bret Parker, an alumnus with two kids in the school. "When I went to HM, the track coach, Walt Beisinger, invited some of the people from the track team to his house. He and his wife. Nothing inappropriate about it. The kids could never do that now. I think that's unfortunate. I understand why but I think it's a loss. It's worth it but there is probably a way you can have some of it and still have a safe place."

"I applaud [Kelly's] efforts and know that my kids are in a safe environment," Marjorie Kaufman wrote. "And yet, there must be an investigation. Because we now know the head of school was one of the predators, we are looking at a gross failure to supervise by the Board at that time. They deserve our collective wrath and blame for presiding over a school staffed and led by predators. It is indeed their bill to pay as fiduciaries. And yet, I doubt any one of them will be held accountable. And I doubt any of them will confess to knowing anything."

Parker agrees, for what it's worth—he is also one of the HM alumni and current parents who question the value of an independent investigation. "What will an independent investigation uncover that hasn't already been disclosed other than make the survivors feel more vindicated?" he asked. "I don't know what the investigation would do. What's the real learning here? What has not been addressed? What could people take from this that will help them going forward?"

In an effort to distinguish itself from the administration and the board, Hilltop changed its website to read "Hilltop Cares is independent from the Horace Mann School and is not in any way subject to the control or input of Horace Mann, its governing body or its administration."

Many critics still wanted to know what had taken so long. Why had it taken some of the world's richest alumni—some worth billions—to begin funneling money to dozens of survivors in need of therapy? Scully pulled away from Hilltop Cares when a private family matter, unrelated to Horace Mann, received negative press. The truth was that providing money for survivors' therapy was easier said than done. There were ethical questions of how to keep a survivor's identity anonymous. There were legal concerns such as how to pay for therapy across state lines and whether Hilltop could be held liable if therapy went awry and a survivor harmed himself. And how could they structure the entity to properly match survivors with licensed therapists? Could Hilltop provide money for someone who wanted alternative therapies like yoga or meditation?

Once the legal hurdles were overcome, Hilltop still awaited its not-for-profit status. Eager to begin funneling money to survivors, Hilltop searched for an existing charitable organization that would act as a fiscal sponsor so that it could accept donations. At that point, Hilltop was approached by Designer Collections, an organization formed by the Horace Mann junior Lucy Golub as a clothing drive to raise money for survivors. Golub's father, Lawrence, an HM alumnus, was the founder of the multibillion-dollar investment management firm Golub Capital.

For some, Designer Collections became a target. "She will ask Horace Mann students to collect gently used designer clothing and accessories" to help pay for therapy, according to an internal Hilltop email, parts of which were published in the *New York Post* on January 24, 2014. The tabloid had fun with the slightly grotesque image of rich kids cleaning out their closets to give abuse victims some help.

Despite the good intentions, many HM alumni felt that putting a teenager front and center was a cynical move and inappropriate as well. "Do you mean to tell me that the grown-ups are too busy to deal with this thing?" Paul said at the time. "And you're going to have a sixteen-year-old handing out money to fifty-year-olds whose lives have been decimated? It's patronizing. What is this, a fucking mitzvah project?"

Golub defended herself and her intentions. "Horace Mann students care about the survivors," she told the paper. "And we are proud to be helping in our own small way."

Kathy Howard, Ben Balter's mom, was asked to join the Hilltop Cares board but declined. "I just didn't feel it was right for a student at the school to be hearing all these stories along with board members. After all I've been through I had no desire to sell old clothes to raise money for a wealthy school. I was tired."

Despite the alumni cynicism, nearly two years after "Prep-School Predators" was published, dozens of survivors finally began receiving money to cover hundreds of hours of individual therapy sessions.

In March 2015, Marjorie Kaufman invited the HM community to a benefit concert for Hilltop Cares to be held on May 1. The evening was the brainchild of the alums Claudia Knafo (HM '80) and Jeremy Bar-Ilan (HM '80), professional musicians who felt that the power of music could help close some wounds. Among the many who agreed to perform was Jon Seiger, known for his ability to mimic the trumpet playing and singing of Louis Armstrong. This would mark Seiger's first return to the school after thirty-six years. Joseph Cumming agreed to play the piano in a reunion of the original Horace Mann Jazz Band. Steve Fife was invited to read from his memoir, *The Thirteenth Boy*.

As the date of the concert approached, Tom Kelly offered Horace Mann's Fisher Hall as a free venue so that more of the money raised could go directly to Hilltop's mission of providing therapy for the survivors. Any good feeling about Kelly's gesture was tempered when word spread that he would be making the opening remarks. It was unclear whether Kelly had asked or even intended to speak, but the mere suggestion outraged some.

"TK [Tom Kelly] should have no role in Hilltop Cares," one alum told a group of survivors and HMAC supporters in an email. "He can send a check . . . His having any public role is grotesque."

Seiger began to regret his decision to participate. "I now wish it wasn't happening," he emailed me. "The school did not set up or fund HTC, nor did TK. His speaking at the benefit concert implies that he and the school had something to do with creating or funding HTC.

When I was asked to perform at the fundraiser, I was not told that TK would be speaking, and I do feel he shouldn't be."

When these concerns were conveyed to Hilltop Cares, Kaufman, Daniel Miller (HM '82), and others decided that any speech Kelly might give would do more harm than good—and they made it clear Kelly would not be speaking.

I still felt ambivalent about attending. I hadn't visited the school since my article appeared, but in the end I figured that if survivors were willing to participate, showing up was the least I could do.

I was quite nervous as Paul, Madeline, and I pulled up to Horace Mann and parked in front of the headmaster's house. We walked across the baseball field and paused to take a picture.

As I entered the reception area of Fisher Hall, Peggy Maresco, a longtime HM staffer, greeted me warmly. "Hi, Amos," she said, and proceeded to tell me how she still remembered my costume (a working shower) from Senior Absurdity Day in 1982. It was a small moment, but one that softened my feelings about the school. I never wanted to forget all the wonderful people—teachers, friends, current parents and students—I'd met.

In the *Law and Order* episode based on the HM scandal, the fictional school embraced the fictional survivors. When I entered the lobby, the scene resembled that episode come to life. In addition to offering the hall, Kelly had paid for the catering, and waiters were walking around with sushi and other hors d'oeuvres. A carving station served prime rib with horseradish sauce. Survivors mixed at the open bar with HM board members, Hilltop Cares members, and current teachers and administrators. Detective Daryl Sims, of the Bronx Special Victims Unit, told those gathered around him of his trips around the country to interview Berman, Blagden, Lin, and others named as perpetrators. "It was probably the most fascinating case I ever worked on," Sims told the small group. "I could have opened up two or three more files for every person I talked to."

The performance mainly featured Horace Mann graduates. Knafo, a concert pianist, played a piece by Manuel Ponce whose title, "Malgré Tout," translates as "Despite Everything." It was inspired by a friend of the composer who continued to create sculptures despite losing his right arm. Knafo played the entire piece with her left hand.

Fife read several moving passages from *The Thirteenth Boy*, reminding the audience of the reason for Hilltop Cares' existence.

The final performance was led by Seiger, who ripped it up. He played piano, vamped, and told jokes. At one point he played the piano and trumpet simultaneously and in different keys. He introduced the jazz standard "Everything Happens to Me" by saying, "Over the years, I've taken this as my theme song—think about it." He injected a little more humor into the evening when he announced that a special guest would be joining the reunion of the original HM jazz band. "Tom Kelly, come on down!"

"It's so nice to see them all up there together," I overhead Kelly, seated behind me, tell his wife.

In the end, it was a classy and strangely pleasant evening. Calling the night "bittersweet," Joseph told *The Riverdale Press* that the concert "was a very important first step in the right direction." He continued to maintain, however, that an independent investigation would be in the best interests of the community. "I hope the board of trustees realize this would be the best way to promote healing," he said.

The evening raised $17,500, which would cover the cost of roughly one hundred therapy sessions.

It was a positive step in the right direction and I wondered if there was any way to leverage the evening's good will. Was there any way to detoxify the situation for the broader community? Was there an approach that would also help the rest of us—the old girlfriends and boyfriends, the nonabusing teachers, those of us who "knew" on some level, those shocked by the revelations, teachers, board members, parents, and students, then and now, grappling with the fallout of everything we now knew? Could anything heal the rift between the warring factions of Horace Mann alumni? Was there a model for that kind of community reconciliation?

I took these questions to Beth Fisher-Yoshida, the academic director of the Negotiation and Conflict Resolution program at Columbia University. Fisher-Yoshida invited Jenny Besch, the director of the Westchester Mediation Center, and the three of us explored the possibility of applying a "restorative justice" approach to the Horace Mann situation.

Fisher-Yoshida and Besch told me about the Albany Archdiocese's efforts. In the early 2000s, it expelled nineteen priests for committing sexual acts over fifty-three years and paid out settlements totaling more than $2.3 million. That same year the retired New York State Court of Appeals judge Howard A. Levine established the Independent Mediation Assistance Program (IMAP). His plan was to assist the victims in Albany. Levine consulted with various experts on the trauma associated with childhood sexual abuse and developed the idea of a mediation process that would provide a safe space to explore creative options for healing individuals who were abused. IMAP took precautions to safeguard the identities of victims while investigating the allegations. The idea was for victims and abusers to be interviewed separately and, if the victim chose, for him to confront his abuser face-to-face. The mediation process would not preclude a victim suing his abuser or seeking a monetary settlement.

Although the Albany pilot provided an interesting experimental alternative community-wide healing process, it has not been widely replicated.

•

The leading contemporary advocate of restorative justice is the criminologist Howard Zehr. "If the traditional criminal justice process seeks to address issues of broken laws, culpability, and punishment, restorative justice asks questions from the victim's perspective designed to lessen the adversarial nature of the criminal or retributive justice system," Zehr wrote in his book *Changing Lenses: A New Focus for Crime and Justice.* "Questions such as, 'Who has been hurt? What are their needs? Who has a stake in the situation? What is the appropriate process to involve stakeholders in an effort to address causes and put things right?'"

In criminal cases, victims can testify about the crime's impact upon their lives, family members can receive answers to questions

about the incident and participate in holding the offender accountable. Offenders might tell their story of why the crime occurred and
how it has affected their own lives. Offenders are sometimes given
the opportunity to compensate the victim directly—with money, the
performance of community service, or an act that is specific to the
offense.

Perhaps the most famous case of the restorative justice approach
was the South African Truth and Reconciliation Commission (TRC).
Victims were invited to give personal statements about their experiences, some of which were repeated in public hearings. Perpetrators
were also afforded the opportunity to give testimony and request amnesty from both civil and criminal prosecution.

Although the TRC was seen by many as a crucial component of a
post-apartheid South Africa, the process was not without its critics,
who felt that it had fallen short of achieving reconciliation between
South Africa's black and white communities. Perhaps the harshest
criticism came from family members of Steve Biko, the prominent
anti-apartheid activist killed by South African security police. The
family opposed amnesty for Biko's killers, arguing that the TRC was
unconstitutional and a "vehicle for political expediency" that "robbed"
them of their right to justice.

Whatever its limitations, could such an approach apply to Horace
Mann? I discussed the question with another restorative justice advocate, Parker Palmer. "The last thing anyone needs for healing is to
treat this as solely a legal or monetary matter," he told me. "In order
to heal a community, this stuff has to be talked about in open and
honest ways. This will legitimate the claims and will allow others
who have been harmed to come forward and seek the help they need.
One of the best things the HM community could do would be to hold
a series of open forums with a third-party convener or mediator, to
help tell stories and heal wounds. It could involve experts in various
arenas of this issue. Ideally it should be done on the Horace Mann
campus in order to exorcise the institution. This stuff has a way of
getting into the walls of buildings. And it can't be one time. It needs to
be an ongoing conversation on this very issue."

Palmer admitted that given what he'd read in the press and seen on HM's website, getting the school to sign on would be difficult. "It's easy to put some child protective measures in place and post on your website that the issue has been dealt with as though it were a magic bullet," he said. "An approach like what I'm suggesting is a challenge to the self-satisfied culture of prep schools in general. It is difficult for them to square this sordid history with their self-image. Individuals and institutions armor themselves in reflexive ways. Trustees wear that as armor. Their self-identity is wrapped up with the school being an incredible place that has given them so much opportunity and a successful life. You need to appeal to them as educators. Make a forum so good that it would be embarrassing for the board not to attend. This is an educational institution. An educational institution's role is the formation of human beings—not the deformation."

12

TRUTH BE TOLD

Mouse, you slayed the dragon," said Eli Chalfin (HM '81), the shortstop on that 22–1 baseball team, of the stormy days that followed the publication of my article in June 2012.

Though the beast was brought down by many, the dragon-slaying image seems apt. Years of hiding or ignoring the truth had come to an end. Maybe it was because the relationships between some teachers and students made us squeamish, or maybe we thought it was none of our business. Then as now, students at Horace Mann worked relentlessly; it was a point of pride to go without sleep in preparation for an exam, to crash in the library or even miss some epic social event— the concert of the year, the performance of a lifetime—because you were writing some paper, making some masterpiece, reimagining the world. We were spartans in our way, and inconvenient truths and unsavory rumors could be ignored in the name of pursuing a greater goal. Horace Mann graduates were owed the world.

But even then, students and teachers alike spoke both openly and in whispers about what we now know was one of the worst recorded cases of sexual abuse in American educational history.

Who were the abusers? The image of Jerry Sandusky being led away in chains is a new archetype: the sexual predator as monster, as deadly and dangerous as Hannibal Lecter. But the men and women who committed hundreds of acts of sexual violence were not simply monsters and no amount of simplification can flatten them. They committed monstrous acts, but part of their allure was that they were also great teachers, wonderful listeners, and excellent coaches. When Whit Sheppard saw the man who molested him in the photos of Deerfield reunions, he wasn't simply attending the celebrations: he was overseeing them as "the much-beloved Czar."

"It's hard to think of Mr. Theodore as a 'monster,' easier with some of the other Horace Mann perpetrators," Kate Geis wrote me about Theo. "If I had been abused, I might not have trouble with the label but instead I see abusers as people who are damaged, and have done horrible acts. Under these labels is a person who was known by part of the community only as a mentor, teacher, or friend, but that same person violated a child, betrayed them, did things that were criminal."

I felt the same way about Inky as I did about Theo. He, too, had loved me like a son and had almost single-handedly changed the course of my life. Although my impression of Inky had been whittled down from savior to pathetic alcoholic and tragic weakling, and then to violent perpetrator and a man presiding over a group of sexual predators, I still cannot bring myself to hate the man who did so much for me. He was warm, gregarious, handsome, charismatic, a wonderful storyteller, and a baseball enthusiast who changed dozens of lives. He also ruined some.

Several of the twenty-two abusers are still alive. Robert Berman still lives in Tuxedo Park. He shares his house with Robert Simon, his former student. (Simon is a specialist in paintings by old masters, and made the newspapers when he helped discover, restore, and sell a Leonardo panel called *Salvator Mundi*, which was purchased in 2013 by a private collector for more than $75 million.)

Tek Lin, who admitted to *The New York Times* that he abused several boys during his tenure, is retired and living in California. So too is F.'s yet unnamed abuser.

I decided it was time to go see one of the dragons.

•

On an icy Sunday in February, I drove to Shoreham, Vermont, a rural town a few miles southwest of Middlebury. A recent nor'easter had buried the quiet valley in snow. I was going to see Crawford Blagden, the teacher who had been named by several female students. My stomach tightened when I saw the name BLAGDEN on a black postbox in front of a typical rustic Vermont home. A few cars were parked in various levels of snow.

Blagden arrived at Horace Mann in 1980 after several short high school teaching stints and a job in admissions at Columbia University, where, for three dollars an hour, he would interview prospective students. He'd been driving a cab in Boston for four years when HM's headmaster, Michael Lacopo, invited him to join the English faculty. The two had met a few years earlier when both were working toward a master's degree at the Bread Loaf School of English, a summer graduate school of Middlebury College.

Back then, Blagden, who was divorced by the time he arrived at HM, smoked a pipe and wore flannel shirts. He fit in easily with the other members of the department, including Tek Lin, Joyce Fitzpatrick, Alan Breckenridge, and Bruce Weber. In addition to teaching English, Blagden coached cross-country and assisted with Searchers—the Outward Bound–style program that Mr. Breck (as we called him) had developed years earlier.

Although I never had him as a teacher, I got to know him through Andrew and Paul and other friends who had taken Searchers. Sometimes he'd pitch batting practice and delight in the fact that he could still get kids out.

I knocked gingerly on the front door and heard nothing. Had he changed his mind about speaking to me? I had hastily packed my family into the car for a "weekend trip to Vermont" the moment Blagden agreed to see me. I knocked a little harder and took a few deep breaths as I heard footsteps inside. When the door opened, I recognized him immediately. His hair was whiter and he was slightly heavier than I remembered him, but the square jaw and the glasses were the same. Whenever I heard Garrison Keillor on the radio, it was Blagden's face I pictured.

"Hey, Crawford," I said, willing my voice into a casual, familiar tone as if we spoke all the time.

"Nice to see you, Amos," he said as he grasped my hand warmly.

Blagden poured me a cup of coffee. (He'd asked me the night before if I preferred coffee or tea.) His relaxing living room was lined with the books, old newspapers, wool blankets, and gentle disorder one might associate with a retired schoolteacher in Vermont. A pot-belly stove warmed the home he shared with Lynn, his wife of eighteen years. He lowered the volume on the Olympic hockey game he'd been watching, offered me the big chair, then sat on the comfortable couch, where he was quickly joined by Rosie, his springer spaniel. His home reminded me of the atmosphere he had worked so hard to create in Room Ten, the classroom he'd turned into a refuge where kids would spend hours lounging on frayed couches listening to jazz and shooting the breeze. Blagden's shepherd-husky mix, also named Rosie, roamed the classroom freely.

"I loved my time at Horace Mann," he told me. "I absolutely loved it. Interesting, smart kids who worked hard. I was extremely happy there."

Blagden encouraged students to write their deepest thoughts in their journals. "I just wanted them to write," he said. "They would write whatever they wanted. I just wanted to cool everything down. The place was so pressured and everybody had to go to Harvard and Brown. Room Ten was a drop-in room for students. They would listen to music, relax. They had enough to worry about."

Blagden carried some of those close relationships with him for decades, including with G., the Wright victim I'd grown up playing baseball with in Riverdale. Blagden had grown very friendly with G.'s mother as well, and for many years he'd sent them Christmas cards. This year, in response, he received a curt cease-and-desist letter that began: "Crawford, it was upsetting to me to receive your Christmas card. I am the person referred to as 'G' in Amos Kamil's article, a member of the HM survivors group, and fully and painfully aware of your role in the abuse of minors at HM."

"I was very surprised to get that letter," Blagden told me. "He threatened to take legal action against me if I ever contacted him again. I called his mother and she doesn't want to speak to me. Breck doesn't speak to me. It hurts. A lot of people don't speak to me anymore. Clearly I hurt a lot of people I didn't mean to hurt. Can you imagine? Some of my closest friends, people I've known for so long, find me so reprehensible they won't even speak to [me]. But I gave people a reason not to talk to me. Clearly I fucked up."

I asked him what he knew of the charges against him.

"I had an affair," he admitted. "She was a student and on the cross-country team. She was very bright. I waited till she was seventeen."

The relationship, as Blagden referred to it at times, with Rebecca lasted four, five, or six years and, according to him, they would get together every two or three weeks or so. Rebecca said it went on for a lot longer and with more frequency.

I had tried for more than two years to gently persuade Rebecca to speak with me. I don't know if it was conscious or not, but it seemed as if she was avoiding me. She would tell me to call her and then miss the appointment. Given what some of the others had said about her volatility, I assumed she simply didn't want to speak anymore about it. Although I understood her trepidation, her behavior did little to ease my sense that she might be an unreliable source. I didn't want to retraumatize her, but given what Blagden had said about her, I felt it was important to at least give her the opportunity to respond. When I finally did connect with her, she seemed thankful to be able to tell me her version of the events.

Rebecca said Blagden's interest in her started when she was in the seventh grade and had first arrived at Horace Mann. "He would say things like, 'I want to be your boyfriend.' Then he would stand behind me and start molesting me." She described her contact with him as going on for nine or ten years. "He would take me into the woods and have sex with me and stuff. He would take me home from school to his house and have sex with me around four times a week. There were times when I slept at his house. My parents would be calling all my friends looking for me. I would tell them I fell asleep at a friend's house.

"The first time he raped me, he took me to his basement apartment and made me take a shower. His shower had two showerheads—one up at head level and one at the level of my stomach. I remember him soaping me up and washing me off."

One night, in the mid-1980s, when Rebecca was a junior, Blagden says, he invited her to an English faculty party. "I had called David Schiller, who was the head of the department, and he said I could bring anyone I wanted. When he greeted us at the door, Schiller gave me that look like, 'What are you doing here with a student?' But nobody said anything to me. She was the only student there. I remember Randal Castleman [HM's much beloved librarian] talking to her for a long time in the kitchen."

"Did anyone give you a signal it was okay?"

"Oh, come! What kind of signal do you need, Amos?" he said, his anger flaring. "Jesus! Look, I was stupid. When I look back, I was sick and bloated. And so corrupt. Nobody ever admonished me. I assumed they all put two and two together. I mean, today . . . it's good that things like that wouldn't fly today."

When I asked Rebecca about her memory of this event, she guffawed. "That is so fucked up. He is mixing me up with another girl. I know who he is talking about. He had multiple relationships. He was telling me I was the only one. That was one of the things that hurt. When I caught him and confronted him, he said, 'They came on to me. They bought me flowers.' I realized he wasn't in love with me. I was just an object. A number."

Whether or not she attended Schiller's party, Rebecca insists that her connection to Blagden was out in the open. "They knew it while it was going on," she told me. "Crawford would take me to concerts, and when other teachers asked who he was with, he'd say 'I'm with Rebecca' and nobody would bat an eyelash. Some teachers definitely knew. They didn't condemn it. They thought it was hot."

Rebecca claims that after she graduated, her parents approached Headmaster Foote, Michael Hess, and other trustees with evidence of Blagden's abuse. "My parents were not seeking revenge or money, but when they found out what I had been through, they wanted to make sure it never happened with anyone else. Every time a new headmaster came, they would contact them," she said. A former teacher and administrator, who wished to remain anonymous for fear of risking his pension, told me he had been next door at the time of one such meeting.

When her parents died, Rebecca says she went through their belongings and came across many items from the period. "I had storage lockers of evidence," she said. According to her, there were dozens of love letters from the English teacher. There were apology letters to Rebecca's father from Blagden, written on school stationery. There were other letters to her father in which Blagden blamed her for the sex they were having.

For his part, Hess claims he was never approached by Rebecca's parents about Blagden. "I didn't know Crawford Blagden. I didn't know there was anything involving him," he said. When it was suggested that he must have known Blagden because his kids attended Horace Mann at the time Blagden was teaching there, Hess said he was not involved enough in his kids' schooling to know the names of their teachers. When pressed, Hess admitted that perhaps he had misspoken about never knowing or meeting Blagden but still insisted he never attended a meeting about him or knew of the accusations.

Rebecca said her parents also approached the Bronx DA, who she said did nothing with the claim.

When Kelly took over from Mullady in 2005, Rebecca says, her parents told him what had occurred so that it wouldn't happen to other kids. She says they never asked for money.

Blagden insists that Rebecca's parents knew about his "relationship" with their daughter all along. "Her parents would call looking for her at my apartment. I went to their house lots of times for dinner. Obviously they knew. But they never said anything."

If taking her as his date to concerts and parties hadn't gotten them noticed, what happened next did. When Rebecca was a junior, she was taking care of her friend Edward's apartment in Manhattan. Edward was not a student at Horace Mann.

"She invited me over and we had sex that night," Blagden said. "We go back there the next day and we were in Edward's parents' bed. When the parents come back to the apartment, they were like 'Who the fuck are you?' and 'What are you doing here?'"

After some ugly back-and-forth, Blagden was forced to admit to Edward's parents who he was.

"Once that happened, I thought I'd be fired for sure," he said. "I was waiting for Michael [Lacopo] to call me in and can me. But it never happened. Lacopo didn't know. That poor guy. He was as straight as they come. He would have fired me immediately. Probably would have kicked my ass first."

According to Rebecca, Blagden was emotionally and physically abusive. "He would hit me across the face so hard that I would fly across the room and land on the linoleum floor with blood running out of my mouth," she said. "I remember staring at the linoleum floor and seeing stars and having him beat me on my back. This was intermingled with him raping me vaginally and anally. He was mentally ill. Out of control. . . . He physically abused me, but I never stood up for myself. I took it. He made me feel like a whore. He would beat me and say, 'You made me do this!' Then in another moment he could be so sweet. And I would totally bond with him. I would go home and remember not wanting to shower because I would have these bruises the size of handprints all over my back."

I asked Blagden about Rebecca's charge that he beat and raped her in the basement of his rented apartment.

"She's crazy, Amos," he said emphatically. "I didn't rape nobody," he said as either a turn of phrase or an odd construction for a former English teacher. "Absolutely not."

"But Crawford, why would she make it up?"

"I have no fucking idea, man. You know me well enough to know that I would never . . . I was stupid and way . . ." He gasped and his voice trailed off. "I didn't abuse her. I think she's fucking crazy. I guess I didn't think she was crazy back then." He laughed. "I cared for her. I was good to her."

"Did you love her?"

"I guess at that time I thought I did. When you're fucking someone, you tell yourself that you love them. What else can you do? But looking back on it now, I'm like, Jesus Christ! What was I doing?"

"If I'm crazy, it's because of him!" Rebecca countered when I told her what Blagden had said. "He got me high, drunk, and physically and mentally abused me for ten years. It destroyed my parents. They both passed away before this all came out, so they never got to see HM held accountable. It destroyed my family."

"Were there others?" I pressed Blagden.

"This is the first time. The only time. But I flirted a lot with a lot of girls."

I asked him if he remembered Alison Pollet.

"Sure, I remember Alison," he said.

I showed him a page in her journal where he had written, "I love you, Alison Pollet" in the margins.

"I wrote stuff like that all the time. I did. But I didn't mean it like that. It wasn't sexual. But we did have a kiss, so I guess it went at least that far. We talked on the phone. She came to the apartment. That's when we kissed. I don't remember how it developed. But if Alison wants to know she should write me directly. I'll answer her."

When I pushed him a little more, he admitted that there had been another girl from HM, but he insisted that it ended well and they were still in touch. I didn't know whom he was referring to and he wouldn't tell me her name.

When Lacopo took a job as the head of Isidore Newman, a day school in New Orleans, he asked his old friend to come down to teach English. In 1992, after eleven years at HM, Blagden went to Newman, where, among other students, he taught Cooper Manning, the older brother of NFL quarterbacks Peyton and Eli.

"I was king of the hill when I left Horace Mann. I had good relationships with the kids. That was part of the program. I was good at my job. I had one parent tell me, 'My kid would have committed suicide if it wasn't for you.' I still have the last evaluation letter that Schiller ever wrote. It was very positive." Blagden got up and rummaged around looking for the teacher evaluation he'd received more than twenty years earlier.

Blagden said that Rebecca, then in college, visited him in New Orleans, where they hooked up again. "It was the last time I saw her."

I asked Blagden if he knew how many teachers and administrators had been named. He shook his head.

"Twenty-two," I told him.

"Wow. That's scary, man. That's fucking scary," he said. It was hard to tell if he counted himself among them. "I had no idea how widespread it was. I had absolutely no fucking idea. I mean, I would have been somebody that somebody would have come to if someone was bothering them. Nobody ever did. But Tek, Kops, Clark, Somary— he was the biggest of them all—I didn't pay attention to them. There was too much shit to do to wonder about who was fucking who. It isn't part of the thing."

As much as he liked his fellow faculty members, Blagden was no fan of Inky Clark. "Inslee was a weird one. He was bogus. He did a great job up at Yale, but by the time he got to HM he was sliding through. Frankly, I thought he was a bit of a blockhead. It was pretty clear to the grown-ups that all he cared about was the baseball team and that he didn't care about anything else.

"Early on at HM I was walking the campus one Saturday when I ran into Inky and Kops," he recalled. "They invited me to the house for a beer. There were two iceboxes, one packed with Heinekens, so I took one of those. Inky then went to the icebox and made himself a martini in a jelly jar. I thought he was going to split it up but he just handed it to Kops and then made another for himself. I remember thinking to myself, 'Man, these guys like to drink.'"

Drinking was a subject Blagden knew something about. I remember hoisting beers with him at the Dublin House or the West End, two Upper West Side bars frequented by HMers where pitchers of beer were cheap and, despite the drinking age of eighteen, the bouncers and bartenders never checked our fake IDs. On more than one occasion I pulled Blagden, blind drunk, out of a bar and deposited him on the floor of his basement apartment a few blocks from my apartment. I wondered aloud if he had simply blacked out during the episode in his basement with Rebecca, but he waved me off dismissively.

"Do you still drink?"

"Yeah, I still drink," he said almost defiantly, almost proudly.

"I didn't know Wright. He was before my time. I had no idea about Somary. He was real pompous, but he was pretty much a genius and the head of the art department. With a school as high pressured as Horace Mann, you really needed a strong arts department. I really admired Somary for his dedication.

"I was amazed by the revelations about Tek. I was very surprised. I learned a lot from Tek. Especially grammar. You have to admire what he did for the school. He planted all those trees. He was like a minor god. It's not like we were buddies, but he did a lot for the school. Do you think they all knew about each other?" he asked me. "I would have thought that there was no collaboration."

I told him that we now knew that Somary knew about both Inky and Tek. And that Clinton knew about Tek. And so on.

He shook his head. "I used to be so proud of Horace Mann, and now I feel ashamed. The closeness I had with the kids was a good thing. We would go to concerts together, I remember going to a Los Lobos concert with a bunch of kids. I used to go down by the river with G. and a six-pack of beer. I just got too involved. I went overboard. I got carried away. I just got too close to the kids. I was really good at my job. I just got stupid. Fat. But it was a different world. I was in a bar recently and ran into a guy who teaches snowboarding, and he was telling me that they get a rap about sexual harassment. That never happened back then. But it's a good thing. But I shouldn't have been drinking with them. I let it get ahead of me. It went too far. And that is what I regret."

Although the conversation was relaxed and friendly, Blagden seemed to be a bundle of conflicting and ever-changing emotions—regretful, defensive, guilty, passive, angry, contrite, and aggressive. Given the circumstances, I was surprised he'd agreed to meet me at all. He told me that his wife wondered what good could come of talking to me. It was a legitimate question—one I'd heard hundreds of times in various forms.

So I put the question to Blagden himself: "Why *did* you agree to speak to me?"

"I can't change what happened at Horace Mann, Amos. That was two lifetimes ago. There's nothing I can do to make what happened at HM any better. If speaking to you is a tiny little step in the right direction, then it's worth doing. I had to tell you. I know you. I would have said 'fuck you' if it were anyone else."

When I suggested that he seemed almost relieved to be speaking with me, he agreed. "'Relief' is a good word. I feel relief. I knew you were straight and trying to do something important. I strongly believe it's worth doing it. I'm glad I spoke to you."

"Are you angry with me?"

"Not at all. I wish you well, man. You did the right thing. I feel like I accomplished a little bit. It's good to say it. I think you'll be fair. It will help some of these people. It's not gonna be a book that sells. But I expect a free copy."

He wasn't joking.

As I packed up my things, I asked about the house we were in. He said it belonged to Lynn. "I could never afford a house," he said. "I've lived in a lot of basements."

We walked to my car, shook hands, and exchanged goodbyes. Blagden guided me as I backed out of his snowy driveway. I drove a mile down the road and pulled over to stare at the picture-postcard rolling white hills of the valley. I called my wife, Madeline, and as we discussed where to meet, I noticed a car pulled over about thirty yards ahead. An older man approached the car. I rolled down the window and realized it was Blagden, wondering if I was lost.

"Just trying to figure out a good spot to meet my wife and kids."

"Follow me," he said. "I'm going to Mr. Up's in Middlebury. It's a great bakery."

As much as I was intrigued by the notion of sharing breakfast with Blagden and my wife and our two teenage daughters, I declined.

I called Andrew not long after my encounter with Blagden. Andrew had been a student of his and today is a psychologist who works with abused and neglected children. Andrew called me back a few days later to tell me that he'd been thinking a great deal about what I told him.

"The one line that kept coming back to me was 'I didn't rape nobody,'" he said. "It has three levels of meaning for me. First and most obvious, it's a pretty ironic grammatically incorrect construction for a former English teacher. Second is that it's consistent with my memory of the image Crawford liked to put forward of himself to us in high school—the outsider and antiestablishment rebel who'd been kicked around by life; the guy who didn't play by the rules. At a third level, and as a psychologist, I couldn't help noticing the literal meaning of his double negative, 'didn't rape nobody.' One way that you can read 'I didn't rape nobody' is 'I *did* rape *somebody*.' I don't really buy into the whole Freudian slip thing. But just like when I read Tek Lin's words in the *New York Times* interview last year, or when Bill Clinton famously said, 'I did not have sexual relations with that woman,' I am struck by the contorted language that perpetrators employ when referring to their behavior. It's often quite disturbing and revealing."

Andrew told me another memory of Blagden from when he was a student at Horace Mann. "I think it was in his classroom on the first floor of Tillinghast. Blagden asked a group of us, 'Boys, have you ever fucked a girl in the ass? At first you push and push and nothing happens. And then, boom! It's like sucking air.' We cracked up. I mean, we were like sixteen—most of us had never even had sex. We joked about it afterwards—it seemed like Blagden being one of the boys. But as I became an adult, it became clear how incredibly inappropriate that interaction was, how misogynistic, and how much it exemplified the unhealthy, sexualized culture of teachers at the school at that time. As a parent of teenagers, I can't even imagine how angry I'd be if I learned that a teacher was talking to my son in that way."

On May 29, 2014, Teo Armus-Laski (HM 2014), the editor in chief of *The Horace Mann Record*, published a lengthy editorial titled "School for Scandal: Talkin' 'bout Our Reputation," that offered a glimpse into how some current students were dealing (or not dealing) with the scandal. It was his last piece for the student paper before graduating and moving on to Columbia University, and in it he explored the reaction on campus to the blizzard of negative press the school had received.

"Everyone is concerned with establishing a superior reputation for the school—yet in most cases, we refuse to take on any individual responsibility to improve this reputation," Armus-Laski wrote. "Throughout my high school career, any time this school has ended up in the press (usually not for positive reasons), I've heard my classmates and teachers . . . embark on tirades about how the media loves to hate our 'elite prep school.'"

Armus-Laski's willingness to identify with the survivors was, in his own assessment, a minority position. He had interviewed many survivors and had grown familiar with the subject matter by virtue of his relationship with Kathy Howard. "Maybe it was because Dr. Howard was my faculty adviser for three years," he told me in a telephone interview. "I would spend time with her while she was going through mediation. I could see the toll it was taking. Every time I tried to bring it up—whether in relaxed conversation or even at an editorial meeting—no one wanted to discuss it. It was 'HM is being attacked' or 'It was a long time ago.' They were personally too identified with the school. I go to the school, but I didn't take it personally. So many students associate themselves so much with the school. They were acting like it was irrelevant to the school today. For me it was very surprising and confusing."

Armus-Laski's editorial continued:

Having been a legal adult for all of two months, I'm not sure I'm qualified to judge how the Board of Trustees has handled the revelations of sexual abuse. But after reporting on the issue for a year, it's pretty clear to me that no front-page magazine article would have been published had the administration in the 1960s through 1990s responded to the many complaints survivors said they took to the school's administration . . . If this school is really to become the kind of intellectual Garden of Eden so many people claim it already is, then it needs to stop blaming the outside world . . . If you don't want . . . the school whose board you sit on to end up on the cover of *The New York Times Magazine*, deal with charges of sexual abuse by meeting the demands of the survivors.

Armus-Laski's editorial, holding true to Headmaster Gratwick's boast in the 1950s that the administration did not meddle in *The Record*'s editorial affairs, was a revelation to the many alumni who no longer maintained a daily connection to the school. Armus-Laski had managed to break the wall of silence that seemed to divide the school into two camps. The wall, to use Kelly's formulation, was between the two Horace Manns—one looking forward and one looking to the past. It was a relief to many of the older survivors and alumni who wondered how closely the current students were following the story or whether they even cared at all. (To be fair, if, when I was a student in the 1980s, I had heard that abuses occurred in the 1950s, I'm certain I would not have possessed the maturity, compassion, and clear-eyed perspective that Armus-Laski brought to bear.)

The Record's supposed freedom of the press was not always extended to the broader HM community. When Charlie Varon (HM '76) wrote a letter to the editor in response to a *Record* article titled "Annual Fund Breaks Record with over $5 Million," the paper's editorial board declined to run it.

Varon went to Processing Horace Mann, where he posted, "Once I was editor of the HM Record. Now I can't get a letter to the editor published there." He then posted the contents of his unpublished letter:

The article touches on the HM sexual abuse scandal and its effect on alumni giving. It notes the decrease in donations from alumni of the 1960s and 1970s, the period of greatest sexual abuse at HM. But the article fails to tackle the moral question facing any prospective donor: "Can I in good conscience support a school that has failed to act decently to those alumni whom it has wronged?" No matter how strong the current faculty and student body, no matter how great the gifts the school has given us, and no matter how far in the past the abuse occurred, that troubling question persists. And it will continue to persist until the Board of Trustees does what so many other secondary schools, facing similar scandals, have done: take the high road and commission an independent investigation. On the matter of an independent investigation, I have heard no credible reason why Horace Mann has failed to act. I have heard only evasions.

Meanwhile, across the hilltop, the Riverdale Country School, HM's longtime rival on and off the field, was turning itself into a world-class institution at the forefront of character-based education. Riverdale students regularly discuss subjects like leadership, communication, vision, and integrity as part of a curriculum that seeks to move beyond the classroom. The school's head, Dominic Randolph, is openly skeptical of the current obsession with testing, telling *The New York Times*, "This push on tests is missing out on some serious parts of what it means to be a successful human." Character is far more important than test scores, he insists, and a greater indicator of future success. Teaching—even defining—character is difficult. But working with the "positive psychologist" Martin Seligman, Randolph came up with a list of twenty-four essential character traits the school seeks to inculcate—traditional qualities like bravery and fairness, as well as more nuanced ones such as self-regulation and gratitude.

Meanwhile, Horace Mann has grappled with several smaller scandals since my article came out. These are the kinds of incidents that have made some parents worry about how much weight the idea of character has on campus. There was a poetry seminar where students read racist and sexist statements from the stage ("I like to go nigger hunting on Sundays"; "I like to fuck Miley Cyrus up the ass"). The teachers in the audience seemed to take it in stride. While many parents, students, and administrators expressed shock and outrage, others were less surprised. In an op-ed piece in *The Horace Mann Record*, Esther Ademola, a black student, wrote: "Words and ideas were thrown around that I've heard expressed in hallways, classrooms and the cafeteria. I personally have been subject to remarks much worse than those shared on stage. The one aspect of this that shocked me was that people had the audacity to get up on stage in front of the entire school with absolutely no regard for our emotions and utter such filth."

In the wake of the event, David Schiller, the head of the school's Upper Division, visited many classrooms to apologize. He also sent a letter to parents in which he took the blame for what had happened. "It was my responsibility to ensure that the presentation to our students was fitting and appropriate. It was not," he wrote. "I should have intervened to stop the assembly, and I did not do so." Schiller also said he hoped that this was the beginning of "a healthful and healing process."

Another incident involved a student who tried to sabotage another's college admission chances by making malicious statements about him to the Ivies he was applying to. The head of college placement, Canh Oxelson (a Harvard grad who also works as a Tiger Woods impersonator), decried the lack of values the incident demonstrated—and then was arrested for threatening to send naked pictures of his ex-girlfriend to her boss. Oxelson denied all the charges, and the matter was later dismissed.

At the beginning, I was under the impression that "all the teachers knew" about the abuse that was going on at Horace Mann and did nothing. As time progressed, I had to recalibrate that notion. I realized there were different levels of knowing—different cliques, different relationships to the school and to other faculty members. Some of the teachers who must have looked the other way were among the people I admired most in the world. People like Alan Breckenridge, the highly respected English teacher and administrator whose daughter, Jodi, remains one of my best friends to this day.

In a world of talkers, Alan Breckenridge was a doer.

As a young man with a tortured relationship to his own father, he provided a model for me of the way a man could be. He did things quietly, with no thought to the importance of his role in the greater scheme of things; he built things—like his house on a lake in Vermont—with his own hands; he eschewed the spotlight with a dry sense of humor; he listened rather than lectured.

For many of us, he was a living example of Hemingway's definition of a hero: "a man who lives correctly, following the ideals of honor, courage and endurance in a world that is sometimes chaotic, often stressful, and always painful." Mr. Breck was stoical, slow to show emotion. He seemed to struggle valiantly with his own tragic faults as well as those of the surrounding environment.

While being a fixture of Horace Mann for more than forty years, he managed to remain an outsider. He created Searchers to give pampered Ivy-bound New Yorkers a taste of independence, freedom, and serenity that only the outdoors could provide. He raised his family of three with his wife, Eva, in a humble house in a modest neighborhood in Teaneck, New Jersey. He drove "the Breck van," shuttling students from New Jersey to Horace Mann and back, to supplement his income. He led "Breck" trips to Vermont as a way of supporting his family's expensive passion for skiing. It was a tradition for those who went on Breck trips to crayon their names on the drywall of the bunk room. To this day, whenever I take my kids to the house, they run up to the room to check on the name I scrawled there circa 1979.

He was rarely at faculty parties or privy to the gossip circles.

The morning after I met Blagden, I had breakfast with Alan Breckenridge at a café near his home in Burlington, Vermont. He had recently turned eighty and, despite heart bypass surgery, still retained the taut physique he had from years of running, skiing, and continuous manual labor. The highlight of his birthday celebration, he told me, was a book put together by his family that included well-wishes from dozens of his former HM colleagues and students, including tributes from me and my brother Daniel.

Mr. Breck was devastated by the revelations that had unfolded over the past few years. As I relayed news of my meeting with Blagden, he still punctuated his active listening with, "Yah, yah, sure, sure"—a quiet, verbal tic that had been the source material for many imitations over the years.

"That sounds like the Crawford Blagden I know."

"Did you stop talking to him after the scandal?"

"No, I haven't spoken with Blagden for years. It has nothing to do with all this."

I told him I was grappling with his lack of communication since the scandal broke.

"I was never angry with you," I said. "And by no means do I put you in the category of the abusers, but, like so many of us, I just don't understand your silence."

"I feel terrible that so many kids were hurt while I was there," he said. "Part of it is, and this is not meant as an excuse, I have a terrible memory. I always have."

He then relayed a story Dick Warren had recently reminded him about. When an inner-city kid went missing on a Searchers trip, they had convened a search party and ultimately found the boy sitting quietly by a tree.

"Dick can tell you every detail about that day," he said. "He even knows the kid's middle name. I didn't even remember that it happened. That tells you something about the way my mind works."

In some ways he was questioning why he didn't know and how he should have known. "I was surprised when they fired Stan Kops, if that gives you any sense of how out of it I was."

He was clearly uncomfortable and saddened by all that had emerged. He was unsure, however, what good it would do to talk about what he did or didn't know.

"If I say I didn't know, they will think I am lying. If I say I knew a little, they will want more."

"But Dick Warren and Joyce Fitzpatrick both wrote letters to the community," I pointed out. "Doc Passow and Bruce Weber, too. And nobody blames them. I think it just lends a little more nuance and dispels the notion that everybody knew."

"I just couldn't formulate the words that I thought might make a difference."

"But isn't saying nothing just as bad?" I asked. "I think people would love to hear from you. It would be healing on some level."

"I just can't think of what to write that would be helpful," he said as he quietly slid the check for our meal over to his side of the table, "or that wouldn't sound self-serving."

Once again, Andrew, who started this avalanche around a campfire at Hell for Sure Lake, showed the way in an email.

Hi Alan,

Too many years have passed since I last saw you. I'm writing now because I wanted to connect with you about Horace Mann. The experiences Amos wrote about definitely impacted my life in a permanent and difficult way. These past months since the article came out have been amazing for me in many ways, both extremely challenging but also healing. What I wanted you to know was that during my time at HM, and in the context of the darkness that existed, you were a light. You provided something crucial to my survival; just by your calm presence and by the things like Searchers that you did, you gave me hope. And of course you did this for so many others. In my life today, I work in the midst of many broken systems (children in foster care, low income community mental health, academia!) that I cannot fix. You have been a role model for me in how to be a force for good in those contexts, in how to look for what I can do to help, and then to do it. I am sure that the information coming out about HM must be painful for you; but for my part, I just want to tell that I am forever grateful for the role you have played in my life.

"I can't believe none of them knew," J. told me. "After a while I decided Alan was too important for me for so many other reasons— I was like an adopted son—and I decided not to hold it against him. It was a classic and complete act of forgiveness."

I felt the same way.

•

HMAC's groundbreaking attempt to crowdfund Judge Snyder's investigation yielded only $17,180, bringing the total amount raised to $57,180, far short of the $150,000 Snyder and her team required to continue. The group quickly pivoted its strategy. It would now team up with Charol Shakeshaft, the educational researcher who studied abuse at schools. She was engaged in a research project aggregating "best practices" and sending them out to educational administrators and teachers around the country so that they could weight and rank-order them in importance. She would then ask schools and other youth-serving organizations to rate the importance of these best practices. HMAC planned to apply Shakeshaft's weighted practices to various independent schools and grade them according to how many of the practices they put into effect.

"We are going to apply the final set of practices to various NYC independent schools," Rob Boynton told *The Wall Street Journal.* The idea, he told me, was to grade them "according to how many they have put into effect. Sort of like those grades that NYC restaurants receive. We'll give an 'A' if a school fulfills, say, 90%, and a 'B' for 70% of them. I think this will be a good way to get more publicity for the practices, and a simple way for a potential parent/student to judge whether a school is safe. The idea is to make it so simple that anyone can do it."

In addition to working with the Shakeshaft report, HMAC decided to put together another survey of independent schools where sexual abuse was revealed during the past five years. It would be the first time anyone had compared the way independent schools behaved after sexual abuse was revealed.

Although HMAC's independent investigation was scaled back for lack of funds, Judge Snyder was still meeting with many people who could shed light on what happened. In some ways, HMAC's smaller-scale independent investigation was more likely to have a practical impact than the original plan for a full-blown investigation. Horace Mann was now going to be used, in classrooms around the world, as an object lesson in what not to do.

HMAC's relentless activity caught the attention of many longtime child advocates. "HMAC is a model for all alums," Marci Hamilton wrote to Peter Brooks of HMAC's efforts. "You all are rewriting the book on what it means to be a responsible adult. Very heartening."

Hamilton would know. A professor at the Cardozo School of Law and a highly regarded scholar and child's rights advocate, she had been in the trenches on the issue for years. Her book *Justice Denied: What America Must Do to Protect Its Children* is one of the seminal works in the field. In June 2014, she issued a report summarizing the statute of limitations reform efforts on a state-by-state basis. "This is another good year for the victims of child sex abuse in a number of states, including Hawaii, Massachusetts, and Florida," she wrote. "It is also the year that the states with some of the worst statutes of limitations and most troubling sex abuse scandals—New York and Georgia—continue to sit on their hands."

On May 13, 2014, Hamilton and Brooks joined a day of lobbying in Albany on behalf of the Markey bill.

"New York is among the worst states in the country for child sex abuse statutes of limitations," Hamilton told those assembled for the rally. "It shares this distinction with two deep southern states, Alabama and Georgia, and two Midwestern states, Indiana and Michigan. While the vast majority of states have been increasing access to justice for victims over recent years, New York continues to block access for the vast majority of New York's child sex abuse victims." Bridie Farrell, the national speed-skating champion, spoke as well. "The statute of limitations needs to change," she said. "I reported it much sooner than most; a lot of women don't come out until they've married and have their own children. So having a five-year statute of limitations is an insult."

Brooks held up a chart showing the results of HMAC's study of the twenty-one independent schools with recent reported issues of abuse, four in New York. Horace Mann had by far the most victims and the most abusers. "We see a hundred and nineteen reasons to enact the Child Victims Act. Sixty-three reasons in my school alone—victims of abuse," he told the crowd. "Many of these victims were created by schools stalling reports that would have stopped abusers. New York's [statute of limitations] promotes a badly tilted system which does not prevent abuse, creates more victims, blocks justice, and re-injures victims repeatedly . . . Administrators at Horace Mann . . . used the current SOL as a roadmap to cover up. Still today Horace Mann refuses to explain, investigate, or cooperate with an investigation into the conditions that allowed sexual abuse to hurt so many for so long—conditions that are systemic obstacles shared by many schools, dioceses, and organizations in N.Y. state."

Although the Child Victims Act, which Markey had first introduced in 2007, had been adopted four times by the New York State Assembly, it had never made it to the floor of the State Senate—largely because of the Catholic Church's lobbying and the Republican leadership's fear of adverse political consequences for supporting it.

Despite some glimmers of hope, supporters of the Markey bill still faced an uphill struggle.

I met one of the heroes of this story late in my reporting. Alvin (HM '76) had surfaced only after "Prep-School Predators" was published in the *Times*. He was one of those who read my story with a sense of shock and relief.

"When I read your article, I was probably the only guy in New York grinning," he told me when we finally spoke. "I was like, 'Yeah, yeah, yeah. I don't have to be in the closet about this anymore.' I always thought I was the only one, but I was shocked by the extent of the racket that was being run."

By the time he was in sixth grade, Alvin was reading at the twelfth-grade level. He was an African American kid from the Manhattanville Houses in Harlem; Horace Mann might as well have been in another galaxy. His mother, recently divorced from Alvin's dad, was elated when he received a scholarship to attend Horace Mann, because the local high school "seemed like a place of idiocy and bullying."

In the fall of 1970, Alvin joined Horace Mann's last all-boys class in the first form (the equivalent of seventh grade). Alvin wondered at his good fortune, and despite the sense of dislocation, he felt honored to be there. Aside from the culture shock that came with shuttling between Harlem and Horace Mann, Alvin says he experienced almost no discomfort about his race or class. He was, however, surprised by the formality. "We called everybody 'sir.' You didn't even have to learn a teacher's name. Everybody was sir."

Despite his academic excellence, Alvin, like many other HMers, struggled under the enormous workload. "The schedule was daunting," he said. "I was cut off in almost every aspect of my life in the projects. In hindsight, I realized it was like working at a corporation. This is a job. I found my best friends among a group of guys who were also struggling and willing to admit it."

Although many of Alvin's Horace Mann friends were white, he often found himself hanging out with the black and Latino students, who banded together both socially and academically. Terrence A. G. Archer, an overweight, authoritarian biology teacher, originally from the Caribbean, became their mentor. (His students joked that his middle initials stood for "Almighty God.")

"Archer taught biology like Professor Kingsley taught law in the movie *The Paper Chase*," wrote Doug Henderson (HM '76) in his memoir *Endeavor to Persevere*. "Many of Mr. Archer's students still speak wistfully of him. Several went on to become doctors, and a few have told me that were it not for him, they would have chosen a different profession. He remains very much alive in my thoughts, and I cherish the many memories I have of a truly remarkable teacher and extraordinary human being. Somehow, I know that he watches over the students for whom he cared so much. Thirty-five years after his death, he still remains the paradigm for academic excellence."

Alvin also had Archer for biology, so it felt natural to join the dozen or so students Archer would invite to his Brooklyn home. The atmosphere was like Blagden's Room Ten, a lodge where students would hang out, study, and sometimes sleep over.

"His game was to be a do-gooder for the minority students," Alvin told me. "He would invite students to his home and tutor kids. He was tasked with getting us through the school.

"In hindsight, I guess I always felt there was something off about him. A biology teacher who didn't give a fuck about his body? In retrospect he was a fat, pain-in-the-ass bitch. He wouldn't just give you an F if you failed something. He'd give you an F to the first, F to the second degree, F to the third degree, and so on. But hindsight's twenty-twenty."

After his parents' divorce, Alvin's father had been mostly absent, and his mother, like so many other adults in his life, urged him to have a positive male role model. Archer fit the bill and soon began taking him alone on trips around the city.

"We'd go to the old Times Square and he'd buy me pornographic magazines. That's how sexuality entered the discussion. We'd look at naked pictures of girls and he'd ask what I would do with this one or that. Other times he would speak about sex in very biological terms. As my body was going through adolescent changes, he would comment on things like my nipples becoming hard or facial growth."

The pornographic magazines and sex talk lasted for months. Then one day, back in his Brooklyn apartment, Archer began performing fellatio on Alvin. Eventually, after several more encounters, Alvin says that Archer asked him, "Will you penetrate me or will I penetrate you?"

"My imagination did not stretch to comprehend what he was suggesting," said Alvin. "As a fifteen-year-old boy, I didn't know that men were entered until dealing with this guy. In terms of the sexual relationship, I always played top and he played bottom. I never saw his genitalia, so it was easy to imagine this was my girlfriend."

By the time he was in eleventh grade, Alvin estimates, he and Archer had between fifty and one hundred sexual encounters.

In the summer of 1975, in between Alvin's junior and senior years, Archer died of cancer. Alvin felt peer-pressured to attend the funeral, where he sat in the back and left as soon as it was over. He learned later that his old teacher had left him $4,000 in his will.

Archer's death triggered the trauma Alvin had suppressed. "There was no one to speak to," he told me. "Not that I would have spoken to anyone about this for two million dollars. And never did for fourteen years. For a teacher at HM, I guess he was a nice-enough guy. But who's comparing rings of hell here? I got a real education in shades of gray. I would trade back that bit of innocence for anything."

Alvin admits that in some ways the abuse made him a better student. "It sounds strange, but I became more intellectual. I turned inward in a way that was beneficial and wasn't. I became more aware of what's on the surface is only on the surface. If I were assigned something about Shakespeare, I would read Spenser and other source material. I would research things beyond the surface to see what was underneath the guise of what was being presented to me. In the long run, it didn't help me."

The sex with Archer also emboldened Alvin in other ways. "I figured if I was fucking my teacher, I could handle anything. I felt empowered. If I can do this, why the fuck can't I lead on the field, or the school, the world? Outwardly I became a leader."

Alvin became the head of the Black Student Union, the football captain, and the star running back, and he joined the editorial board of *Manuscript*, HM's prestigious literary magazine. In Inky's urban studies class, Alvin began to stand up to his fellow students.

With his projection of togetherness, Alvin sailed through HM and into Yale, where, once again, on the surface, he excelled. But on the inside his life was in turmoil. "I'd spend a lot of time wondering if I was gay," he said. "And I couldn't relate to the problems of my fellow students. People would tell me about their girlfriends or something of that nature and I was thinking to myself, 'I was fucking a man for two years.'"

Alvin managed a solid academic career and in his senior year was asked to join an elite secret society—not Skull and Bones, he says. "When I was asked to speak about my personal life, I spoke in vague generalities about my time at Horace Mann and then went totally blank about the whole Archer deal." Although he knew he should have felt honored and enjoyed himself more, Alvin was starting his lifelong battle with depression. When he left New Haven, his life began careening. "I really blew away the '80s on drinking and risk taking. Drugs came later." Drugs, alcohol, depression, unemployment, and promiscuity became the themes of his adult life.

"I don't have a profession. I find it horrible to deal with authority," he said. "Everyone thought I'd be in the president's cabinet or a billionaire. I was a sales manager for a while selling temp services to Wall Street firms, but I've had a checkered work life with long stretches of unemployment. Whenever I was let go I fell into a severe depression. And all of this has its roots in this deal at HM."

Eager to prove to himself and the world he wasn't gay, Alvin became a serial monogamist, clinging to heterosexual relationships for as long as possible. But he never married. "I could never trust women. I just don't trust."

At some point in the 1990s, a therapist with whom he'd shared his secret suggested that, as a healing mechanism, Alvin volunteer at Horace Mann to face his demons head on. He joined the Alumni Council and ultimately HM's Board of Trustees during the time that Eileen Mullady was the head of the school.

"One bright spring day, before a board meeting to talk about fund-raising and building additions, I sat with Mullady on a bench facing out toward the field," he recalled. "I told her what happened to me. She just didn't want to hear about it. She kept making a distinction between the school then and the school now. She wasn't interested."

Mullady's brush-off was the last straw, and Alvin severed all ties with the school. "No shame at the breaking of the social contract. Moral leadership? You won't find it there. They took smart people and said that they shaped them. Place has made me dumber in a lot of ways. In the end I felt like a pawn's pawn's pawn. 'Fuck Horace Mann' was my attitude at that point. They didn't care about students then. I doubt if they care about them now. Blow it up as far as I'm concerned."

Alvin was one of the few survivors at peace after the mediation. "I deserved millions for what happened to me," he said. "I was happy to get what I could because of the statute of limitations. I am using the money for psychotherapy. I will use some of it to go to a dry-out farm and take away drugs and alcohol as a palliative."

Alvin also became a patient of Louise Lipman, the therapist he'd met at the mediation. "I'm thinking about going to get an MSW and eventually hang a shingle. I think I have something to offer people who have been sexually abused. That would be a humble and honorable way to make a living given what I've been through."

He is fifty-six years old.

ACKNOWLEDGMENTS

Bringing this story to light took a village. There are thousands of people who shared stories, comforted friends, and encouraged me and others to stay the course. I can't possibly thank (or even remember) everyone, but here's my best attempt. A deep, full-hearted thank-you to:

Everybody who paved the road to publication: Ariel Kaminer, Hugo Lindgren, Jillian Dunham, Julie Tate, Steve Hirsch, the folks at the MacDowell Colony, my wonderful agent Todd Schuster. Jessica Greenbaum, the brilliant and no-drama Alex Star, Jonathan Galassi, and everyone at FSG who enabled this truth to see the light.

The many lawyers and mental health professionals who helped me to understand the complex issues of treating and legislating cases of sexual abuse, including Dr. Phil Fisher, Dr. Richard Gartner, Geoff Genth, David Godosky, Dr. Laurie Gordon, Andy Hyams, Paul Mones, Kevin Mulhearn, and Michael Rinzler.

The hundreds of members of the Horace Mann community, former students and teachers alike, who joined me on this sad and painful journey. A partial list of "strangers met in friendship" includes Rob Adler, Dan Alexander, Alan Ampolsk, Kate Aurthur, Charles Balter, Ed Beck, Susannah Blinkoff, Ed Bowen, Robert Boynton, Alan Breckenridge, Jodi Breckenridge, Nicole Brown, Eli Chalfin,

Nick Chen, Joseph Cumming, Louise Elton, Ben Field, Steve Fife, Marc Fisher, Joyce Fitzpatrick, Marge Frank, Jon Frankel, Jeff Franklin, Dr. Nina Freund, Kate Geis, Josh Gelman, Dr. Laurie Gordon, Peter Greer, Ele Hamburger, Doug Henderson, Rob Hollander, Dana Baum Hopper, Dr. Kathy Howard, Bill Hughes, Bill Irwin, Dan Kamil, Ariel Kaminer, Martin Kaminer, Marjorie Kaufman, Claudia Knafo, Dom Kulik, Lorraine Kayton Kulik, Ron Lombardi, Jody Lewen, Jackie Lowey, Josh Malina, Josh Manheimer, Daniel Miller, Rob Nisonoff, Erica Modugno, Peter Oppenheimer, Jennifer Rosenfeld Pileggi, Alison Pollet, Dr. Christina Propst, Lynn Richmond, Dr. Deborah Rovine, Dr. Shira Sanders, Mitch Schonfeld, David Seide, Jon Seiger, E. Noach Shapiro, Chet Slaybaugh Sr., John Slaybaugh, Rich Smyth, Betsy Spanbock, Dr. Alice Swenson, Jordan Thomas, Charlie Varon, Mike Vatis, Dick Warren, Bruce Weber. A few others will go unnamed but not unappreciated for what they contributed to this story. A special shout-out to Peter Brooks, the Cairo Genizah of any and all information regarding the events related in this book.

My mother and the three best brothers a guy could ask for.

My four miraculous children—Maia, Lea, Abi, and Itai—who often wondered why I was "always talking about Horace Mann."

Madeline, who listened, prodded, questioned, pushed, read, and reread, all while carrying so much water on the family front.

INDEX

A NOTE ABOUT THE AUTHORS

Amos Kamil is a playwright, screenwriter, and investigative reporter. His 2012 cover story in *The New York Times Magazine* brought the Horace Mann scandal to light.

Sean Elder has written for *Newsweek*; *New York*; *National Geographic*; *O, The Oprah Magazine*; and numerous other publications. He lives in Mill Valley, California.

CPSIA information can be obtained
at www.ICGtesting.com
Printed in the USA
LVOW03s2037271217
560975LV00005B/526/P